P9-DGE-128

DATE DUE

NOV 2 6 1995		
NOV 2 1 1995		
APR - 9 1996		
APR 1 2 1996		
DEC 2 1996		
MAY - 4 1997		
APR 2 6 1997		
GAYLORD		PRINTED IN U.S.A.

RACE AND ETHNICITY IN RESEARCH METHODS

OTHER RECENT VOLUMES IN THE
SAGE FOCUS EDITIONS

RACE AND
ETHNICITY
IN RESEARCH
METHODS

John H. Stanfield II
Rutledge M. Dennis
editors

SAGE PUBLICATIONS
International Educational and Professional Publisher
Newbury Park   London   New Delhi

For information address:

 SAGE Publications, Inc.
2455 Teller Road
Newbury Park, California 91320

SAGE Publications Ltd.
6 Bonhill Street
London EC2A 4PU
United Kingdom

SAGE Publications India Pvt. Ltd.
M-32 Market
Greater Kailash I
New Delhi 110 048 India

Printed in the United States of America

Library of Congress Cataloging-in-Publication Data

Main entry under title:

Race and ethnicity in research methods / edited by John H. Stanfield II,
  Rutledge M. Dennis.
      p.   cm.—(Sage focus editions; 157)
    Includes bilbiographical references and index.
    ISBN 0-8039-5006-3. — ISBN 0-8039-5007-1 (pbk.)
    1. Ethnic relations—Research.   2. Race relations—Research.
  3. Ethnology—Methodology.   4. Sociology—Methodology.
  I. Stanfield, John H.   II. Dennis, Rutledge M.
  GN496.R33 1993
  305.8'0072—dc20   93-9489

93 94 95 96 97 10 9 8 7 6 5 4 3 2 1

Sage Production Editor: Astrid Virding

Contents

PART I

Introduction and Epistemological Considerations

1

Methodological Reflections

An Introduction

JOHN H. STANFIELD II

During the 1984 meetings of the American Sociological Association, I organized a roundtable titled "Methodological Innovations in Race Relations Research." The purpose of the roundtable was to bring together several leading sociologists to reflect on the relevance of various methodological approaches for testing and modifying theories in race relations research and to recommend new approaches. Out of that stimulating intellectual exchange came an April 1987 issue of the *American Behavioral Scientist* that included several revised papers from the roundtable.

I organized the present volume three years ago in an effort to encourage race and ethnic studies researchers in American social sciences to think critically in epistemological and theoretical veins about methodologies. Two of the chapters here first appeared in the aforementioned *American Behavioral Scientist* issue, but the others were written expressly for this volume. During the preparation of the manuscript, Rutledge Dennis was kind enough to hold the fort while I was abroad for a year and a half and to assist me upon my return.

As almost 10 years have elapsed between the 1984 roundtable and the publication of this volume, I should mention the genesis of my interest in this subject and why I have persisted so long in thinking about it. Ever since my graduate school years at Northwestern in the early to middle 1970s, I have been struck by the lack of methodological imagination in racial and ethnic studies. Indeed, the logical positivist tradition that has dominated so much American social scientific logic of inquiry has encouraged a general absence of critical reflection on how and why social scientists study empirical realities as they do. When epistemological and theoretical questions are raised about methodology, usually such inquiries are divorced from substantive subfield concerns and discussed in a vacuum, as philosophy of social science considerations.

The absence of critical reflection about methodology in racial and ethnic studies is not the only result of the discouraging pervasiveness of logical positivism in social scientific research. As a graduate student, as a budding sociologist of knowledge, I took a race relations seminar during my first year, and I became both intrigued and disturbed by how politically and culturally biased many classical racial and ethnic studies were. For me, race relations was a new area of study, and I became more than concerned as I read the prefaces of classical studies and began to get into the history of social science literature. I became increasingly aware that much of what went under the guise of objective study, owing to the presence of statistical tables or lengthy ethnographic excerpts, was actually an ideologically determined and culturally biased production of knowledge.

By *ideologically determined and culturally biased production of knowledge,* I mean that discourse orientations were rooted firmly in historically specific folk notions of socially constructed racial differences and their sociological, political, and economic consequences. This is to say that, much like other subfields focusing on sensitive status and norms issues with significant moral implications (such as gender inequality and deviance), the study of racial and ethnic issues in the social sciences has remained deeply grounded in societal folk beliefs. Thus conceptualizations of research problems and interpretations of collected data in racial and ethnic research often have been preceded by a priori ideological and cultural biases that determine the production of "objective knowledge." For this reason, the gathering and interpretation of statistical and ethnographic data in racial and ethnic research frequently serves to lend a professional gloss to what are in reality nothing more than cultural and social stereotypes and presumptions derived from historically specific folk wisdom.

My favorite classical example comes from the Chicago school of sociology and its intellectual descendants, such as Robert E. Park's

(1950) race cycle. Although it is true that Park eventually called his race cycle model into question, its influence on generations of race relations scholars is a classical example of the institutionalization of dogma in social science research: Although the master researcher may move away from or even discard the seminal idea, those who follow continue to use it to model research questions.

When one grasps the historical context in which Park lived and wrote, it is more than apparent that his race cycle was a reflection of liberal racial idealism of the time, rather than a model grounded in the empirical realities of an urbanizing biracial industrial society. Liberal racial idealists such as Park believed that despite Jim Crow laws and their economic and political manifestations and consequences in American cities and countrysides, Afro-Americans would eventually assimilate into the host society at least culturally. The word *eventually* is important, because assimilation is actually a timeless process that is rooted more in liberal ideals regarding the inevitable goodness of U.S. democracy as a utopian belief than in empirical realities.

Cultural assimilation as the immeasurable outcome of the Parkian race cycle was a liberal folk belief that shaped the way sociologists viewed race relations for decades. Despite Park's eventually changing his mind, his students, such as Charles S. Johnson and E. Franklin Frazier, and disciples, such as Gunnar Myrdal, continued to use the race cycle and its outcomes as a paradigm that guided their data collection and shaped their interpretations of findings. After the 1970s, William J. Wilson's (1978) *The Declining Significance of Race*—which, despite its Marxist and Weberian cosmetics, is premised on Parkian race cycle ideas—rejuvenated race cycle thinking in a totally different historical context.

The ideological underside of Parkian thought comes to the surface, of course, whenever there is a resurgence of racial violence and racial movements from the left or from the right that remind us that although Afro-Americans and other people of color may culturally assimilate more or less, race continues to be a primary issue rather than a tragic moral contradiction in U.S. society. As the civil rights movement and the race riots of the 1950s and 1960s delegitimated the validity of the Parkian race cycle model, the resurgence of racial violence and the expansion of racist populist movements in the 1980s and 1990s have discredited the "declining significance of race" perspective as a scientific statement.

What is most interesting, and this is finally the point of all this, is to observe the continuation of folk wisdom-derived dogma in professional social science circles specializing in racial and ethnic studies despite empirical evidence to the contrary. As much as classical and neo-Parkian thought has been called into serious question and shown to be grounded obviously in wishful thinking, social scientists who study race and ethnicity continue to hold on to such ideologies and cultural biases. This is because ethnicity and (especially) race are emotion-laden issues; these are difficult matters for scholars to confront honestly, because scholarly reflection cannot force most Americans and other Westerners to engage willingly in introspection about these topics. Despite Los Angeles's burning twice since the 1960s, it has been more comfortable for social scientists to allow folk wisdom about assimilation, the culture of poverty, and democratic ideals to remain as intrusive ideologies and biases in their analyses than to face the music of what is really going on in the United States and other race-centered societies.[1]

The ideological and cultural biases that encumber social science research concerning race and ethnicity in the United States and indeed in other Western nations have made the issue of methodological adequacy quite problematic. Because confirmations based in folk wisdom have taken precedence over the pursuit of truth in this research area, it is not surprising to find that rules of procedure and evidence that usually apply to other less ideologically charged subfields are broken, bent, or ignored when ethnicity or race is the subject matter. There have been cases, such as Frazier's *The Negro Family in Chicago* (1932) and Wilson's *The Declining Significance of Race* (1978) and *The Truly Disadvantaged* (1987), in which race-related works have been rewarded professionally and in public culture more for their conformity to dominant ideologies than for any methodological adequacy. It has been instructive to observe how quickly the scholarship of Black conservative social scientists has been publicized and popularized in the 1980s and 1990s because of its anti-affirmative action and anti-civil rights tones, even though such works may have serious methodological flaws.

With all this said, there is a great need to begin to treat racial and ethnic studies as a serious area of inquiry, worthy of epistemological and theoretical reflection and innovation. When it comes to methodology as it relates to conceptualization and testing of concepts in real worlds, we have to begin to search for ways to make our tools relevant. The dramatically changing world in which we live demands that we cease to allow well-worn dogma to keep us from designing research projects that will provide the data necessary for the formulation of adequate explanations for the racial and ethnic dimensions of human life. If we do not do so, the social sciences in the United States and abroad will become increasingly marginal as ethnicity and race become increasingly dominant in the problems faced by U.S. society and the world in general.

What this implies is that if we can rethink traditional methodologies and revise them, and design and apply new ones, we will begin to see racial and ethnic matters as they really are. The pictures may not be pretty, but at least they will be telling the truth, and certainly that is what doing social science is supposed to be all about—telling the truth, even when it hurts pretty badly.

On the other hand, I should add, in some cases, the ideologies and cultural biases to which I allude have also on occasion prevented us from seeing or understanding social and cultural episodes that provide evidence that people are actually more plastic and fluid than we wish to believe. As much as U.S. social scientists have made interracial interaction into a human dilemma, we rarely develop the methodological tools to probe the countless cases of people who look different phenotypically and yet still get along and live their lives—marrying, having kids, engaging in work relationships, making friends—with no difficulty whatsoever. Indeed, given the race centeredness of this society, with its racially saturated media, political, economic, and educational systems, it is difficult if not impossible for many Americans to realize that race is problematic in human relations because it is made into an issue, not because it is a natural bone of contention and source of tension. That most American social scientists have a hard time understanding this can be seen in the fact that studies of prejudice and racism are much more pervasive than studies of interracial harmony in race relations research. We ask more questions and record more observations to document patterns of intergroup dislike and discord than we do to document positive bonding and cooperation.

Given the climate of deepening conservatism that marked the 1980s and early 1990s, this negative trend in how we go about identifying and pursuing research questions may continue, because the study of racism and racial conflict has an expanding market. In a race-centered society such as that in the United States, with a mass consumer culture, images of whites and Blacks throwing stones at each other in print and on television are a more profitable commodity than images of whites and Blacks hugging and kissing each other.

The chapters that follow represent what I hope is the beginning of a much-needed effort to address seriously the issue of how to improve the methodological basis of research into race and ethnicity. The contributing researchers were selected from three different methodological spheres: qualitative, quantitative, and historical/comparative. Each was asked to lay out the traditional parameters of a methodology used in social science research, to discuss how it has been applied to race and ethnic studies, and to suggest how the methodology could be improved. Each contributor was asked to concentrate as much as possible on the epistemological and theoretical aspects of the methodology he or she discusses. As in any anthology, there is some unevenness in the achievement of the goals laid out for the contributors. However, generally speaking, the mission of bringing together a thoughtful group of scholars to stimulate further, more comprehensive discussion on the methodological reflections in racial and ethnic research was accomplished.

Rather than offering descriptive overviews of each chapter here, I believe it would be more instructive to use the essays to develop an inferential grounded theory (Glaser & Strauss, 1967) of sorts regarding methodological reflections on race and ethnic research. This is one more advantage of organizing the essays into three methodological spheres, qualitative, quantitative, and historical/comparative. Discussing such a grounded theory of methodology will be useful because it will help to fill in the conceptual and substantive gaps in this volume as well as place points made by the contributors in proper perspectives and contexts.

As in any social science subfield, in racial and ethnic research methodological issues include concerns about researchers and their interactions with human beings (subjects) under investigation. In qualitative studies, the researcher is recognized as being the data collection instrument, as the ethnographer, participant observer, content analyzer, or oral history interviewer. Because subjective experiences constitute the paramount data to be extracted from human beings under study, effective qualitative researchers spend much of their time worrying about rapport with subjects and the impacts their values have on the research process. These worries are written up in personal experience terms.

The personal experience focus in qualitative research is particularly problematic in racial and ethnic research. In a race-centered society, it is not surprising to find that, historically, Euro-Americans have constructed the rules of procedure and of evidence. Thus, even though there are classical cases of, say, Afro-Americans doing participant observation studies, the ethos guiding how they collect experiential data and interpret those data is rooted in Eurocentric hegemony. But, that aside, there is the basic question of whether or not Euro-Americans can penetrate the intersubjectivity of people of color and, if so, what strategies they should follow to minimize inevitable biases flowing from being reared in a different, dominant racial or ethnic population. In Chapter 3, Margaret Andersen attempts to address this most important question.

Rutledge Dennis (Chapter 4) and Elisa Facio (Chapter 5) remind us of an important footnote to Andersen's observations and suggestions regarding the problems and prospects involved in the practice of members of the racially dominant group doing experience-based research on those in racially subordinate populations. Namely, what do we do about the class as well as racial hegemony that marks the ideological and institutional characteristics of the social sciences? The dilemma of outsiders studying "the Others" does not stop at the threshold of research projects involving the racially dominant attempting to pierce the cultural and social veil of the racially subordinate. It also involves the perplexing fact that, given their credentials and the norms of professional community membership, researchers of color who study their own communities are also outsiders, owing to the class divide. The class gap between the researcher of color and subjects of color, who are more than likely poor as well as racially oppressed, is a particularly touchy issue for those who view themselves as liberators of the oppressed.

Of course, quantitative and comparative/historical researchers are also concerned about their relationships with human subjects, although in ways different from qualitative researchers. In the quantitative social research literature, there is a vast logic of inquiry and technical store of knowledge about designing questionnaires and strategies for interviewing, drawing samples, and using secondary data sets. Most of this literature grapples with issues concerning interaction with subjects, randomization of data collection, and data analysis; little of it explores the role of researchers' life histories in the shaping of research designs. In fact, it is presumed that surveys, census reports, and other sources of statistical data yield objective results if the researcher follows certain technical procedures. Seldom are issues raised about the human faces and consciousness behind the development of such methodological tools and their outcomes (such as statistical tables). Carole Marks (Chapter 8) and A. Wade Smith (Chapter 11) remind us in their unique ways of the importance of putting human faces on demographic and survey approaches to the study of Afro-Americans. Both methodologies tend to minimize the relevance of people of color in developing generalizable conclusions about the character of American society.

The human, that is, the cultural, basis of quantitative methodologies and their intellectual products is the root of numerous controversies in the social sciences. Critical historians of social science, for instance, argue that the use of IQ and Eurocentric standardized test scores represents a pseudoscientific effort to concoct statistical arguments that justify the sorting out and stratifying of populations along racial lines. Chapter 10, by James Patton, is an interesting attempt to demonstrate how culturally sensitive methods of testing can be valuable for identifying gifted Afro-American youngsters. In reading his arguments, one is reminded of the great need for comprehensive research on how the consciousness and interests of quantitative researchers produce culturally biased methodological tools and outcomes hidden behind the guise of objective data presentation.

In Chapter 9, Samuel Myers brings to the table another important Pandora's box. Fashions in quantitative research, and their applications, are not only culturally derived but may also be premised on obsolete worldviews. Many assumptions about race relations built into law and public policies during the 1960s and 1970s were certainly not all that adequate. What has aggravated the matter is that legalized conceptions of what racial discrimination is and eradication strategies have not kept up with relatively recent societal shifts. There are, simply, new forms of racial discrimination, and there must be new ways to measure and quantify it. More than that, we should realize that the original legalized concept of racial discrimination has fatal flaws that make suspect what has been measured and quantified by government formulas and institutional standards. To understand why, we must come to terms with the life histories of the personalities responsible for constructing the legalized concepts of institutional racial discrimination.

Historical/comparative researchers remind us how ethnocentric and ahistorical American social sciences are. The traditions in the racial and ethnic subfield do not deviate from such intellectual trends. Sociologists and other social scientists investigating issues in Western industrial countries have become more historical and comparative, but this work has been done more in the area of Eurocentric class analysis than in investigating ethnic and especially racial issues. Thus most research in the areas of ethnicity and race, particularly that done in and about the United States, has yet to be grounded in sophisticated notions of historical process and is centered on singular cases with no domestic or cross-national comparative perspective. This is why the contributions to this volume of Duane Champagne (Chapter 12) and Charles Ragin and Jeremy Hein (Chapter 13) are so crucial; they help us think about the value of comparative and historical analyses in theorizing about racial and ethnic issues and trends.

There are two matters that cut across the various methodological spheres, and these are addressed in one way or another by most of the contributors: discourse problems, and data validity and reliability. I will conclude here with third and fourth matters that are not discussed as extensively but deserve at least brief mention: ethics and human values, and the creation of new epistemologies. How elites talk and write in race-centered societies, as Teun van Dijk informs us in Chapter 6, certainly has a profound role in reproducing the racial order of things. Social science discourse involves an elite way of talking and writing that in race-centered societies creates public images of the dominant and of the oppressed that appear to be objective and value free. In qualitative research, the leeway given to subjects to speak their minds, to speak from their hearts, is translated and reproduced in the language of the academic elite, and so are the rough notes of the ethnographer in the field. In quantitative research, the reproduction of the low status of the racially oppressed is even more brutal in the transformation of human beings into manipulated statistical categories. And as much as historical/comparative researchers attempt to reach across cultures and societies, they still have the problem of having to return to home base—researchers must report their findings using professional discourse styles that are understood and rewarded by their peers.

Writing in the discourse style of the racially oppressed is viewed as unprofessional, as popular literature. This is tragic, because the conservative character of professional jargon, particularly about racial issues, often stifles if not outright destroys the passion that is an important element for understanding the complex depths of race, racism, ethnicity, and ethnocentrism. It is no wonder that during the course of this century, during the rise of the modern social sciences, many of the most important, sobering analyses of racism have been written by journalists and novelists, such as Carl Sandburg, Richard Wright, Ralph Ellison, Terry Wallace, James Weldon Johnson, Toni Morrison, James Baldwin, and Studs Terkel. One often forgets that the most influential race relations statements made by William E. B. Du Bois, Zora Neale Hurston, and Robert E. Park were found in their literary work rather than in their empirical scientific research. (We forget, for instance, that Du Bois's double consciousness concept was a literary construct in *The Souls of Black Folk* [1903/1961], not an empirically tested phenomenon.) Meanwhile, through the generations, the voices of critical-minded professional social scientists studying race relations continue to be compared to journalistic and literary accounts, hesitant utterings edited by conservative communal norms.

As I argue in Chapter 14 of this volume, no matter what the methodology is, data validity and reliability are crucial issues, although in different ways. This point is especially important in race and ethnicity research for the reasons given at the beginning of this essay. That is, the ideological intrusions and cultural biases that have shaped the development of the racial and ethnic studies field have made data validity and reliability questions quite problematic and controversial. If the field is going to become more than a dumping ground for ideological displays disguised as scientific reasoning, there is a great need to reflect on how to confront data validity and reliability problems honestly. Meanwhile, we continue not to check our cultural biases, to base data interpretations on obsolete worldviews, and to design studies with no historical grounding or comparative dimension. As a result, we continue to produce soothing ideological rationales in the academy at the expense of increasing ignorance of a world in which the primacy of race and ethnicity, both in the organization of U.S. society and in the global community, is growing at an accelerating pace.

Problems and dilemmas in the areas of ethics and human values are also critical issues in research concerning race and ethnicity. It is not unusual to find historical and contemporary cases in which the human rights of racially oppressed and white immigrant subjects have been violated. The desecration of Indian graves in the advancement of anthropology and the use of the inner-city poor in public health research projects are merely two of the more blatant examples of the normative ways in which the humanity of people of color has been degraded in research processes. More than that, the exclusion of people of color, both as researchers and as subjects, from playing significant decision-making roles in research projects involving members of their racial/ethnic populations is legendary. The recent controversy over the decision-making composition of the National Academy of Science's group assigned to study the status of Black Americans echoes similar exclusionary practices that occurred in Myrdal's (1944) *An American Dilemma* project.

The routine ways in which people of color are excluded from significant decision-making roles in race and ethnicity research processes or are included on ideological rather than scholarly grounds have profound implications for the value of the produced knowledge. Such exclusionary and ideologically influenced (rather than scholarship-oriented) practices extend to elite professional social science journals and invisible colleges. One wonders, then, for instance, whether the absence of radical critiques of American racism (which go beyond vulgar economic reductionism and deal with touchy cultural and socialization issues) in the most prestigious American sociology journals is the result of the fact that there are no sociologists thinking and writing along those lines, or whether such scholars cannot get their work through the peer review process. My own experiences in professional associations, as well as conversations I have had with sociologists of color, convince me that the there is more than a grain of truth in the latter possibility (Stanfield, 1988). It has gotten to the point where sophisticated radical sociologists and other social scientists of color in the 1990s are forced to publish in either relatively marginal American professional journals or more accepting European professional journals, where leftist thinking is not viewed as deviant, as it is in much of the United States.

This issue of the cultural conservatism of American professional social science journals when it comes to racial and ethnic issues is an important point for another reason: It loops back to the discussion on discourse. Ironically, as elite American sociology and other social science journals continue to maintain peer review networks that exclude radical and otherwise critical discourses on ethnic and especially racial issues, the well-established fields of history, literature, and American studies are beginning to diversify their canons through publishing sobering accounts of American racism and ethnocentrism. Indeed, it is coming to the point where some of the best sociology of race is to be found in literature and history journals rather than in social science journals.

The exclusionary practices of academic social sciences along racial lines have maintained a cultural hegemony that has monopolized the construction and legitimation of methodological perspectives. The proof in the empirical pudding that the cultural hegemony I allude to exists is found in the textbook methodology literature. As a marginalized methodology, it is true that ethics and human values are discussed in the "how-to" ethnographic literature. But in the dominant quantitative mainstream, little attention is paid to well-institutionalized cultural biases in the construction of instruments, manipulation of secondary aggregate data, and construction of statistical tables and graphs. Raising such questions can prove to be dangerous political business, especially given the fact that the growth of large-scale quantitative research that includes racial and ethnic variables is proving to be a lucrative career path. But even as researchers who embrace such methodological perspectives become well published in the top journals and are otherwise rewarded by their professional colleagues, the disturbing question remains, given the cultural hegemonic biases of their aggregate data manipulations, are they really explaining anything all that relevant outside the walls of their cozy offices and computer labs? For instance, can we really learn something about the complexity of social stratification in the United States as a plural society when we drain the factor of subjective experiences of different populations and construct standardized statistical categories such as white and Black for making statistical comparisons and coming up with correlations? As I ask in Chapter 2, What are "whiteness" and "Blackness," anyway?

Historical/comparative research is not, of course, immune to ethical and human values considerations. Indeed, such research involves some very cumbersome and complex issues in the areas of ethics and human values. In historically grounded social science research in the race and ethnicity field, there is the problem of cultural biases dictating the selection of archival materials and other historical documents. In comparative research there is often the dilemma of language and cultural differences between the researcher and subjects. When comparative race and ethnicity research has a historical twist, questions of ethics and human values become even more bewildering.

Moving forward in racial and ethnic research requires more than reconsidering concepts and methodologies. Much more basically, we must begin to create new epistemologies to ground our theories and test them through methodological applications. By *epistemology,* I refer to the meaning of life and the physical environment that undergirds how we think and what we think about and how we interpret what we think about. Also, in terms of research, epistemology includes ethics, human values, and politics, involving how researchers structure relationships with collaborators and with subjects.

Perhaps the major epistemological revolution that must occur in racial and ethnic research in this country and in other Western nations is a transformation of the evolutionary arrogance that has impeded understanding of the normality of pluralism and cultural difference. Until that happens, no matter the theoretical or methodological perspective, race and ethnicity researchers will continue to pursue the wrong questions or incomplete questions about important issues, such as intergroup relations and the impact of social mobility on ethnic and racial identity (e.g., asking how mobility decreases racial identity rather than transforms it or pluralizes it within a given upwardly mobile subordinate racial population).

Further, as Margaret Andersen, Melvin Williams, and I point out in our epistemological reflections, researchers need to rethink their mundane acceptance of the autocratic power relations of the research process. Sharing knowledge and professional rewards with subjects of color, beyond symbolic gestures, should be viewed as enhancing rather than tarnishing the relevance of studying the institutions and communities of people of color. The more researchers of the 1990s and beyond view cross-cultural and cross-class research as a shared human experience rooted in mutual respect and empowerment, the more knowledge for the good of all will advance well beyond the usual rhetoric regarding the enlightened virtues of science.

I wish to thank Mitch Allen, Sage Publications executive editor, for patiently waiting for this manuscript. The contributors also should be commended for sticking with this endeavor, particularly during my long absence from this country. I extend special thanks to my coeditor Rutledge Dennis, who kept this project together during my absence and provided stimulating feedback during the final phases of manuscript preparation. Last but certainly not least, many thanks to my research assistants Crystal Lyles and especially Darlene O'Dell.

Note

1. In race-centered societies (Stanfield, 1991), races are created as social and cultural constructions and used as political weapons. Generations of societal residents are socialized into the belief that it is "natural" to assume that real or imagined phenotypic features predict values, personality, intellectual attributes, moral fiber, and leadership abilities. In this sense, race is not only a category but an organizing principle of everyday life, because it facilitates decision making in such matters as self-concept, concepts of others, residential choice, hiring and firing in labor markets, and selection of mates and friends.

2

Epistemological Considerations

JOHN H. STANFIELD II

Race and ethnic relations is a subfield that has been shaped greatly by political expediency and cultural ideologies (Ashley Montagu, 1952; Gossett, 1963; Gould, 1981; Hymes, 1972; Ladner, 1973; Rich, 1986; Stanfield, 1985). As a result, little systematic thought has been invested in epistemological questions concerning methodologies employed in race and ethnicity research. When epistemology has been explored it has usually been through the lenses of the mundane logical positivism that has grounded most race and ethnic relations research in American and European social sciences (Ladner, 1973; Rich, 1986).

This chapter addresses a fundamental question: What are some essential epistemological considerations that researchers in race and ethnic relations should take into account, regardless of methodological approaches? That is to say, whether researchers take a quantitative or a qualitative approach, there are certain epistemological universals in race and ethnic relations research that must be considered in the design and execution of research processes.

First is the question of category construction. Research in race and ethnicity is essentially inquiry into particular categories of humans. This point is worthy of emphasis, because quite frequently the construction of races and ethnic populations is a taken-for-granted attribute in social research. This operates on at least two levels. First, in race-centered societies such as the United States and other Western nations that dominate social science research production (Stanfield, 1991), citizens are socialized to view self and others in terms of race and ethnic categories. This is because, in general, everyday vocabulary is race saturated (Essed, 1991; van Dijk, 1987a). Race-saturated everyday language (verbal and nonverbal) reflects and determines how Americans describe themselves and others, especially others with distinctly different phenotypic attributes. Thus the tendency for descriptions of the phenotypically different other to be more socially intense, often negatively so, is the result of historical cultural traditions that encourage citizens to link phenotypic differences with presumptions about moral character, personality, interpersonal behavior, and intelligence.

We do not and should not expect social scientists to be any different from other citizens in having been socialized to accept race-laden assumptions about the nature of the world and human nature; social scientists and their disciplines are also products of a race-centered society. But the presumptuous embrace and utilization of such categories by social scientists generates a number of dilemmas. Perhaps the major one is that racial categorization in everyday life is usually overly simplistic. Given the highly race-centered content of dominant U.S. history, society, and culture, most Americans lack a sophisticated approach to the issue of race and racial categorization. For this reason, everyday terms such as *white* and *Black* actually have little empirical meaning, except in the most stereotypical ways. So, unless one is studying stereotypes, these terms have little utility for adding to our understanding of the complex empirical realities of populations that are socially constructed racial groups.

Few social scientists realize that the mundane racial categories they use in their research are actually grounded in folk beliefs derived from precolonial era thinking about the inherent superiority and inferiority of populations along phenotypic and genetic lines. Racialist thinking and categorization was, of course, at its height during the nineteenth century, when European and American enlightenment required explicit references to the nonhumanness of people of color to rationalize their oppression in the eras of human liberation movements. Progressively during the twentieth century, reputable anthropologists and biologists have demonstrated the fallacies in categorizing human populations along racial lines, especially when such categorization has been linked to presumptuous predictions of human qualities and character. Nevertheless, there is a significant discrepancy between what the reputable world of the human sciences knows about the mythologies of racial categorization and how societal members are socialized into self-concepts and into concepts of others.

Second, on a more technical level, social researchers have tended to treat race categorization data as unproblematic. While qualitative researchers record subjects' experiences of feeling or being white or Black or of some other racial categorization, quantitative researchers embrace uncritically the statistical categories derived from government documents and survey coding. In qualitative research, to construct meanings of "whiteness" or "Blackness" is to interpret interview or observational data, usually drawn from subjects who have been well socialized into the racial norms of society. One norm is the assumption that everyone in America has a racial identity. It is either objective, as seen in phenotypic attributes, or subjective, in terms of self-admission. From census interviews to job applications to school reports to affirmative action reporting, Americans are bombarded with presumptions about their racial identifications. The media and schools teach racial categorization through visual and written language.

Thus the qualitative researcher who encounters an informant with no racial identity experiences difficulty, because racelessness has no meaningful category in American experience. Quantitative researchers have yet to construct raceless statistical categories.

Another problem is that researchers, no matter their methodological orientations, have no way of distinguishing whether an informant's expressed racial identification is a response to objectified categorization derived from learning experiences in a race-saturated society or merely a subjective admission. Besides the basic problem of categorization as a social and political construct, the dilemma of possibly confusing objective and subjective racial identifications is one of the major perplexities of census data. Furthermore, there is the historical problem of census takers who actually select racial identifications for respondents. The problems inherent in that approach to data gathering are too obvious for me to take up space and time discussing them here.

The point of the above discussion is that social categorization along racial lines is an American norm that prevents needed epistemological and theoretical questioning regarding the nature of identity and consciousness in race-centered societies. The vast majority of literature on racially defined populations in the United States is rooted in taken-for-granted objectified conceptions of racial identity. This has resulted in a number of fallacies in the meaning of racial group membership that have functioned more to legitimate ideologies regarding objectified notions of racial differences than to offer accurate empirical evidence regarding the complexities of human identity in race-centered societies.

I will discuss two of these fallacies: the fallacy of homogeneity and the fallacy of monolithic identity.

The Fallacy of Homogeneity

The historic race relations literature in the social sciences and humanities is dominated by homogeneous examinations of people of color. Terms such as *Afro-American, Latino,* and *Indian* connote internal sameness. This tradition flows from the Afro-American model that has influenced the construction of cultural lenses through which social scientists and humanists have viewed people of color. Recently, as a result of the writings of Latino and Native American scholars who are reinterpreting their cultural heritages and the rise of the new cultural diversity emphasis in literature and in history, the homogeneity fallacy has begun to erode.

There is still much work to be done, however, not only in exploring the present and future phases of the new American pluralism but also in reinterpreting classical texts and traditional data sources that have produced a conventional literature on people of color that includes homogeneous interpretations. For instance, take the historic Afro-American communities literature in sociology, which includes seminal works by Du Bois (Blackwell & Janowitz, 1974), Frazier (1932, 1939, 1949a, 1949b), Drake and Cayton (1945), Johnson (1934), Park (1950), and Myrdal (1944). With the exception of class distinctions, this classical community studies literature does little to draw analytical status distinctions (for instance, gender, ethnoregionism, age, and, especially, ethnic differences) among Afro-Americans.

The absence of ethnic differentiation in this literature has more to do with the cultural assimilationist worldviews of pre-World War II prominent sociologists of Afro-American experiences than the empirical realities of Afro-American social life. A reexamination of even the slave narrative literature with a critical cultural eye would reveal the presence of ethnic differences among slaves based upon their tribal backgrounds, their status histories in such backgrounds, and their experiences on different plantations (E. T. Thompson, 1975) and in urban settings as spheres of acculturation and sociocultural diversification.

The migration of southern Black folks to northern cities prior to World War II was not merely an economic or sociological process of community formation. It was also a complex cultural process involving the synthesis of Afro-Americans from similar and different ethnoregional backgrounds, creating new forms of institutions and transforming old ones (Marks, 1989). As obvious as this observation may seem in the new diversity studies in history and literature, the presence of historical ethnic distinctions in Afro-American communities is still a novelty yet to be entertained in American sociology and other social sciences.

From this vantage point, for instance, one is hard pressed to consider Drake and Cayton's (1945) *Black Metropolis* as a complete or final analysis of urbanizing Afro-American experiences in Chicago. One wonders where ethnoregionism and Caribbean immigration fit into the neat status categories and institutional analyses of Bronzeville. The same can be said regarding Frazier's (1957) *Black Bourgeoisie*. What were the class and Black immigrant effects on the formation of the values and identity of Frazier's new Black middle class? At most, Frazier discusses the intricate issue of ethnoregionism in terms of the intergenerational absorption of prosperous southern migrants into old Afro-American families or the displacement of such first families by new arrivals.

Frazier's evolutionary and assimilationist frame of reference pre-vented him from considering how and why certain kinds of Black ethnoregional experiences and other Black ethnic experiences derived from Caribbean and African experiences created class values and tradi-tions that made so many members of the Afro-American middle class fit into the genre of Veblen's (1927) American leisure class. This point has some degree of relevance when we consider the data available in many major Afro-American communities in the form of biographies, narratives, newspapers, voluntary association records, oral traditions, and school records that document the invidious differences of being from rural Georgia or rural Alabama and from Kingston or Lagos and sociological consequences such as the formation of community-based institutions, status systems, and traditions when Black migrants from different places arrive and settle in the same geographical space.

I am reminded of a fascinating passage in Kwame Nkrumah's auto-biography that chronicles his arrival in New York City from Ghana in 1935 to attend college at Lincoln University in Pennsylvania. The first president of Ghana recalls:

I knew nobody in New York but had been corresponding with a Sierra Leonean who had graduated from Lincoln University. He was not expecting me so I called a taxi and directed the driver to the address in Harlem that he had given me in his last letter. Luckily he was in and he made me very welcome. I felt immediately at home in Harlem and sometimes found it difficult to believe this was not Accra. (Nkrumah, 1973, p. 24)[1]

The Fallacy of Monolithic Identity

An outgrowth of homogeneous descriptions of people of color in social sciences and humanities literature and in dominant public culture is the assumption that people of color have no differential identities. Certainly it is in keeping with racial stereotyping to assume that because someone looks a certain way he or she has X or Y identity characteristics. It has even been assumed in the literature that individuals or groups who deviate from objectified identities because of cultural or biological mixture are either marginal persons or in pathological identity crisis (Park, 1950). The possibility of a broad range of identities within populations of people of color that are healthy and well integrated is the antithesis of what dominant racial populations presume about people of color. In fact, the reproduction of a singular monolithic identity as objectified reality is a must if people of color are to remain oppressed second- and third-class citizens. To recognize that people of color have ranges of identities is to acknowledge their humanity in a way that is threatening to the status quo, in that it disturbs the social, political, and economic arrangements of the dominant group. This is why the most powerful dynamic of the movement led by the Reverend Martin Luther King, Jr., in the 1950s and 1960s was its demonstration to the American public through the mass media that Afro-Americans were not the one-dimensional, passive personalities portrayed in popular culture and in academic scholarship.

Identity questions—such as "What is a white person?" or "What is a Black person?"—become problematic when one considers the extensiveness of ethnic mixing that has occurred in the United States in reciprocal acculturation and cultural assimilation processes, if not in miscegenation experiences. It is difficult for many researchers to understand this point, because usually acculturation and assimilation are assumed to be asymmetrical processes involving subordinate populations' internalization of the cultural attributes of the dominant population (the "host society"). As distasteful as it may be for Euro-Americans or Afro-Americans who view themselves as racially and culturally "pure," more than 300 years of colonial and national development in the United

States has involved extensive cultural intermingling with conquered and enslaved subordinate populations. It may not be readily acknowledged, but the United States has always been dominated by a syncretic culture. It is only the power of denial embedded through socialization and mythological constructs such as the concept of a host society that have prevented most Americans, including social researchers, from seeing or understanding the rich syncretic flavor of dominant American culture.

This observation does great injury to conventional concepts of race-based identities even when such identities are self-reported. This is because few Americans are actually taught what they really are, in terms of cultural composition. This is especially the case for those in the dominant population whose ancestors include members of oppressed populations.

The two-tiered racial matrix in American society has also made identity issues problematic. Each person is supposedly *either* Euro-American or Afro-American, Euro-American or Asian, Euro-American or Latino. Where to place people from mixed backgrounds has always been a dilemma, both for keeping official records and for constructing everyday identity categories. The problem is exacerbated by the fact that what "mixed people" call themselves is a matter of choice and in many cases is dependent upon situation and historical circumstances. The self-identification of mixed persons can also be dependent upon life-cycle phases and regional and environmental locations. What all this means is that it is conceivable that the fluctuations in numbers of, say, "Blacks" and "whites" reported in the U.S. Census from decade to decade may actually be in some significant sense more a function of mixed persons' changing their racial identity declarations than of real increases and declines in population numbers.

The entire fascinating issue of mixed persons leads us into the matter of skin color and other phenotypic characteristics. Objective racial identity, in terms of counting populations officially and everyday inter-group interactions in the United States, is very much based on skin color. One is readily defined as an Afro-American if one has dark skin color, woolly hair, broad nose, and other particular physical characteristics. The problematic objective identity comes into play when the Afro-American's skin color is white and his or her other phenotypic features are those stereotypically associated with populations of European descent. This is, of course, the same when it comes to other people of color. As long as light skin color is associated with European descent, a person with light skin may "pass" for white.

We really have no way of knowing how many people of color who have white skins pass for Euro-American every year. We do know it happens, however, and that it is easy for some, especially in large cities and in regions of the United States that have no critical mass of the subordinate population the person passing is escaping from. There are also, of course, cases of, say, light-skinned Afro-Americans or Latinos who never reveal their identities to their children, who consequently grow up thinking they are Euro-American.

On the other extreme is the problem that those in many populations, particularly from southern Europe and Latin American and Puerto Rico, have experienced: being identified as and interacted with as Afro-Americans because of dark skin color. For this reason, years ago, dark-skinned Italians were forced to go to segregated Afro-American schools in the South. Many dark skinned Puerto Ricans and Cubans have long resented being mistaken for Afro-Americans and subsequently have gone out of their way to distance themselves from the archetype of American racial oppression by proclaiming loudly their Latino heritage.

Monolithic notions concerning the identities of people of color are further muddled if we consider the intricate influences correlated and convergent statuses have on identity formation in such populations. Class, gender, religion, age, region, and language in historically specific contexts all complicate "what identity is and means" for individual people of color. Although, as Marxists and feminists have demonstrated, there are certain experiences that bind members of status categories across racial categorizations, such as being poor or being women together, one should not forget the ways in which racial inequality and ethnic variation within constructed racial categories create identities that deviate greatly from the status norms students of class and gender articulate.

There is also, I should add, a danger of viewing white identity as a monolithic phenomenon. The Euro-American immigration literature, with its melting pot emphasis, at most considers ethnic diversity among whites as a temporary phase prior to inevitable assimilation. In contrast to the literature on involuntary and voluntary immigrants of color, studies of Euro-American immigrants acknowledge the cultural contributions of white immigrants to "mainstream culture" much more readily. Nevertheless, at least in race and ethnicity studies, there is a tendency to view white identity in a monolithic fashion. Phrases such as *white racism* and *white people* beg the bewildering question, Which white people?

This point is important, because when identity problems are dealt with in the race and ethnicity field as experiential phenomena, they usually concern people of color—the racially oppressed. As in so many other social science fields, the powerless rather than the powerful have their heads examined. This observation is offered as constructive criticism of the new approaches to literary analysis and historical research, which are diversifying notions of identity only as far as they relate to the racially oppressed and not to the racially dominant.

The neglect of the collective and individual identities of Euro-Americans in race and ethnicity research discourages understanding of the sociological aspects of identity formation as an intergroup phenomenon. That is to say, racially dominant and subordinate populations both influence how both groups develop identity and consciousness. Indeed, this is the way in which the structures of multiracialism in race-centered societies are reproduced and transformed.

This is all offered as prelude to an intricate epistemological problem. How do we conceptualize identity issues in race and ethnicity research that go beyond reified, simplistic stereotyping? How do we use official data sources with care in exploring racial identity questions, realizing the problematics of aggregate data and the ill-defined circumstances of self-reporting versus actual self-identity? If we have to categorize people to understand who they are and how they define themselves, how do we do so in this area of research more in terms of self-definitions than in terms of what popular cultural folk wisdom dictates? How do we incorporate understanding in research designs regarding the interactional aspects of identity formation in dominant and subordinate populations that would make such considerations much more sociological?

Aside from the two fallacies discussed above, there are a host of other epistemological considerations in doing race and ethnicity research. Two major ones that come to mind concern comparative analysis and ethical concerns. The best social scientific work is comparative. This is because, whether we are trying to explain something about the world or to predict future trends and tendencies, our arguments are strongest when we are able to bring to the table evidence drawn from more than one case.

In race and ethnicity research, comparative analysis can go any number of ways, some more obvious than others. There are, of course, internal group comparisons, which explore similarities and differences across status and social organizational categories. External comparisons usually involve presenting data analyses that exemplify similarities and differences between comparable status categories of Euro-American samples and samples of people of color. Unfortunately, we do not have enough studies that examine comparisons and contrasts of status and social organizational issues across categories of people of color, because of styles of research that have become entrenched in the race and ethnicity field. Given the acceleration of the demographic coloring of America, such comparative studies involving categories of people of color are going to become critical research design considerations in future years.

Perhaps the race and ethnicity area requiring the most work is that of cross-national comparative studies. Except for the prospering international migration field, few race and ethnicity researchers conduct cross-national research. Indeed, as many scholars have noted, the study of race and ethnicity has tended to be nation bound in contexts such as the United States, Great Britain, France, and South Africa. The growing closeness of the global community requires that the national walls of race and ethnicity research be broken down. In many ways, ethnic bonds and their social organizational expressions (institutions, communities, languages, ecosystems, networks) have always mattered more than national boundaries, and certainly this is becoming truer by the day.

Ethics and Human Values

Issues of ethics and human values are central to any research enterprise. They are especially sensitive when it comes to status-related research. In race and ethnicity research, questions of ethics and values are especially prone to controversy, because race and ethnicity problems raise emotional concerns in the public cultures of race-centered societies. Researchers in mainstream disciplines rarely if ever reflect seriously on the effects their racial and ethnic identities and consciousness might have on what they see and interpret in race and ethnicity studies. It has been easier for researchers to rationalize and legitimate their logical positivistic claims by constructing supposedly value-neutral methods of data collection and interpretation than to acknowledge the intrusions of their life histories and cognitive styles in research processes in race and ethnicity studies.

It is for this reason that epistemological considerations in racial and ethnic research in the social sciences cannot be divorced from concerns regarding the functions of cultural hegemonic domination in knowledge production and dissemination and in the selection and rewarding of intellectual careers. For decades, white males and females have been viewed as the authoritative voices on racial and ethnic matters. Social scientists of color have found acceptance in their professional communities to the extent to which they have embraced status quo versions of empirical realities concerning racial and ethnic issues. It has been difficult, if not impossible, for scholars of color with truly radical, liberating views on racism and its eradication and on the validity of cultural difference as a normative human attribute in the industrial world to be heard, believed, and rewarded within academic communities and on the outside (Hymes, 1972; Ladner, 1973; Stanfield, 1988).

The persistence of white male authority in interpreting racial issues, particularly those of national significance, was more than apparent in who became the public experts in the aftermath of the 1992 Los Angeles riots. Although during the 1980s Black race experts from the left and the right were invented and promoted by the media and political institutions to fill a gap when discussions about race were unprofitable, all of a sudden we had a rash of white, usually male, race experts appearing out of nowhere to discuss the Los Angeles situation authoritatively. Even apparent Black giants such as William J. Wilson from the left and Thomas Sowell from the right were unceremoniously waved to the sidelines as white male authorities stepped forward to take center stage.

In social science graduate programs in the 1990s, there is still a movement toward the political right in what professors prefer to teach their future colleagues about race and ethnicity. The 1992 Los Angeles riots will probably encourage a greater shift to the right, because Americans have yet to demonstrate that they have mastered lessons of the 1950s and 1960s very well. In fact, if anything, the quickness with which the riots disappeared from the front pages and the prime-time talk shows of the national media indicates how indifferent, if not hostile, dominant cultural influentials are toward resolving daunting racial crises. More than that, we can point to the actual content of media coverage of the riot, which was obsessed with making good copy, getting sensational film footage, and conjuring up social stereotypes of rioters invented in the 1960s (such as creating the impression that the rioters were for the most part Black, solely responding to the "white racist" motivations behind the not-guilty verdicts in the trial of four Los Angeles police officers accused of beating Rodney King). In their efforts to commodify race as profitable product for mass consumption in the media marketplace, journalists in the most influential media did little to simply tell the truth. Nor did most try to encourage constructive discussion going beyond warmed-over arguments that were inadequate even in the 1960s, especially the "culture of poverty" explanations touted by politicians and by self- and media-anointed race experts.

All of this is tragically related to the value basis of race and ethnicity research. The failure of social scientists who dominate discourse in their disciplines to understand or care about the realities of racism beyond simplistic solutions from leftist or rightist perspectives has led to the continuation of a number of disturbing value biases in race and ethnicity studies. These value biases have greatly impeded the development of a clear understanding of the meaning of the United States as a pluralist society.

For instance, much of our thinking about race in the United States is rather obsolete, stemming mainly from turn-of-the-century evolutionary cognitive styles. These cognitive styles are apparent in the presumptions researchers often make regarding the imperatives of comparisons of whites and people of color and cultural standards of data generalization. For example, it has been viewed as both appropriate and normative for social researchers to select Euro-American populations or samples for discussion, with no or little regard for populations or samples made up of people of color. Too many studies are published claiming to be "American studies" that are rooted in white populations and samples, with, perhaps, short notes explaining the reasons for excluding people of color, whose presence in the study would just complicate the analysis (I am not referring to studies of topics in which people of color are statistical rarities).

On the other hand, it has been commonplace for scholars, particularly scholars of color, to be criticized for conducting studies with no comparative white samples or populations. The subtle evolutionary presumptions underlying such criticism are more than apparent: People of color in many social science circles are not relevant enough to stand on their own two feet in analysis; unless they are compared with whites, they have no value in important social science circles.

Cultural standards of data generalization are the basis of researcher presumptions regarding the racial or ethnic population source of constructing universal statements. It has always been the norm in the social sciences to assume that Eurocentric empirical realities can be generalized to explain the realities of people of color. In most presumptuous fashion, for decades, researchers steeped in Eurocentric norms have applied Eurocentric concepts of families, deviance, social movements, psychological development, organizational behavior, stratification, and even spirituality to the experiences of people of color. This has occurred to such an extent that our social science knowledge of the indigenous senses of people of color is actually quite sparse and superficial.

Intellectual movements that claim to use indigenous logics of inquiry, such as Afrocentrism, have, with very few exceptions, actually romanticized more than empirically studied the realities of indigenous peoples of color. Indeed, it is important to keep in mind that the major inroads Afrocentric reasoning has made in academic circles have been more in the humanities and history rather than in the social sciences. In the humanities and history, it has been legitimate and important to raise Afrocentric issues regarding meaning as a diverse experience in fiction, art, narrative, and music. But such inquiries do not need to be subjected to rigorous tests of empirical relevance to be acceptable in professional humanistic communities.

It is interesting that the situation opposite to that noted above is a nonissue in social science inquiry. That is to say, the realities of people of color are never considered as legitimate standards of generalization to Eurocentric realities. Imagine having a social science with cultural standards of generalization that encourage researchers to apply what they have found in the process of studying Afro-Americans to white populations. Unfortunately, this is not viewed as a legitimate rule in cultural standards of generalization. But the thought does bring to mind instances in social scientific research in which the researcher meant his or her empirical findings among a sample or population made up of people of color to be generalizable to "Americans," only to have the study pigeonholed as, say, "Afro-American research."

Whatever the researchers' motives, it is rare for mainstream scholars to select empirical observations about people of color, such as female-headed family structure or religious behavior, to explain Eurocentric realities, although it has been instructive to watch researchers relabel the "deviant and pathological" patterns of the poor and of people of color and normalize such trends when they become dominant middle-class Euro-American patterns. For instance, during the past 20 years, as an increasing number of professional Euro-American women have chosen to have children out of wedlock and are experiencing divorce in record numbers, scholars have begun to discuss "alternative family structures." Meanwhile, poor Afro-American single mothers are still viewed as moral and social problems, with broken homes and children fathered by a multitude of males. As uneasy as it may make family researchers feel, there is actually a great deal to be learned about alternative family structures by investigating such family patterns in Afro-American communities rather than pretending, intentionally or unintentionally, to create a completely new field of inquiry.

On the paradoxical other hand, there is also the dilemma of the work of scholars of color being shrugged off as mediocre or otherwise irrelevant as a defense mechanism exhibited by those who wish not to acknowledge the importance of the empirical findings or claims of these researchers. After all, once again, the study of ethnicity, and especially of race, is a highly controversial enterprise that runs up against Baconian idols of the mind or Freudian cultural taboos if empirical observations are thought to be stepping on tender toes. One defense mechanism is the claim that whatever is found is found among all groups, including whites. Thus the response to the claims the researcher is advancing is often, So what?

This is precisely what happened to E. Franklin Frazier when his *Black Bourgeoisie* was translated from French to English in the late 1950s, only to be attacked by insulted middle-class Afro-Americans and sympathetic Euro-American liberals. Frazier, who was surprised by the force of the initial negative emotional public response to *Black Bourgeoisie*, attempted to head off the typical defensive response some reviewers used to minimize the importance of his findings, which he felt did not warrant a comparative white sample. He wrote this shortly before his death (this quote also nicely sums up several points I made earlier):

Another criticism which deserves attention was that this study did not reveal anything peculiar to Negroes. This was a criticism offered not only by Negroes who are sensitive about being different from other people, but by white people as well. Some of them were the so-called liberal whites who, when any statement is made which might be considered derogatory concerning Negroes, are quick to say that the "same thing is found among whites." Other whites pointed out what is undoubtedly true: that this book dealt with behavior which is characteristic of middle-class people—white, black, or brown. Some of my Jewish friends, including some young sociologists, went so far as to say that the book was the best account that they had ever read concerning middle-class Jews. Here I might repeat what I stated in the book: that the behavior of middle-class Negroes was an American phenomenon, and that in writing I was tempted to make comparisons with middle-class whites, but that the book was essentially a case study of the new Negro middle class. It was not my intention to make a comparative study. As a case study of middle-class Negroes, it does show the peculiar conditions under which a middle class emerged among the Negro minority and the peculiar social and cultural heritage of the Negro middle class which was responsible for its outlook on life. (Frazier, 1964, p. 310)

The presumptions in the American social sciences regarding the imperatives of comparing the experiences of whites and people of color and Eurocentric cultural standards of generalization and interpretation are value biases embedded in evolutionary epistemologies regarding racial relevance and irrelevance. They remind us of the folly of divorcing logic of inquiry and explaining from the hegemonic cultural politics that shape knowledge articulation in what only appear to be value-free social sciences.

Questions regarding human values in social research and their political functions are among the many ethical considerations in the structuring and operations of research processes. By *ethical considerations,* I mean the moral questions and dilemmas that may or may not be thought about regarding researcher treatment of human subjects. Although scandals in social science during the past 20 years have forced some degree of government and academic regulation of the treatment of human subjects, certain areas of social research have become such lucrative sources of career enhancement and life-style aggrandizement that the business of disrespecting the rights of subjects goes on as usual. This is especially the case in research on poor people in which subjects receive services in return for consenting to be part of a research study or clinical practice for budding professionals. In such cases, if subjects want needed medical services, they must cooperate. Such abuse of human subjects is what I call legal unethical behavior, because although it may pass the standards set by university human subjects committees, it still involves taking advantage of the marginal resources and communities of the poor by developing exploitative exchange relationships— the exposure of their bodies before strangers, for instance, in exchange for free access to inner-city teaching hospital clinics.

Needless to say, the moral dilemmas in race and ethnicity research are numerous. Much research on people of color has been based on researchers' asking subjects ridiculous or embarrassing questions that the researcher would never answer him- or herself and certainly would not ask his or her own relatives, friends, or colleagues. There is a disturbing naïveté in the folklore of Eurocentric social science that people of color are stupid, that they cannot process what the researcher is really trying to say, and that they do not realize they are being used. There is also the absurd presumption that because people of color smile easily and allow researchers into their homes and communities readily (at least they used to), it is easy to gain access to the lives and minds of these subjects. It has rarely occurred to many researchers, owing to the arrogance that their status and craft have encouraged, that there is a possibility that not a few people of color merely have different, more subtle ways of deceiving strangers and holding back information. Many researchers would be surprised, if not angry, if they could see the Afro-American respondents who so politely answered their questions and then kindly closed the door after them, only to have a good laugh. Or consider the anthropologist in the African village who writes a great book and becomes *the authority* based upon data generously given to him or her by the natives, not because they were gullible, but because they enjoyed the researcher's gifts or because saying no or disagreeing is not tolerated in certain African cultures.

In thinking about the epistemology of ethical considerations in research on people of color, the cultural and/or class and/or gender differences between researchers and subjects requires special sensitivity about the discrepancies in moral character between researchers and subjects. Rarely do researchers consider the fact that ethnically and especially phenotypically different subjects are moral beings just like themselves, and that subjects' moral character is quite different from their own if there are noticeable gender, cultural, and class gaps (one can argue that the class gap is a constant, given the professional status of the researcher, regardless of gender or racial/ethnic background or consciousness).

There is another moral issue seldom addressed in social science research that is distinctly pertinent when applied to race and ethnicity research; namely, the research processes of the social sciences involve power relationships between dominant (researcher) and subordinate (subject) parties that can be studied empirically, like any other form of social inequality. Defining the research processes of the social sciences as involving power relationships raises a number of intriguing questions that have been addressed at most in piecemeal, technical ways. For one thing, as alluded to, we can learn a great deal about structuring research processes in the social sciences through considering the literatures on social oppression. Particularly useful are studies addressing the complex issues of the cultural and political nature of domination and subordination, the cultural stereotyping of the dominant and the subordinate in the structuring of relationships, and the politics and sociology of exclusion and marginalization in relationships between the dominant and the subordinate.

Second, both the dominant (researcher) and the subordinate (subject) have human rights that can be recognized totally, selectively, or not at all. Usually what happens is that the researcher recognizes and exercises his or her human rights, usually defined in academic freedom and professional credentials terms, whereas the human rights of subjects are at best defined in the bureaucratic guidelines of academic institutions and funding sources. Human subjects and/or the populations they represent have rarely been consulted or, better yet, included in the decision-making processes that produce guidelines for research on human subjects. This tendency for researchers and their institutional sponsors to define the human rights of subjects is indicative of the hegemonic power relationships that undergird research processes.

From this perspective, research in the social sciences is one of the last areas in U.S. society in which social inequality is treated as a given. It is assumed that researchers have expertise that is beyond the comprehension of those they study. This may be true in some cases, such as in research involving infants or adults who have lost their capacity to communicate. For the most part, however, social scientists have tended to be quite protective of their privilege in designing research processes. It is often too threatening to include in this process human subjects who may call into question the theoretical assumptions or methodological strategies of the researcher. When it comes to doing research in communities surrounding a university, there is always the fear that human subjects will raise questions regarding the right of the researcher to enter the community. This is especially problematic in cities where relationships are tense between the local communities and an aloof university.

My comments on applied ethics may seem utopian to some, but I believe strongly that if the social sciences are going to be of any relevance in the next century, their human creators and maintainers must democratize how they structure, interpret, and distribute their work. This involves understanding the complex structure of research processes in terms of who is involved and the ways in which their rights must be protected. This liberation of research processes also requires the breakdown of and breaking away from status barriers that more often than not prevent scientific work from being defined, carried out, and distributed adequately. This is especially the case in research involving culturally different researchers and subjects.

Unless we find adequate ways of liberating the research processes in the social sciences, there will be mounting public questioning of the relevance of scientific inquiry, especially from the empowering institutions and communities of people of color in the United States and abroad. No longer can social scientists hide behind the ivy-covered walls of academia and their research laboratories, assuming they can study whomever they want to, whenever they please.

The changing ethnic demographics of the United States and the politicization of various groups are making it more than apparent that the arrogant manner in which dominant human scientific research has been done in the past will not be tolerated in the future. Already there is growing resistance in nonwhite American communities as well as in the Third World toward the dominant research approach, which tends to confer hegemonic authority on the researcher and offers human subjects only a few symbolic crumbs.

Conclusion

This essay on epistemological considerations has been premised on a number of assumptions worthy of review. First, logics of inquiry are cultural and political constructs. Thus the study of methodology must begin with questions concerning the life histories of researchers and the embedded norms, values, and beliefs of the institutions, communities, and movements they build, stabilize, and transform

This approach to the study of methodology is especially important when we consider the history of race and ethnicity as a field of study. This is because, no matter the logic of inquiry preference or its technical capabilities, researchers who engage in racial and ethnic studies are involved in a highly controversial venture. For decades, much potential sobering knowledge about racial and ethnic issues has been either lost or distorted because researchers have failed to reflect on the implications of their life histories and cultural backgrounds as ideological intrusions in this emotion-laden field of study.

Second, when we examine the production of race and ethnicity research in disciplines originating in race-centered society from the critical cultural studies perspective, it becomes apparent that much of our thinking about race and ethnicity is convoluted and otherwise blurred by ideological intrusions encouraging the use of folklore in collecting and interpreting data. The use of homogeneous and, I should add, reified terms such as *white* and *Black* buys into and indeed reproduces traditional racial stereotypes more than it facilitates adequate data collection and interpretation. The survival of evolutionary cognitive styles in the mundane levels of paradigm formation in race and ethnic studies prevents sophisticated understanding of the formation of structures and the structuring of processes in plural societies. Evolutionary cognitive styles have inhibited the asking of interesting and important questions regarding the historical and contemporaneous influences people of color have had in shaping dominant U.S. culture and society as well as their own indigenous life worlds. More than that, well-entrenched evolutionary cognitive styles have legitimated logics of inquiry that only appear to be scientific. If we understand science to be the pursuit of tight fits between concepts or conceptual systems and empirical realities, then evolutionary cognitive presumptions such as asymmetrical generalizations from ethnically and racially dominant experiences to those of the ethnically and racially subordinate impede the development of scientifically adequate explanation in racial and ethnic studies. In fact, the acts of imposing the experiences of the dominant on the subordinate as a logic for explaining their attributes and ignoring the relevance of subordinate experiences for explaining those of the dominant extend the parameters of folk racial ideologies in society more than do advances in scientific knowledge production.

The political sensitivity of racial and ethnic issues has resulted in a host of ethical problems. This is because in race-centered societies there has been a long history of disregarding the humanity of the racially oppressed and ostracized ethnics that has encouraged the routinization of human rights abuses in the use of such populations as research subjects. Also, career-making authority relations in social science disciplines in general and especially in racial and ethnic studies have made it difficult for people of color to compete successfully for authoritative voices in defining what research is and is not and setting the rules of evidence and debate. At most, people of color who have been anointed in social science fields as significant men and women have been loyal to the political right, left, or middle among the accepted community of scholars. As the roles of such "foot soldiers" are essentially those of tokens, and they serve to legitimate the dominant cultural views of their Eurocentric disciplinary establishments, their truncated prestige is based on their producing group-specific knowledge presumed to have little or no relevance for more general human nature issues. Thus, for cultural consumption purposes in academic and public marketplaces of ideas, what these foot soldiers have to say is neatly packaged in race relations statements, usually confined to race-specific sessions in professional meetings, racial topics on talk shows, and textbook chapters on race issues. Their historical immortality is defined in racial terms, as when Frazier is described as "the great *Black* sociologist who was famous for his studies on *Black* people" (as opposed to the more general portrait of Frazier as a brilliant student of American class stratification and of gender and family studies).

Whether a social scientist examining racial and ethnic issues prefers quantitative or qualitative methodological approaches or a combination of both ("triangulation"), there are daunting epistemological problems that he or she needs to think through. The critical historical period we have entered requires that we reexamine what has been taken for granted in racial and ethnic studies. Although the racial and ethnic studies field has always been afflicted with a host of epistemological difficulties, this is even more the case today. The radical changes in this country and in world society require that we not only critique traditional epistemological assumptions that have always been suspect but establish new ones that would encourage refreshing and more adequate logics of inquiry.

For instance, there is a great need for epistemological traditions such as participatory research strategies that would assist research subjects in improving their quality of life, as opposed to the impersonal, exploitive conventions of logical positivism. As another example, relativistic and pluralistic meanings of cultural difference, rather than evolutionary meanings, would encourage more complex research into how populations in their various stratified positions come to create, maintain, and change a society through reciprocal processes of interaction and separation.

If the problem of the twentieth century has been, as Du Bois put it, the problem of the color line, the problem of the next century will be the deepening complexities and contradictions of that color line. This observation cannot be appreciated until we pour new wine into new bottles through creating new ways of thinking and explaining a new world; this can best occur if we revolutionize the epistemological considerations of racial and ethnic studies and the social sciences in general.

Note

1. It is no wonder that a few pages later, Nkrumah (1973) remarks while reflecting on his academic experiences in the United States in the late 1930s: "At that time I was interested in two sociological schools of thought in the States, one represented by the Howard Sociologists led by Professor Fraser [*sic*], and the other led by Dr. M. J. Herzkovits, Professor of Anthropology at Northwestern University. The Howard school of thought maintained that the Negro in America had completely lost his cultural contact with Africa and the other school, represented by Herzkovits, maintained that there were still African survivals in the United States and that the Negro of America had in no way lost his cultural contact with the African continent. I supported, and still support, the latter view and I went on one occasion to Howard University to defend it" (p. 36).

PART II

Qualitative Methods

3

Studying Across Difference

Race, Class, and Gender
in Qualitative Research

MARGARET L. ANDERSEN

Sociological studies of race have often been distorted by having been centered in the perspectives and experiences of dominant group members. This has resulted both from the exclusion of African American, Latino, and Native American people from the general frameworks of sociology and from the application of ethnocentric concepts to the study of racial-ethnic groups. As Ladner (1973), among others, points out:

> Blacks have always been measured against an alien set of norms. As a result they have been considered to be a deviation from the ambiguous white middle-class model, which itself has not always been clearly defined. This inability or refusal to deal with Blacks as a part and parcel of the varying historical and cultural contributions to the American scene has, perhaps, been the reason sociology has excluded the Black perspective from its widely accepted mainstream theories. (p. xxiii)

AUTHOR'S NOTE: An earlier version of this chapter was presented at the International Interdisciplinary Congress on Women, University College, Dublin, Ireland, July 1987. I would like to thank Maxine Baca Zinn, Sandra Harding, Peggy McIntosh, Howard Taylor, and Lynn Weber for their comments on an earlier draft.

Like its sister discipline, women's studies, Black studies seeks to build more inclusive research through incorporating the experiences and perspectives of traditionally excluded groups. One way to accomplish this has been to encourage studies of race and ethnic relations by minority scholars themselves, on the assumption that they are better able to understand the nuances of racial oppression. This assumption is best stated by Blauner and Wellman (1973):

> There are certain aspects of racial phenomena, however, that are particularly difficult, if not impossible, for a member of the oppressing group to grasp empirically and formulate conceptually. These barriers are existential and methodological as well as political and ethical. We refer here to the nuances of culture and group ethos; to the meaning of oppression and especially psychic relations; to what is called the Black, the Mexican-American, the Asian and the Indian experience. (p. 329)

Blauner and Wellman's argument underscores the point that research occurs in the context of power relationships, both between the researcher and research subjects and in the society at large. As they point out:

> Scientific research does not exist in a vacuum. Its theory and practice reflect the structure and values of society. In capitalist America, where massive inequalities in wealth and power exist between classes and racial groups, the processes of social research express both race and class oppression. The control, exploitation, and privilege that are generic components of social oppression exist in the relation of researchers to researched, even though their manifestations may be subtle and masked by professional ideologies. (pp. 314-315)

This position, largely articulated during the early 1970s in sociological writing, poses important questions about the social construction of knowledge about race and ethnic relations. Particularly, the question is raised: How can white scholars contribute to our understanding of the experiences of racial groups? Can dominant groups comprehend the experiences of outsiders and, if so, under what conditions and with which methodological practices?

Doing research in minority communities poses unique methodological problems for members of both minority and majority groups. Baca Zinn (1979), a Chicana sociologist, has described the methodological problems she faces when doing research on Chicano families. She directly acknowledges that her relationships with research subjects are never equal and that, as a researcher, she cannot alter the political context in which research takes place. She argues that minority scholars may generate questions that are different from those asked by majority group researchers. Minority scholars are also less likely to experience distrust, hostility, and exclusion within minority communities. At the same time, however, the accountability and commitment of minority scholars to the communities they study pose unique problems for their research practice. In a different context, Cannon, Higginbotham, and Leung (1988) have shown that qualitative studies are also easily biased by the greater willingness of white middle-class subjects to participate in research. Because dominant groups have less reason to expect they will be exploited by researchers, they are more likely to volunteer as research subjects.

The problems of doing research within minority communities are compounded by the social distance imposed by class and race relations when interviewers are white and middle-class and those being interviewed are not. For white scholars wanting to study race relations, these conclusions in the research literature are daunting. How can white scholars elicit an understanding of race relations as experienced by racial minorities? How can white scholars study those who have been historically subordinated without further producing sociological accounts distorted by the political economy of race, class, and gender?

John Gwaltney, a blind Black anthropologist who studied the experiences and beliefs of people in his hometown community, has written eloquently about the obstacles white researchers should expect when doing research in Black communities. The Black men and women he interviewed strongly expressed their mistrust of white social scientists. They reported, "I wouldn't want to talk to any anthropologist or sociologist or any of those others if they were white because whatever I said they would write down what they felt like, so I might just as well save my breath" (quoted in Gwaltney, 1980, p. xxv). Another said, "We know white folks but they do not know us, and that's just how the Lord planned the thing. . . . Now they are great ones for begging you to tell them what you really think. But you know, only a fool would really do that" (p. 102). Given these problems, how can white researchers study Black and Latino subjects or, for that matter, how can men study women? Although the focus in this chapter is on studying across racial differences, the theoretical discussion applies to the relationship between any dominant group researcher and his or her minority group subjects.

Feminist scholars have argued that members of subordinated groups have unique viewpoints on their own experiences and on the society as a whole. Known as standpoint theorists, these scholars argue that race, class, and gender are origins of, as well as objects of, sociological knowledge. According to this literature, a feminist standpoint is distinct from a perspective or bias because it "preserve[s] the presence of the active and experiencing subject" (D. E. Smith, 1987, p. 105). Standpoint theorists understand that researchers and their subjects are located in specific social-historical settings. Because there is a social relationship between researchers and their research subjects, research cannot be construed as a process of eliminating the presence of the researcher. Yet, the claim of objectivity often assumes that the researcher has no presence or that to be objective is to remove oneself from the situation at hand. Considering this argument, feminist standpoint theorists have argued that research must be seen in context. Politically engaged standpoints are not simply the result of biological identity. Rather, standpoints are achieved; they are not inherent in one's race, sex, or class. But how are such standpoints accomplished by dominant group members wanting to construct liberating knowledge about race, class, and gender relations?

Standpoint theorists argue that those who maintain an interest in reproducing racist and sexist relations are least able to see the social construction of race, class, and gender relations. Indeed, "there are some perspectives on society from which, however well-intentioned one may be, the real relations of humans with each other and with the natural world are not visible" (Hartsock, 1983, p. 285). Feminist standpoint theorists draw from Marxist theory the idea that material life structures and sets limits on the understanding of social relations; thus the vision of the ruling class, race, and gender is partial, because it not only structures the material relations in which all are forced to participate, but also takes for granted the labor, indeed the very existence, of oppressed groups.

Patricia Hill Collins (1986) argues that the marginality of Black feminist scholars gives them distinctive analyses of race, class, and gender. She sees Black feminist scholars as best generating Black feminist theory, but also suggests that all intellectuals can learn to read their personal and cultural biographies as significant sources of knowledge. As "outsiders within," Black feminist scholars use the tension in their cultural identities to generate new ways of seeing and new sociological insights. Likewise, majority group scholars can develop and utilize tensions in their own cultural identities to enable them to see different aspects of minority group experiences and to examine critically majority experiences and beliefs.

This understanding recasts earlier arguments that only minority scholars can produce knowledge about racial-ethnic groups. It suggests that white scholars doing research on race and ethnicity should examine self-consciously the influence of institutional racism and the way it shapes the formulation and development of their research, rather than assume a color-blind stance. This is a fundamentally different posture from that advocated by the norms of "unbiased, objective" scientific research, in which one typically denies the influence of one's own status (be it race, gender, class, or other social status) in the shaping of knowledge. It requires that we see ourselves as "situated in the action of our research" (Rapp, 1983), examining our own social location, not just that of those we study.

Elsewhere I have argued that white feminist scholars can transform their teaching and thinking through centering their thoughts in the experience of women of color (Andersen, 1988). Feminist scholarship has shown that moving previously excluded groups to the center of our research and teaching produces more representative accounts of society and culture. Building more inclusive ways of seeing requires scholars to take multiple views of their subjects, abandoning the idea that there is a singular reality that social science can discover. Minority group members have insights about and interpretations of their experiences that are likely different from those generated by white scholars. The question is not whether white scholars should write about or attempt to know the experience of people of color, but whether their interpretations should be taken to be the most authoritative (Hooks, 1989). Furthermore, how, in constructing sociological analyses, can dominant group members examine their own racial identities and challenge the societal system of racial stratification in which what they observe is situated?

The Setting

These issues are examined here in the context of a community study of race relations. In this study, I (a white scholar) wanted to know how changes in the political economy of race relations were experienced by African Americans in this community. What meaning do African Americans in this community give to their experience? And how do they define the class, race system in which they live? I studied a small community with a historically rigid racial division of labor and a history of paternalism persistently defining contemporary relations between whites and Blacks— hardly a social structure conducive to the trust and empathy desirable for building a sociological research project. I entered this project knowing the particular limitations that my own racial status would create.

The community is located on the Eastern Shore of Maryland—a peninsula on the eastern shore of the Chesapeake Bay. The community appears prosperous and alluring and in many ways seems to be an ideal American town. There is a central village green. Church spires are the highest points in the city skyscape, and the main street is dotted with chic boutiques. Those who walk on the streets seem to know each other; they stop to chat and, in their conversations, they inquire about each other's families and exchange news about others in town.

Because this is a waterfront community, it can also be approached by boat. On the shore, one sees expensive waterfront estates—so many of them that one might wonder how so many people became so rich. Many of these estates are invisible from land; from the bay, their long docks can be seen—many with multiple yacht slips. Sailboats fill the rivers and coves surrounding this town, and motor yachts twice the size of the average American home (and full of more than the usual amenities) are common. One of these yachts displays a flag at the bow: "He who dies with the most toys wins!"

Yet there is a dual reality here—one hidden in small, all-Black hamlets that do not, in many cases, even appear on the road maps and that do not front the bay waters, as do the privileged acres of the rich. The dual reality is perhaps no better described than by Frederick Douglass, himself a slave 150 years ago on the estate of Edward Lloyd, the Eastern Shore's largest slaveholder. The sailing ships that contemporary visitors today covet and admire were, to Douglass, symbols of the oppression of Black people. Standing on the shores of the Chesapeake, he wrote, "Those beautiful vessels, robed in white and so delightful to the eyes of freemen, were to me so many shrouded ghosts to terrify and torment me with thoughts of my wretched condition" (Douglass, 1962, p. 125).

Sociological descriptions of the county in which the Eastern Shore lies reveal great inequality in the experiences of whites and Blacks living here. Slightly more than one-third of Black persons live below the poverty line, compared with less than 5% of white families.[1] (Nationally, 16.1% of Black families in the same year lived in poverty.) Median income for white families here in 1980 was approximately $21,000; for Black families, it was less than $7,500—only 35% of white family income. (Nationally, Black family income in 1980 was 60.2% of white family income.) Inequality between whites and Blacks in this county is further demonstrated by the skewed character of income distribution. Nearly 40% of Black households in this county have incomes less than $5,000 per year (nationally, this figure is 2.5%), compared with less than 13% for white households. No Black households in this county have incomes higher than $35,000, and only 2% have incomes between $25,000 and $35,000, compared with one-fourth of white households.

The persistence of such striking inequality on the Eastern Shore, with its historical past based on a plantation economy, makes it a region rich for sociological study. Less than 100 miles from Philadelphia, Baltimore, and Washington, D.C., the region seems like an anachronism in that the yachts, fashionable shops, and luxury automobiles are clearly symbolic of contemporary class relations, but the juxtaposition of rurally segregated Black communities and paternalistic relations between whites and Blacks evokes a strong feeling that the past is still present. The Eastern Shore remains predominantly rural, agricultural, and geographically isolated. It is here that slavery originated in the United States, although slavery is more typically associated with states further south. Until 1790, two-thirds of the slave population lived around the Chesapeake Bay, where tobacco and wheat crops dominated production. In 1660, Maryland was the first state to enact laws defining slavery as a legitimate institution. Now, former plantations are owned by elites and, in some cases, multinational corporations. Patterns of residential segregation are characteristic of the living arrangements between whites and Blacks.

Two questions framed my research on the Eastern Shore: What has been the experience of African Americans in this community? and What are their understandings of how race relations have changed in their lifetimes? Pursuing the answers to these questions demanded data different from those that could be gathered through secondary sources. My questions were both historical and qualitative, each involving different methodological problems that ultimately will shape what is known from this study. The absence of firsthand accounts reflecting on and describing African American experience in this community limits sociological understanding of the development and persistence of racism. The methodological problems posed by the historical analysis are similar to those posed by contemporary qualitative research. Historians have been overly dependent on historical records left by members of the dominant group, usually elites. Other available historical documents are typically those left by philanthropists or government agencies, documents often characterized by images of Black Americans as pathological (Uya, 1981).

Although I used primary historical evidence from archival and personal documents to understand the historical experience of African Americans in this community, contemporary accounts of race relations through the eyes of Black Americans are rare. This is precisely the kind of information that the literature suggests is most inaccessible to white researchers. Wondering whether I could reliably collect such information, I proceeded to do field research and to conduct extended interviews with low-income, elderly (mostly in their 80s) women, both Black and white, who had little formal schooling. As a white, middle-aged, middle-class researcher, I knew I was crossing not only racial boundaries but also those of class, age, and education. Because of the high degree of racial and class segregation in this community, these boundaries seemed potentially even more clearly marked. Ideally, I could have hired Black interviewers to conduct these interviews, but without research funding, this was impossible.

Interviewing Across Race and Class

The subjects for this study were poor elderly women, both Black and white—women whose lives have perhaps been the most distorted by social scientific research. These are women whose experiences have been underrepresented, at best, in the social science literature. More typically, they are excluded and ignored in sociological studies, even though their lives provide a rich portrait of the fabric of social life and, especially, race, class, and gender relations. My interviews with these women reveal that the scientific framework of social science research actually obstructs the formation of relationships essential to achieving an understanding of these women's lives.

The interviews were designed to produce open-ended oral histories of the women's work and family histories and their perceptions of how relations between whites and Blacks in their community had changed over the course of their lifetimes. Although qualitatively based, interviews are typically guided by the same principles of detachment and neutrality characteristic of quantitative research analyses. As Oakley (1981) has argued, conventional reports of interview data typically include the following information about the interviews: how many there were, how long they were, how they were recorded, and whether the questions followed a standard format. Researchers typically do not report the characteristics of interviewers, nor do they discuss interviewees' feelings about being interviewed, the quality of the interaction between the interviewer and interviewee, or the reception and hospitality extended to the interviewer. Routine methodological instructions tell interviewers to control the interview by directing their questions and the answers of those with whom they are speaking. This method of research procedure is, as Oakley argues, fundamentally hierarchical. It manipulates those being interviewed as objects of study and suggests that there should be minimal human contact and no emotional involvement between the research subject and the researcher. In fact, researchers are warned that the

> interview is designed to minimize the local, concrete, immediate circumstances of the particular encounter, including the respective personalities of the participants. . . . As an encounter between these two particular people the typical interview has no meaning; it is conceived in a framework of other, comparable meanings, between other couples, each recorded in such fashion that elements of communication in common can be easily isolated from more idiosyncratic qualities. (Benney & Hughes, 1970, pp. 196-197; quoted in Oakley, 1981, p. 32)

Oakley concludes that sociologists are routinely instructed to interview research subjects by manipulating them as objects of study. According to conventional methodology, the best data are those that are produced through minimal human contact and minimal interrelationship. Researchers are admonished not to get too emotionally involved with subjects. Such a method assumes the passivity of respondents and forces them to adapt to the situation as defined by the interviewer. Moreover, researchers are told never to inform interviewees of their own beliefs and values.

My research suggests that this conventional methodological approach is counter to that required for white scholars to produce more inclusive and less partial and distorted accounts of race, class, and gender relations. To begin with, it is impossible even to count the exact number of interviews in my project and to report the amount of time they took. Many of the women included in this research refused to be interviewed formally, but were willing to talk with me for hours. One woman asked that the tape recorder be turned off at various places in our conversation. With the tape recorder off, she spoke freely about information she thought should remain confidential, although it revealed important, yet sensitive, information about race and gender relationships in the community. Another woman told me her long and intriguing life history and talked openly about class and race relations in the community, but refused to be taped. We sat in my car for most of an afternoon, in subfreezing winter temperatures. Other important information and ideas in this project came from many days and hours of informal discussion with these women at the local senior center. Thus the field research for the project and the actual interviews blur, with no exact number of interviews to be reported, but, nonetheless, with these conversations/interviews providing rich data about race and gender relations in this community.

As found in other work on race and ethnic relations, the women in this study were savvy to the potentially exploitive character of academic research. Many told stories about past researchers who had come to study them but who had not, in their eyes, done a very good job. They talked at length about what was wrong with the researchers' approaches, personalities, and attitudes. They scoffed at the presumption of many researchers that they could come to this community and learn about women's lives from a distance. The women also clearly understood that the research was more important to me than it was to them. They knew it would have little effect on them, and it would not change their lives. They made themselves helpers for my purposes, but did not let themselves be exploited. Moreover, within their accounts of previous research projects were clues about the grounds on which they would trust me—despite the clear differences between us.

Several talked at length about how my "personality" made them more trusting, open, and willing to speak with me. These comments made me think about what I was doing—consciously and unconsciously—to elicit their reported trust. Primarily, I did not pose myself as an expert in their lives. Quite the contrary, I introduced myself as someone who was interested in learning about them particularly because their lives were unreported and undervalued by teachers and scholars. Most responded by being honored that someone was going to "write a book about them." One woman reported talking with her daughter following the interview, saying how helpful it had been because now she and her family were talking about their racial histories. She said, "I really liked talking with you. You know it's helpful to us talking about our backlives. It helps you start to think about your backlife. You talk plain and understanding. It helps me think about my backlife."

Most of these women thought of themselves as "just ordinary." When they were reluctant to be interviewed, it was often because they did not understand why anyone would take an interest in them. Defining their experience as important to know and understand, especially in a context where their age, class, gender, and, in some cases, race left them undervalued, increased the cooperation and rapport I was able to generate with them. More important, for many, seeing their life as of interest to a "teacher" affirmed them and made them feel positively valued. Throughout the process of meeting and interviewing them, I was reminded of the humility with which I had to work. I could not assume the role of expert, and I needed to be willing to talk about my life as a woman and as a white person in my conversations with them. It was important that I did not think of them as victims of racial, sexual, and class oppression, but wanted to learn how they valued their own experience. I was actually aided by the fact that I had no research funding and was not representing an agency. Although in some ways the research suffered from my being unable to hire Black interviewers, it also was important to the women that the research was not sponsored by any organization. They particularly wanted assurance that I was not from the Social Security Administration—a key agency in their own feelings of economic dependence and frustration with bureaucracy.

As other field researchers have found, engaging myself in their world was critical to my research. I was an active volunteer in the senior center that these women regularly attended. Although it was difficult for me to contribute as much time as I did, given other demands on my time as a scholar-teacher, my participation in the center reassured the women of my commitment to them. During the interviews, many talked explicitly about the fact that I spent so many hours there and worked with them on their projects. I was careful to disengage from my role as a professional scholar-teacher while at the center, sharing in their activities, including senior exercises, music, and crafts.

My participation in the everyday activities of the women's culture, both in the center and in their homes, greatly facilitated this research. I threaded needles for those with failing eyesight, glued sequins on pipe-cleaner butterflies in preparation for an annual yard sale, delivered sandwiches during the yard sale, helped make Christmas ornaments and pottery, and discussed cooking, knitting, sewing, and crafts. Often, while doing these things, the women provided the most telling comments on their relationships with each other, their pasts, their feelings about their community, their families, and their work. During these times, I also learned how the women felt; their conversations were filled with emotion, humor, gossip, and play.

In sum, what seems to have made these interviews possible was my direct violation of the usual admonitions to social science researchers. During the interviews, I answered questions about myself, my background, my family, and my ideas. In the interviews and during the field research, the women and I exchanged our feelings and ideas about many of the subjects we were discussing. At times, I showed the emotion I felt during very moving moments in their accounts of their experiences.

Other feminist and qualitative research shows that emotion, the engagement of self, and the relationship between the knower and the known all guide research, just as they guide social action. For example, in her book *Street Woman,* on women's crime, Miller (1986) writes of being afraid, intimidated, and uncomfortable, and, as she learned more about the women's lives, angry and depressed. But she concludes, "For reasons I do not know, these emotions, as paralyzing as they could have been, were rather motivating forces with regard to the research" (p. 189). In my project, despite my trepidations about crossing class, race, and age lines, I was surprised by the openness and hospitality with which I was greeted. I am convinced that the sincerity of these women's stories emanated not only from their dignity and honor, but also from my willingness to express how I felt, to share my own race and gender experiences, and to deconstruct the role of expert as I proceeded through this research.

Conclusion

Some of the methodological practices that emerged in this research are common to more qualitative research methods. For example, qualitative researchers have typically noted the importance of rapport in establishing good research relations. But, as Reinharz (1983) has suggested, research is an act of self-discovery, as well as a process of learning about others. Self-examination of my own privilege as a white scholar facilitated this research project, allowing me to challenge the arrogance that the stance of white privilege creates. Although the structure of sociology as a profession discourages such engaged work, I am convinced that this self-reflective method of constructing knowledge is more compelling and reliable than standard, detached ways of knowing. I know that my understanding of these women's lives will always be partial, incomplete, and distorted. I also know that the Black women did not likely report the same things to me as they would have to a Black interviewer, but that does not make their accounts any less true. If the task of sociology is to understand the multiple intersections between social structure and biographies, then the many ways in which we see ourselves and our relationships to others should be part of sociological accounts.

Feminist scholars have argued that the reconstruction of knowledge from a feminist standpoint necessitates studying the world from the perspective of women (McIntosh, 1983, 1988). Because androcentric scholarship has imposed on sociological observations categories, concepts, and theories originating in the lives of men from dominant groups, we have created an incomplete and distorted knowledge of social life. Studying women on their own terms is more likely to engage the subjective self—that of both the actor and the researcher. Yet, when our research remains too tightly bound by the framework of scientific methodology, we miss much of the texture and nuance in social relationships.

Feminist discussions of research methodology have focused on discovering the social relationship between the knower and the known, arguing that the attempt at scientific neutrality obfuscates and denies this relationship (Harding, 1986). Contrary to the scientific image of the knower as a neutral and objective party, feminist epistemologists have argued that the relationship between the researcher and her subjects is a social relationship, and is bound by the same patterns of power relations found in other social relationships.

My study with the women of the Eastern Shore, as well as the above discussion, suggests that we should develop research practices that acknowledge and take as central the class, race, and gender relations in which researchers and research subjects are situated. At the same time, we should question assumptions that the knower is the ultimate authority on the lives of those whom she or he studies. We should not assume that white scholars are unable to generate research with people of color as research subjects, but we must be aware that to do so, white scholars must work in ways that acknowledge and challenge white privilege and question how such privilege may shape research experiences. Developing analyses that are inclusive of race, class, and gender also requires that discussions of race, class, and gender be thoroughly integrated into debates about research process and the analysis of data. This requires an acknowledgment of the complex, multiple, and contradictory identities and realities that shape our collective experience. As whites learn to see the world through the experiences of others, a process that is itself antithetical to the views of privileged groups, we can begin to construct more complete and less distorted ways of seeing the complex relations of race, class, and gender.

Note

1. Data are taken from 1980 U.S. Census materials. Because the respondents were promised anonymity, data are given in approximate terms so as not to disclose the exact identity of the town.

4

Participant Observations

RUTLEDGE M. DENNIS

The main objective of research is the exploration of ideas, issues, or problems so that we may better understand and/or solve them. Throughout the history of the natural and social sciences, various methodological strategies have been established to enable researchers to comprehend and address the art and science of problem solving. In the social sciences, interest has centered on the dimensions and dynamics of human relations. In the area of human relations, the politics, economics, and culture of race have been major concerns for social scientists during the past 90 or more years. Because of the history of race in U.S. society, the manner in which race relations research is conducted takes on special significance, for strategies involved in race relations research determine the kinds of analysis possible. This chapter explores both the philosophy and the methodology of participant observation in the area of race relations research. I begin with a brief history of my own personal "discovery" of the procedure during my undergraduate and graduate education. Second, I examine some epistemological issues crucial in understanding the methodology of participant observation, and, finally, I briefly review the important participant observation studies in the area of race relations and present some contributions of participant observation to race relations research.

In a previous paper, I discussed the evolution of participant observation in race-related research, examined the ethics of fieldwork, discussed the role of validity in participant observation research, and made a few observations regarding my life in the field while engaged in the

Black Middletown Project (Dennis, 1988). The Middletown Project provided me with my first opportunity to utilize the participant observer method, although the procedure, and its importance as a data source, was not entirely new to me. In fact, I was introduced to the philosophy and technique of participant observation while an undergraduate in an urban sociology class, where we read excerpts from Drake and Cayton's *Black Metropolis* (1945), Hylan Lewis's *Blackways of Kent* (1955), and Lynd and Lynd's *Middletown* (1929). At the time, I was probably less interested in the intrinsic merits of participant observation per se; rather, I viewed it then as a methodological approach that might be less complex than the survey method, which required accompanying statistical knowledge. The idea that participant observation is a noncomplex form of research seemed correct at that time, but I have since come to view that position as incorrect. Later, while in graduate school, I explored the possibility of using the procedure to conduct a study for my master's degree. Having read Carter Woodson's *A Century of Negro Migration* (1918) and Thomas and Znaniecki's *The Polish Peasant in Europe and America* (1918-1920), I thought of studying the migratory patterns of South Carolinians to New York City. More specifically, I was interested in tracing the migration of those from the Charleston area and the friendship and family networks they constructed or reconstructed as they settled into the large metropolis. I spent the summer of 1967 in New York City, where I met and spent some time with many of the "homeboys," many of whom had migrated northward during the past 15 to 20 years. I made note of their close living proximity, and visited the churches, bars, social clubs, and restaurants frequented by Charlestonians. Initially, the project appeared sound and doable. Later, with much reluctance, I shelved the idea. First, I intended to receive my master's by June 1969, and scrutiny of the project indicated that it would be larger in scope than I had anticipated. Second, I had not yet made provisions for funding (either from my university or from private funding agencies), so I was unsure of how to provide for my living expenses, as well as how to acquire the funds to pay for the costs associated with the study.

Although the Black Middletown Project would be my first field study, prior to this experience I had read all of the early major race relations research utilizing participant observation. Indeed, the technique was crucial to the legacy of success in early race relations research, a success that became questionable as complex statistical analyses came into vogue in sociology and the social sciences in general. A look at some of the epistemological issues that justified approaching the social world from new perspectives will enable us to understand how and why epistemological concerns are important in participant observation.

Epistemological Issues

Epistemological concerns are at the heart of any discussion of participant observation. Such concerns include concepts such as materialism and idealism, objectivity and subjectivity, and natural and cultural sciences. Maurice Cornforth (1947) examined the relationships among empiricism, logic, and science, and their relationship to knowledge and knowing, through the work of Bacon and Hobbes as early materialists or naturalists, essentially adhering to the idea that "all knowledge is furnished through the senses. That is to say, we can know nothing except what we learn through our senses, we can form no significant ideas that are not derived from experience, and theories which cannot be experientially verified are worthless" (p. 21). But Hobbes, more than Bacon, believed that the only reality was "matter-body," and that it existed "objectively" in the world, independent of our thoughts and feelings. John Locke, according to Cornforth, continued in the materialist vein of Hobbes, with an emphasis on knowledge as a product of "sense-experience"; however, he moved the knowledge base partially out of the realm of the external by proposing that the object of knowledge is the world of our own ideas and, in a theme later emphasized by Kant, speculated that the substance of objective things is the unknowable.

The "primitive" positivism and naturalism of Bacon and Hobbes and the other English empiricists was challenged by Kant, who introduced the idea (which became the core of German idealism) that the key to understanding and interpreting sense data or sense-experience is the existence of the mind, which arranges and organizes and makes sense of the data; moreover, the principles governing the arrangement and organization of data are inborn and related to human consciousness (Burrell & Morgan, 1979). Kant's attempt to associate consciousness with sense data opened the philosophical, later the sociological, doors to ideas relating to the psychological—thought, will, and feeling, called subjectivism (D. Martindale, 1960).

The key to understanding Kant is the recognition that he does not *deny* the existence of the natural world. He only insists that our knowledge of that world can never be objective knowledge inasmuch as whatever we know of that world is filtered, shaped, and interpreted by a consciousness generated from the mind. Kant is, therefore, partially an empiricist and partially a rationalist. In posing the issue as he did, Kant placed the question of epistemology as a starting point of German philosophy. In emphasizing human consciousness and the concomitant ideas of thought, will, and feeling, Kant paved the way to a demarcation of the natural or scientific and the spiritual or the social, and it was only a short step from the epistemological problem posed by Kant to one of the major philosophical issues of the late nineteenth and early twentieth centuries: the development of two worlds—one the natural, the other the cultural—and how each could be studied, and whether the methodology used to study one could be used to study the other. Burrell and Morgan (1979) state the epistemological impasse in the following manner:

> The major intellectual figures of the 1890s "were obsessed, almost intoxicated with the rediscovery of the nonlogical, the uncivilized, the inexplicable." (H. S. Hughes, 1958:35). This interest in the subjective and irrational was reflected in the work of writers widely diverse as Freud, Weber, and Husserl, each of whom responded in his own distinctive fashion. . . . the work of this generation of theorists returned to the basic problems of epistemology identified by Kant, which confronted both the natural and social sciences. The positivist position came to be seen as increasingly unsatisfactory and problematic on at least two counts. First, within the natural sciences (Naturwissenschaften) it became clear that human values intruded upon the process of scientific inquiry. It was evident that scientific method could no longer be regarded as value-free; the frame of reference of the scientific observer was increasingly seen as an active force which determined the way in which scientific knowledge was obtained. Within the realm of the cultural sciences (Geisteswissenschaften) a second set of difficulties were also seen as arising, since their subject matter was distinguished by its essentially spiritual character. It was realised that man as an actor could not be studied through the methods of the natural sciences, with their concern for establishing general laws. In the cultural sphere, it was held, man was "not subject to law in the physical sense, but was free." (p. 228)

Dilthey was one of the first theorists to address, systematically, the methodological difficulties inherent in the Kantian objectivist/subjectivist dilemma. While protesting the use of a natural science methodology for the cultural sciences, Dilthey contends that any methodology developed for the cultural sciences should have scientific validity. Thus, according to Dilthey, the cultural sciences had to be studied just as scientifically as the natural sciences, but it was to be, according to

Hughes (1958), a *different* type of science, a science that, in Dilthey's view, had to emerge from the inner world of the creative subject into the objective outer world of historical reality. The key concept around which Dilthey organized his methodological approach to the cultural sciences was his use of *Verstehen* (understanding). Dilthey's use of the formula "experience-expression-understanding" explained how he would use *Verstehen* to acquire social knowledge (Remmling, 1967). The concept would enable the researcher as objectivist "to understand human beings, their inner minds and their feelings, and the way these are expressed in their outward actions and achievements. In short, the outward manifestations of human life needed to be interpreted in terms of the inner experiences which they reflected through the *method of verstehen*" (Burrell & Morgan, 1979, p. 229). This method meant that the researcher would analyze the social world and the particular events of that world by an ability to relive or reenact symbolically the experiences of others.

Weber focused on the objectivist/subjectivist and natural/cultural sciences debate by utilizing the *Verstehen* of Dilthey, but he moved beyond Dilthey. According to Weber (1949), the logic of the cultural sciences, and the impetus toward an understanding, consists of the researcher having the ability to utilize empathy to form an accurate and objective "sense of the situation," which then permits the researcher to "uncover causal connections" (p. 175). However, what was new in Weber's assessment was his emphasis on *Verstehen* in conjunction with concepts of subjective meaning and individual action. That is, the central feature of Weber's sociological methodology was his desire to perceive objectively the subjectively intended meaning of an action. Weber did not see this process as being highly esoteric or abstract. Rather, the key to understanding the meaning of any action, in his view, was simply the knowledge, and acceptance, of "established patterns of thought and behavior" (Munch, 1957).

This apparent pragmatic orientation to understanding the nuances of inference as a means of defining what is correct and appropriate in specified situations has been analyzed by none other than the widely acclaimed philosophic objectivist, Karl Popper (1972), who, in his discussion of objective mind, contends, like Weber, that the idea of understanding others is "based on our common humanity. It is a fundamental form of intuitive identification with other men, in which we are helped to expressive motions, such as gestures and speech. It is, further, an understanding of human actions. And it is, ultimately, an understanding of the products of the human mind" (p. 183). Unlike Weber, however,

Popper does not believe that "understanding" should be confined only to the cultural sciences. Instead, it may also apply to the natural sciences.

Popper's (1972) attempt to explore the theoretical and practical realms of "understanding" is consistent with his desire to elucidate the parameters of his three worlds, in which "we can call the physical world 'world 1', the world of conscious experience 'world 2', and the world of the logical *contents* of books, libraries, computer memories, and suchlike 'world 3'" (p. 74). Popper makes no rigid distinction between the methodologies of the cultural and natural sciences because he believes world 2, the world of our conscious experiences, to be a crucial link in the knowledge process. Moreover, Popper believes that we can understand the natural world, especially the world of higher animals: "We can learn to understand the expressive movements of higher animals in a sense very similar to that in which we understand men" (p. 183).

In stating the shared methodological parameters of the cultural and natural sciences, Popper quotes Einstein and uses Einstein's statement to exemplify the objective and subjective realms of knowledge and, by inference, the similarities between the cultural and natural sciences:

"You believe in the dice-playing God, and I the perfect rule of law within a world of some objective reality which I try to catch in a wildly speculative way." I am sure that Einstein's wildly speculative attempts to "catch" reality are attempts to *understand* it, in a sense of the word "understand" in which it has at least four similarities with understanding in the humanities. (1) As we understand other people owing to our shared humanity, we may understand nature because we are part of it. (2) As we understand men in virtue of some rationality of their thoughts and actions, so we may understand the laws of nature because of some kind of rationality or understandable necessity inherent in them. . . . (3) The reference to God in Einstein's letter indicates another sense shared with the humanities—the attempt to understand the world of nature in the way we understand a work of art: as a creation. And (4) there is in the natural sciences that consciousness of an ultimate failure of all our attempts to understand which has been much discussed by students of the humanities and which has been attributed to the "otherness" of other people, the impossibility of any real self-understanding, and the inevitability of over-simplification which is inherent in any attempt to understand anything unique and real. (pp. 183-184)

Weber and Popper, given the analysis presented above, are alike in their view that the realities of the natural and cultural worlds constitute "objective" realities. They would also agree that the "taken for granted-ness" of these objective realities would be affected by our interpreta-tions (Weber) and conscious experiences (Popper) in and of these realities. We are greatly indebted to Dilthey and Weber, especially Weber, for opening the subjectivist window that enabled researchers to view the objective cultural world. Weber perhaps stands between two polar extremes—one a radical positivism and the other a subjectivism that is abstract and metaphysical. So, fearful of Dilthey, of the possibil-ity of a radical immersion into subjectivity that sought to dismiss its importance, Weber instead sought to grapple with all the nuances, strains, and tensions inherent in the dialectics of the objective/subjec-tive dichotomy. It is this tension with which we live in the cultural world today, for the validation of a logic of the cultural sciences is no more a certainty today than it was in Weber's day. We still debate, hotly, methodologies in the natural and cultural sciences with their offshoots, discussions of "hard" and "soft" sciences (the physical versus the social) and the relative merits and demerits of qualitative and quantita-tive data. At least, one of Weber's legacies would be a theory and procedure specially oriented toward a methodology of the cultural and social sciences. As Popper (1972) notes, those in the social and cultural sciences need not suffer from feelings of methodological or scientific inferiority owing to perceptions of their inability to define a world of certainty. On closer inspection, the claims to certainty of the physical and natural sciences, he asserts, are generally groundless.

The Interpretive Framework: From Theory to Practice

One searches in vain for evidence of the causal chain linking the early theoretical and methodological framework of Weber to the early anthro-pological and sociological studies of his interpretive and *Verstehen* schema. That is, the early anthropologists and sociologists did not cite Weber, although they were clearly using his interpretive research phi-losophy in their studies. For example, in his study of the Trobriand Islands, Malinowski (1922) advocates the methodological approach that would serve as a model for all future participant observation research. It is a model reflecting the use of the researcher's interpretive skills as well as the concept of *Verstehen* and is, therefore, reminiscent of Weber's writing on the topic:

This goal [the goal of ethnographic fieldwork] is, briefly, to grasp the native's point of view, his relation to life, to realize *his* vision of *his* world. We have to study man, and we must study what concerns him most intimately, that is, the hold which life has on him. . . . To study the institutions, customs, and codes or to study the behavior and mentality, *without the subjective* desire of feeling what these people live, or realising the substance of their happiness— is, in my opinion, to miss the greatest reward which we can hope to obtain from the study of man. (p. 25; emphasis added)

Also true to the Weberian spirit is Malinowski's (1922) contention that the objectivity of the ethnographic technique is possible to the degree that the researcher can "clearly draw the line between, on one hand, the results of direct observation and of native statements and interpretations, and on the other, the inferences of the author, based on his common sense and psychological insight" (p. 3). Malinowski and the early anthropologists confined themselves to studies of small communities in the South Seas, Africa, and Asia, for it might be one thing to study a foreign culture, yet another to study one's own. Even before Malinowski, Du Bois (1899) conducted the first community study, focusing on the residents of the Seventh Ward in Philadelphia, and although the model for his study was Charles Booth's (1902) study of poverty in London, Du Bois had neither a clearly delineated theoretical nor a methodological framework, as these remarks from his autobiography indicate:

Of the theory back of the plan of this study of Negroes, I neither knew or cared. I saw only here a chance to study an historical group of black folk. . . . I started with no "research methods" and I asked little advice as to procedures. The problem lay before me. Study it. I studied it personally and not by proxy. I sent out no canvassers. I went myself. Personally I visited and talked with 5,000 persons. (Du Bois, 1968, pp. 197-198)

This was a remarkable feat given the funds available for the study. The point is, this virtually turn-of-the-century community study contributed immensely to literature on race relations, prejudice, urban institutions, and the like. Du Bois had no clear guidelines because there were none for the type of study he conducted at the time he conducted it; we can only say that he represented research movements in the direction of participant observation.

The two Middletown studies by Robert Lynd and Helen Lynd (1929, 1937) advocated a more direct participant observation approach, and they are classics, not only because of their depth and scope, but also because they represent the first attempts by sociologists, *qua* sociologists, to conduct community research using the technique of participant observation, which up to that time was viewed essentially as a tool anthropologists used in studying Africans, Asians, and populations living on small islands in the Pacific Ocean. Although unique, Lynd and Lynd's studies (where class was central) were, for our purposes here, surpassed by Hortense Powdermaker's (1939) study of the consequences of racial domination and exclusion in a small Mississippi town (Indianola). Hers was the first anthropological study of a racially divided modern community in the United States that used participant observer methodology to analyze citizens and their interactions and relationships in microcosm in order to draw conclusions and make statements about the larger (national) community.

Though different in many ways, the studies by Malinowski, Du Bois, the Lynds, and Powdermaker had one central theme in common. They were all primarily concerned with similarities and variations in human behavior caused by the existence of certain values and institutions; the researchers all believed that direct participation and observation, with an accompanying use of *Verstehen* to provide insight, when coupled with a rational interpretation of ongoing sociocultural realities, would enable them to understand more fully the persistent patterns of community life.

Those who advocate participant observation seek a "holistic" and "dynamic" approach to community studies and emphasize the importance of analyzing social change; one can understand social change only if one has data from the past with which present data may be compared. This is why, for example, historical sketches of the study areas are offered in Du Bois's (1899) Philadelphia study in the 1890s, Powdermaker's (1939) history of Indianola in the 1930s, and later Davis, Gardner, and Gardner's (1941) study of Natchez, Mississippi, St. Clair Drake and Horace Cayton's (1945) study of Chicago in the 1940s, Hylan Lewis's (1955) study of Kent in the 1950s, and Morton Rubin's (1951) study of Wilcox County in Alabama in the 1950s. If these studies had omitted the early histories of the importance of race and the particular forms of race relations that evolved over time, it would have been impossible for readers to understand the conflicts, tensions, and fears the researchers described.

In explaining social change, participant observers must *reconstruct* community life as it may have been in the past as the basis for examining certain issues and relationships in the present. In the Black Middletown Project, for example, we sought to reconstruct the Middletown of 1924-1925 to serve as a baseline for analyzing Middletown in 1980-1981. In addition to newspaper files, census reports, city directories, letters, diaries, maps, and records of religious, political, and social organizations, one of the most important sources for this reconstruction consisted of taped histories of citizens who were 12 years old or older in 1925. With this array of data, we had many levels from which to corroborate a variety of events, both private and public.

The reconstruction of the community in each of the studies cited above provided an opportunity to trace the development of two concepts highlighted by Weber (1968) and key to any discussion of race relations: community formation and community closure, and group domination. In his "bourgeois" critique of Marx's class theory, Parkins (1979) refers to community formation as "solidarism" and to community closure as "exclusion," and he cites Weber's extensive critique of these concepts:

> By social closure Weber means the process by which social collectives seek to maximize rewards by restrictive access to resources and opportunities to a limited circle of eligibles. This entails the singling out of certain social or physical attributes as the justificatory basis of exclusion. Weber suggests that virtually any group attribute—race, language, social origin, religion—may be seized upon provided it can be used for the "monopolization of specific, usually economic opportunities." This monopolization is directed against competitors who share some positive or negative characteristics; its purpose is always closure of social and economic opportunities to *outsiders*. (pp. 44-45)

In a statement almost tailor-made for minority groups in the United States, Parkins (1979) notes that Weber's "closure strategies would thus include not only those of an exclusionary kind, but also those adapted by the excluded themselves as a direct response to their status as outsiders. It is in any case hardly possible to consider the effectiveness of exclusion practices without due reference to the countervailing actions of socially defined ineligibles" (p. 45). This last quote is crucial for an understanding of minority community development and institution building and is the logic undergirding participant observation studies by Du Bois, Powdermaker, Drake and Cayton, and Lewis. When participant observers know the evolution of community development, they are in a good position to be a part of this community *reconstruction*; they can also be part of the continuing and ongoing *construction* of the community, for they are in a position virtually to *see* the construction and reconstruction process in the making. In the Middletown study the construction-reconstruction process was evident in attempts by churches and social clubs periodically to reanalyze their past and to use that past to make more meaningful their contemporary objectives. In some instances, the participant observer's emphasis on analyzing a group's history serves as a reminder to the group that its history is important and should not be neglected. Moreover, a researcher's interest may very well prompt organizations to devote greater attention to keeping more accurate and systematic records. In the Middletown Project, we found that, until we began to emphasize the importance of historical records, the members of some organizations viewed organizational records simply as something rather dull and dreary—mundane, but necessary.

One of the main assets of participant observation is that it links interpretive understanding of social behavior with explanations of causes and effects. These features are brought together within the context of understanding the "totality" or "social unity" of situations as seen and analyzed in institutional interaction. This explains the heavy emphasis on historical contexts and theories of migration in virtually all race relations community studies. The historical contexts permit discussion of ideas such as push-pull factors governing migratory decisions. This is why, for example, in Black Middletown, it is important to know the state from which Middletown residents migrated and the economic, political, and racial conditions that precipitated the urge to migrate. It is likewise important to know the state of race relations in Middletown, just as it is important to know the impact of the Ku Klux Klan in the area, as well as Catholic-Protestant relations. We cannot have an accurate interpretive understanding of the behavior of Middletown residents, then and now, without knowledge of specific facts surrounding these issues. It is in the process of conducting fieldwork in which life histories are collected that the participant observer can "connect" histories and memories of birthplaces to what it was like when members of a community in-migrated years ago. The survey technique does not permit us to see linkages that can better explain the many dimensions of human behavior. Using survey methodology, we do not see, as we can in participant observation, human behavior *in motion*. More important, as participant observers we see and listen to human emotion in progress— love, hate, fear, envy, shock, dismay, happiness, joy, and more.

The main point mentioned above is that it is possible to *understand* some features of behavior based on causal explanation of cause and effects, but this understanding is not automatic. Rather, this understanding requires that particular interpretive skills be present and interwoven with knowledge of historical facts and combined with an understanding of how citizens act on and react to issues in their daily lives. These interpretive skills emanate partially from the intellectual and scientific "standpoint" from which the researcher approaches the study. From this view, every research project has a heavy element of subjectivism in that the researcher enters the community or reviews the data armed with certain assumptions based on available data. In an earlier paper, I emphasize this point by citing two sets of studies (the Tepoztlan studies by Redfield [1955] and Lewis [1955] and the Pruitt-Igoe studies by Ladner [1971], Schulz [1969], and Rainwater [1970]) to illustrate how and why researchers can draw different conclusions from studying the same communities (Dennis, 1988); I quote Redfield's (1955) attempt to explain this:

> The two accounts of the same community do give these contrasting impressions: the one of harmony and a good life; the other of a life burdened with suffering and torn with dissension and corroding passion. . . . I think we must recognize that the personal interests and the personal and cultural values of the investigator influence the content of the description of the community. Whatever be the intellectual form chosen for the description, or if no clear guiding conception is employed at all, the village or band will be described in a way in some significant degree determined by the choices made, perhaps quite unconsciously, by the student of the community. . . . there is no one ultimate and utterly objective account of a human whole. Each account, if it preserves the human qualities of the creator—the outside viewer and describer—are one ingredient. (pp. 133-134, 136)

I would like to clarify the assertion that presuppositions regarding a particular community will assist the research. Why would such presuppositions not prove fatal to a research project? First of all, the presuppositions made about a community are not made abstractly. For Middletown, for instance, we relied upon previous data from the two Lynd and Lynd studies and the youth study by Fuller (1938) (see Dennis, 1991). These studies and the monograph by Goodall and Mitchell (1976) documented the history of race relations in Middletown from the vantage points of conflict, domination, and power, and Black Middletown emerged as a small and virtually powerless racial enclave. Therefore, in entering the community, we were already aware of historical as well as contemporary racial issues. What we had to do was examine personal and institutional behavior as they related to both the internal dynamics of institution building in Black Middletown and the current and past contexts of collective racial exclusion, racial domination, racial conflict, and power inequality. It is through familiarity with the internal dynamics of the community that we can understand Ralph Ellison's (1964) assertion that a great part of comprehending Afro-American life and culture involves an understanding of the many strategies Afro-Americans used to create a life for themselves "on the horns of the white man's dilemma."

To understand this "process" of community construction was in effect to view Black Middletown as a "totality" or a "sociocultural unity." This does not mean that we ignored or neglected the impact of one subcommunity over another subcommunity, but only that we looked at Black Middletown, *sui generis,* as constituting a reality unto itself and not having to be explained totally through inferences from White Middletown. We sought to capture a part of this reality, and in so doing to understand the dynamics of the community, by collecting data on key aspects of community members' lives: earning a living, family life, marital relations, religious life, cultural activities, race relations, and community activities. Thus, as participant observation studies demonstrate, the sharp eyes, ears, and intellect of the participant observer must all operate collectively like an antenna, such that the "known" history of the community—based on written documents as well as various recorded life histories—serves as a structural backdrop against which contemporary events are compared and juxtaposed along with community members' ongoing observed behavior. For example, the racial tension present when I entered Middletown to conduct fieldwork was a result of several issues then cojoined. One was the reemergence of the county Ku Klux Klan and another was the bombing of the home of a family that had moved into a previously all-white neighborhood. Yet a third issue was the election of a Republican mayor who insisted that he owed Afro-Americans nothing because they had not supported his bid for election. Charges and countercharges filled the daily newspapers. These three events were challenged by the NAACP and by a very small but highly organized Muslim association. These three issues, however, were set against an ongoing and daily scenario in which racial exclusion was present.

The community's immediate response to the events must be explained by the past and present history of race relations—conflict, exclusion, domination, and power inequality. As a participant observer, I sought to make sense of the contemporary conflicts by "understanding" how

Black Middletowners viewed their past and, therefore, interpreted present events with an eye on that past. Thus the advice given by members of the dominant group, that oppressed groups "forget" about the past and attempt to forge new relationships based on the present, has no real meaning inasmuch as the past is also the present. So I was constantly sifting information from historical contexts into contemporary institutional and personal contexts. This was particularly true whenever I held extensive interviews with elderly citizens, who constantly moved, in their own unfolding of their life histories, from the personal to institutional levels and from the past to the present. I was there as a participant observer, Simmel's "stranger" in their midst, mentally reconstructing the geography of the city, but, more important, their stories allowed me to construct mentally their extensive networks of relationships, which served to bind the community together, past as well as present.

As an Afro-American sociologist I was welcomed into the community—by some with open arms, by others with some suspicion. The members of the Afro-American cultural elite had enthusiastically endorsed the project, and some nonelites assumed that the project's findings might represent elite interests. On the other hand, many members of the cultural elite were very clear in their intent to have their particular version of the history of Black Middletown recognized as *the* version. I was, therefore, somewhat ambivalent in my relationships with these individuals, as I was interested in having the acquired information filtered and/or censored through my own sociological lenses. I understood, however, why they wanted their own history to be told as they desired. Class interests and competition among the cultural elites were major considerations. However, we were welcomed by citizens because most had heard about the two Lynd and Lynd studies as well as the study by Caplow, Bahr, Chadwick, Hill, and Williamson (1982), Middletown Three, and were very eager to have *their* stories told, because the Lynds excluded Afro-Americans, and Caplow et al., following the format of the Lynds, did likewise. Thus we were showered with attention from well-wishers as the team visited churches, community functions, family outings, weddings, funerals, and so on.

Throughout my year in Middletown, there was never any possibility of my "going native," for I was widely recognized as a university professor spending a year in the field in order to examine their community. My most important role was that of "stranger," one who was not one of them, or a part of the community, and whose presence would terminate at the end of the study. As such, I was privy to information that longtime residents may not have known. This meant that, in some instances, I had to act as a quiet sleuth—in Sherlock Holmesian fashion—trying to decipher whose version of the truth stood up under intense scrutiny when compared with other available data. There were occasions, however, when individual interpretations of past events were so much at odds that it was impossible to decide whose position was accurate. In such cases the issue may not have been one of deliberate attempts to deceive the researcher, although that is also a possibility; rather, and especially with recounting events of the past, memories fade, vital facts and key individuals are forgotten, and we may have the reconstruction of history as forcefully dictated by one individual or by one group. This is why it is crucial as a participant observer to have informants from as many class and organizational levels as possible. What I found in Middletown was that each competing faction, group or individual, elite or nonelite, has its historical slant. It is therefore up to the researcher to inject his or her logic and critical analysis in order to dissect each version.

The researcher must be able to "live" in the divergent worlds of the community, and therefore would be wise not to permit any group to dictate terms of his or her association with any other group. For example, on several occasions I was informed by members of the upper elites that I should not be seen too often in the bars in the "lower end." I simply informed them that the bars in the area were a part of my study. Likewise, the "Dodge City" guys (those from the "lower end") would kid me when they saw me traveling with the elites. "I saw you with the 'big boys' yesterday. Traveling high, eh?" An effective participant observer must move successfully, and simultaneously, among all groups in the community under study.

Participant observation is not a passive research method; researchers are confronted with issues in the field to which they must respond if they are to maintain good relations with all segments of the community—and this is not always an easy task, as I've just demonstrated. In Black Middletown, it was far easier to side with residents against White Middletown than it was to escape entanglements within the competing groups in Black Middletown. In such matters, simple common sense is a vital tool.

Above and beyond all the issues raised above, there are larger concerns for those engaged in participant observation. These issues involve the ethics of fieldwork and the questions of validity and reliability. I have written about these at length elsewhere (Dennis, 1988), and will now merely summarize my positions.

The Ethics of Participant Observation

In the role of participant observer, the researcher moves in and out of the lives of the members of a community, and the nature of this role mandates a high level of trust. The researcher is privy to information, some of which may be extremely private and therefore extremely sensitive, and some of which may already be in the public arena. It is therefore imperative that information gathered from informants or by the researcher him- or herself remain solely with the researcher. The ability to keep secrets and an understanding of the need to remain closemouthed are important parts of the participant observer role.

The first issue in information gathering is that one must constantly reflect upon the reasons people share their secrets. Information may be shared from the perspective of a friend. Indeed, in some cases, information sharing may help to forge the links in friendships. On the other hand, information may be shared as a means of "getting back at" individuals and groups. The two positions may not be mutually exclusive, but whatever the circumstances surrounding the sharing, the researcher must critically analyze the incoming data, log it in his or her field notes, using coding devices if possible, and seek to determine, based on other information, whether the data might be accurate and how much they may have been fabricated or embellished. The researcher should not, under any circumstances, share information given by one respondent with another.

The protection of informants and respondents is crucial to the research enterprise. In the course of my fieldwork in Middletown, I encountered situations in which individuals sought to pump me for information about other individuals. Researchers must handle such circumstances with care, otherwise their role can become a point of controversy and their effectiveness as researchers nullified. There were times when I was in the presence of individuals who were incorrect in their assessment of an incident or two involving other individuals. I had to remain quiet and merely listen rather than inject information that I knew, and that the speaker would know could come only from the person he was discussing. In other words, fieldwork is often fraught with informational and emotional land mines between which and around which the researcher must maneuver. Choosing sides is not the issue here, although there is much documentation by Du Bois (1899), Powdermaker (1939), Lewis (1955), Drake and Cayton (1945), and Ladner (1971) to demonstrate the efficacy of choosing sides, and the need to choose sides, when the issue is one of justice and fair play. In such cases, when issues involve racial justice, for instance, there is no question but that the researcher should be on the side of the excluded and oppressed. Those who emphasize a "pure" objectivist stance, if such is ever possible, may have ulterior motives. For example, Dollard's (1937) declaration of objectivity is simply an attempt to hide his utter disdain for the Afro-American community in his study. In Middletown, I identified with the community, and although that community was fractionalized, it tended to be unified in its opposition to control and domination by whites.

Another side of the ethics of participant observation concerns the need to protect informants and respondents in publications based on the research project. The community uproar surrounding the "Springdale case" (Vidich & Bensman, 1968) should alert us to the need to ensure a high level of anonymity to community residents. Researchers have an obligation to remain true to certain research objectives and an obligation to tell the stories of the communities they study. However, they also have a bond of trust with the people who welcome them into their communities and entrust them with intimate details of their personal and communal lives. As Colvard (1967) notes in his discussion of factors to be considered in reporting field research, we must constantly weigh the various interests at work in the research process: "There are many parties of interest in research and its public presentation. And in this society, the author of a field study continually encounters competing values: the advance of scientific knowledge, the protection of personal privacy, and the preservation of political responsibility" (p. 319). As measures to protect the privacy of respondents and informants, Colvard suggests that researchers implement the following procedures: (a) Request postresearch permission for publication, (b) delete names, (c) report statuses rather than positions, (d) paraphrase quotations, and (e) edit evidence acquired more personally than in the researcher-respondent roles (pp. 338-355).

Finally, I wish to examine issues of validity and reliability as they relate to methodological concerns in participant observation research. Both H. A. Becker (1958) and Deutscher (1969) have lamented the lack of attention devoted to the problem of validity in the social sciences, especially in qualitative research. According to Deutscher, validity "addresses itself to the truth of an assertion that is made about something in the empirical world" (p. 34). Validity can be divided into external validity and internal validity. External validity, according to Manheim (1977), relates to the extent to which the generalization of the participant observer of one community (e.g., Middletown) may apply to other populations and other localities. That is, to what extent do race relations and internal community concerns of Afro-Americans in Middletown reflect patterns of race and community in other medium-sized cities (with small minority populations) across the country? There are ample data in community studies to demonstrate that, for example, social exclusion, degrees of racial conflict, and the ubiquity of racial denomination have persisted as variables governing group relations in many cities. The comparability issue was even more vital in the Black Middletown study, because, in sticking close to the Lynds' assumptions, researchers for Black Middletown assumed that the interracial characteristics of the city would reflect the nation's, given that Middletown was chosen as a research site in the first place because it reflected, in its population, class, and racial dimensions, the "average" American city. Problems of averages aside, our reading of community studies of race would indicate the generalizability of data to other locales, especially in the broad areas of racial domination, power inequality, and divergent group interests. This is so despite the variations in race relations that might be attributed to the peculiarities of local and regional history or to differences in social class. Studies by Du Bois (1899), Drake and Cayton (1945), Powdermaker (1939), and Lewis (1955) show great consistency in, for example, the relationship between exclusion and domination and institution building among Afro-Americans.

The issue of internal validity concerns whether data recorded in the process of participant observation can be taken to represent actual differences among group members or whether they indicate differences caused by the peculiarities of the observation process. Manheim (1977) notes that of the two validities, internal validity is more important, for, he adds, "without it even the highest level of confidence in generalizations would be worthless." One of the problems I encountered in the field was in deciphering roles certain informants and respondents had allocated for themselves. Because they were aware that the study would eventually be written up in book form, I got the impression that many were interested in "image creation" or "image control," putting forth their versions of their vast contributions to the "Black cause"—often against great odds—and asserting that those who wore the crown of leader were not worthy of the title. Once they had adopted these roles, the individuals felt compelled to behave in ways consistent with the roles. Others sought to create a stage on which they would be the central characters. That is, they were conscious of their position in the community and often "staged" events that would reflect their importance. There was then the question of whether the events and activities could be viewed as "normal" and "ordinary" within the context of community activities. In other words, would they have occurred had I not been there? Likewise, I am sure that my presence at certain events and meetings had an effect on the responses of many individuals.

Reliability focuses on "the degree of consistency in the observations obtained from the devices we employ," according to Deutscher (1969, p. 34). In a situation where there may be a participant observer team in a community, several members of the team may have records of different and inconsistent statements from the same individual. It has been suggested that individual inconsistencies may be caused by "maturation and historical or situational factors" (Denzin, 1970). In any case, the responses by that individual at any point in time might be viewed as unreliable. The reliability issue is clouded by the differences among participant observers as they relate to individuals in the field. Thus how a participant observer presents him- or herself to a respondent may influence the reliability of the responses given. Respondent inconsistency may reflect differences attributed to those participating and observing. For example, a respondent who has shifted from the Democratic party to the Republican party twice within a two-year period and has also moved in and out of the Black power movement may not be viewed as a reliable informant. In this example, the issue is not that the person should not have made the ideological moves, but rather that the moves represent a level of inconsistency such that the individual's responses may be questionable.

Clearly, validity and reliability issues are two sides of the same coin. Deutscher (1969) concurs, viewing the two as "asymmetric":

> When reliability is high, validity may be high or low, but when reliability is low, validity must be low. Empirically observed cases of low reliability associated with high validity must be attributed either to chance or to a hidden (unrecognized and unintended) dimension of reliability in the instrument. . . . Joseph Gutenkauf has convinced me that, in fact, whether a problem is one of reliability or of validity depends on the purpose of the investigator. (p. 41)

Participant observation studies involve complex analyses of individuals, groups, and communities. It is more than, as many claim, an unfocused, nondirected, and theoretically and methodologically barren procedure. At the same time, I do not argue that it should be the only technique in community or small group research. It is simply an important approach that has proven to be successful in providing us with much-needed data in the area of race relations. For example, had we relied upon the survey method, we would not have had the classical community studies of the 1930s, 1940s, and 1950s. Participant observation studies opened the Afro-American community to the scholar and the nonscholar and justified the study of that community as a valuable research enterprise. These classical community studies constitute a legacy in social research of which we are now sociological inheritors. This is not to say that we should conduct community studies using only participant observation. In Middletown, for example, participant observation was only one of many research strategies used.

Conclusion

This chapter has explored some of the methodological issues surrounding the use of participant observation in race relations research. It can be said with certainty that some of the richest and most provocative data in race relations research have been "captured" via the method of participant observation. No other sociological research method has been as successful in uncovering the webs of institutional and interpersonal networks that have been instrumental in the survival and development of Afro-American communities.

In the first part of this chapter, I examined some epistemological concerns, first in the philosophy of science from Hobbes and Locke to Kant. Then I explored the issues from a sociology of knowledge perspective, as it relates to differences in the natural and cultural sciences as explained by Dilthey and Weber. Dilthey and Weber, using their neo-Kantian logic, provided the impetus and justification for the philosophy and theory of participant observation, through their concepts of *Verstehen*, social interpretation, and social meaning. Weber's neo-Kantian assumptions and his concepts of exclusion, domination, power, and conflict were related to the importance of participant observation in race relations research and the advantage of this method over more positivistic approaches: One gets at the heart of the community as a participant observer, and although there are obvious limitations, one gets a closer, inside view of community institutions, individuals, and groups than one could ever get using, for example, the survey method. As a result of my fieldwork in Middletown, for example, I can say that I "know" more about the community and its members than I could have learned through any other research method. It is because early participant observers have dissected and analyzed Philadelphia, Chicago, Kent, and Cottonville that we return to the classics with great frequency for intellectual, emotional, and methodological sustenance. In an era in which number crunching and rapid statistical analysis are unsurpassed, Du Bois, Drake and Cayton, Lewis, and Powdermaker beckon us to march to different methodological drums—more time-consuming and, in some ways, more exhausting, but sociologically and intellectually rewarding. These scholars demonstrated the importance of the single case (community) study via participant observation in which the validation of Afro-American community life could be affirmed; in which the struggles of ordinary citizens could be documented; in which the Euro-American claim to superiority could be challenged and fought; in which, by their own institution building, Afro-Americans asserted that they would continue to survive against the odds. Participant observation permits us to see, hear, and feel, in the studies cited, the stories and histories Afro-Americans never before had the opportunity to tell. As one elderly woman said to me when I told her we intended to study Middletown: "Young man, the whites have told their side of Middletown so many times over. Now we will tell ours. We, too, have a story to tell."

Finally, I close with a list of the advantages derived from the use of participant observation in the Black Middletown study:

1. It was possible to acquire firsthand experience about intimate facets of individual and group life.
2. It was possible to gain a greater awareness of complex and multiple-network linkages among individuals and groups in the community.
3. It was possible to see and understand the consequences of historical and contemporary ethnic exclusion and domination.
4. It was possible to assess the strategies and tactics racial communities create in order to coexist in a nonegalitarian setting.
5. It was possible to acquire an enormous data base about one community that could be of some value in making comparative analyses with similar-sized communities.

6. It was possible to understand the dynamics of conflict and change in closed community settings.

7. It was possible to understand the complex manner in which national values and ideas penetrate the local community ethos.

8. It was possible to understand how racial exclusion and domination shaped the personal development of all sectors of the community.

9. It was possible to witness institutional and organizational change in the making.

10. It was possible to understand the many dimensions of institutional and organizational power in community settings.

5

Ethnography as
Personal Experience

ELISA FACIO

The voices of older people of color are nearly obsolete in the social sciences.[1] The various factors that contribute to this reality could be debated. In this chapter, however, I attempt to rediscover the voices of older Chicano women through the method of ethnography. This work can be considered a step toward providing arenas where such voices are generated, heard, and ultimately transferred into a political form. The methodology involved in gathering information on communities of color is discussed here through a description of an ethnographic study conducted among older Chicano women.[2] Fieldwork took place during a two-year period among Chicana aged affiliated with a senior citizens' center in Northern California.

Because of my commitment to rediscovering voices and the existence of a rich oral tradition associated with Chicano culture, 30 oral histories were collected. In addition, during my two-year tenure in the field, I acted as a participant observer. These methods were selected based on cultural communication patterns and the accessibility to in-depth information that these techniques make available to the researcher.

I entered the field interested in the lives of older Chicanas, the conditions under which they lived, how they felt about their aging process, and the attitudes of the Chicano community concerning older people. At the time of the study, the average age of the women participating was 72. Of the 30 respondents, only 2 are married; the remaining 28 are widows.

The household compositions of the respondents vary. One woman lives with her daughter, and the 29 other respondents live alone, in senior housing complexes, in housing projects, or in homes acquired some 30 to 40 years previously. The average monthly household income among respondents is $420.00, with income derived from a spouse's pension, social security, or social supplementary income (SSI). Only 2 of the women receive social security. Many of the other women have working histories, but they were employed as farm workers, domestics, and the like—jobs that do not usually accrue social security benefits. Of these women, 20 rely strictly on survivor benefits, and the other 8 are dependent on SSI.

Of the 30 respondents, 28 are Mexican immigrants; the other 2 were born in towns along the Texas and New Mexico borders. Their families were either working-class or members of the rural poor. Their average length of residency in the United States is 30 years. Many of these women immigrated to the United States to pursue economic betterment. Interestingly, however, most of these women immigrated after they had married. Only 3 had immigrated to the United States as young children along with their families or extended familial networks.

Sampling Procedures in Older Chicana Communities

Deciding what is to count as a unit of analysis is fundamentally an interpretive issue requiring judgment and choice. It is, however, a choice that cuts to the core of qualitative methods, where *meanings* rather than *frequencies* are important.

Initially, I tried to generate a sample according to traditional methods and standards of the social sciences. The researcher is expected to seek out "random samples." Contacting credible associations, agencies, and community organizations has been established as a way to find legitimate resources or contacts. However, this criterion assumes equality in accessibility of populations. In other words, seeking out a sample consisting of a nontraditional group such as Chicana elderly is not a straightforward task. Thus the "purposeful" character of this sample was established prior to and built into the actual selection process.[3] In order to explore Chicana old age, I relied on my own personal judgment in selecting an appropriate sample, sometimes referred to as a "purposeful sample" (see Pesquera, 1985, pp. 32-33).

My foremost concern was to generate a sample of Chicana elderly who were physically and mentally capable of taking part in the project. Accessibility was an issue that also influenced my decision to seek potential participants from senior citizens' centers and the Catholic church. This decision alleviated much work in generating a sample from social agencies and professional associations that act only as referral and "selective" data centers. I did have accessibility to many such agencies; however, many of them were ill informed about the Chicano aged. Therefore, I sought information on services allocated to Chicano aged from agencies that dealt specifically with the Chicano community (Tobias, 1986).[4]

After contacting the major social agency serving the Chicano community, I was informed that there were two senior citizens' centers serving the Chicano aged in Tiano County. I chose to generate a sample from the senior citizens' center that specifically met social and nutritional needs of Chicano elderly. Additionally, I selected this site because it had a long-standing reputation as providing services aimed at the Chicano elderly population. This senior citizens' center (which I will refer to here simply as the Center) was primarily funded for nutritional and transportation services.

I contacted the Center director to discuss the possibility of my conducting research at the Center. Fortunately, the Center director was an invaluable contact and resource person. She voiced her awareness and concern about the problems faced by Chicano elderly, and about the limited amount of research addressing these issues. After this brief meeting, she granted me permission to pursue my investigation.

In order to become familiar with the Center and its members, I requested to work as a volunteer. My responsibilities included keeping daily attendance records, collecting money for noon meals, and leading exercise classes three times a week. Once a certain rapport had been established, I proceeded to select respondents.

My intentions were to interview approximately 30 to 35 Chicana elderly. Eligibility of potential respondents was determined on the basis of three basic criteria determined by the research design. Respondents were to be female, 60 years old or older, and of Mexican ethnic identity, born in Mexico or the United States. Marital status was not a determining factor in the selection process, given that more than 95% of the women in this age bracket were widows.[5]

The method of selecting respondents for the study depended largely on personal rapport. It was not until I had completed seven months of participant observation that I felt comfortable and competent to ask selected women for their participation in the recording of a life history. There was no set pattern or schedule determining who would be interviewed and when the interview would take place. Scheduling depended on whether they happened to be at the Center when I was also there. Again, based on personal rapport, I intentionally sought out those women I felt would agree to be interviewed. Given that I intended to collect 30 to 35 life histories, and that I sought the most accurate, free-flowing, and intimate accounts possible, I spent a tremendous amount of time and energy in trying to establish a sense of trust with as many Chicana elderly as possible.

The Politics and Ethics of Fieldwork

Entry and departure, confidence and distrust, elation and despondency, friendship and desertion are as fundamental to fieldwork as are academic discussions on the techniques of observation, making field notes, analyzing data, and writing the report. Punch (1986) adds:

> Acute moral and ethical dilemmas may be encountered while a semi-conscious political process of negotiation pervades fieldwork. And both elements, political and ethical, often have to be resolved *situationally,* and even spontaneously, without the chance of "armchair" reflection. (p. 71)

The social and political processes inextricably surrounding fieldwork can be crucial in scrutiny of the method itself. Additionally, issues of politics and ethics that surface during the research process are subtly intertwined with both the outcome of the project and the nature of the data.

The reader may ask why I include such a personal account of the social, ethical, and/or political aspects of this research in the following pages. Primarily, I offer my experience here because students as well as researchers involved in qualitative research are exposed to methods and techniques in a dispassionate and detached manner. Descriptions of personal involvement in the field are usually found in methodological appendices, as they are thought to be superfluous and lacking any "scientific value." On the contrary, in reality, many encounter fieldwork as a solo enterprise, with relatively unstructured observation, close involvement in the field, and deep identification with the researched. This is an important point of discussion, as personal dynamics are an intricate component of ethnographic research.

Whyte (1943), for example, owes much of his richly deserved reputation for *Street Corner Society* to his frankness and honesty in discussing his initial stumbling approaches in Cornerville and also to his willingness to speak of his "foolish errors and serious mistakes" (p. 359). Until Whyte's work, there simply were not many detailed accounts available on the dilemmas, stumbling blocks, and ambivalence associated with fieldwork. Since then, however, serious and insightful material on this area has been published.[6]

Thus sharing the more personal (and realistic) aspects of fieldwork may inform the potential researcher of the personal dilemmas that may be encountered. The investigator quickly learns that fieldwork is not an idealized method in which the research process is neat, tidy, and unproblematic. Additionally, the researcher's social and emotional involvement in the research setting constitutes an important source of data. In other words, personal experiences provide information that can be useful in the analysis of the data, and can help the researcher understand and appreciate the data more thoroughly. I chose to avoid the error of omission to which Clark (1975) refers when she states, "This large area of knowledge is systematically suppressed as *non-scientific* by the *limitations* of prevailing research methodologies" (p. 96).

In the following sections, I will discuss some of the dilemmas I encountered in conducting fieldwork among Chicana aged. First, a detailed account of my entrance to the community studied is provided. In particular, issues of honesty and consent are discussed, as well as establishing rapport and remaining emotionally balanced. This section concludes with a discussion of the processes that took place as I gathered life histories among Chicana elderly.

Participant Observation: Siendo Fisgona

Most researchers who embark on fieldwork in a new setting experience an abundance of anxieties. The biggest fear is whether the members of a community will accept and allow one to probe into their lives for the sake of "scientific knowledge." The type of anxiety experienced, however, depends largely on the community being observed. Communities of Chicano elders have not often been targets of investigation, thus entry into such a community can be complicated by the subjects' lack of exposure to researchers seeking information about their private and social lives. Such anxieties can influence decisions and affect the dynamics of honesty and consent.

My first day of actual fieldwork took place during a monthly birthday celebration. I was initially introduced, by the Center director, as a volunteer and then as a student. Being introduced as a volunteer somehow indicated I had a more sincere appreciation for the elderly than a university student. This is not meant to imply that Chicano elders have negative images of university students, but my being a volunteer simply meant that I was likely to be sincerely interested in them as individuals and not solely for research purposes.

The first Friday of every month, birthdays were celebrated with a special meal and a dance. The inside of the Center resembled a small school auditorium, with a kitchen, stage, and partitioned office spaces. On this particular day, banners decorated the walls, saying "Happy Birthday" in both Spanish and English. Three senior members who make up the Center's band were set up on stage. Many of the seniors were dressed in their "best" clothes, although few were able to coordinate the colors of their clothing because of limited wardrobes. Jewelry was displayed as though of great monetary value. Some, of course, were wearing heavy antique jewelry pieces. Nonetheless, the array of mixed and matched patterns and colors, evidence of economic scarcity, in no way affected the projection of a very solid image.

Feeling hesitant and apprehensive, I sat and observed, trying to remain anonymous. However, my youthful appearance quickly made my presence quite noticeable. Within minutes, my conspicuous appearance provoked baffled, curious glances, mumbling, and many questions. I sat next to a woman named Rita. She immediately smiled, making me feel a little less nervous. She asked, "Are you a visitor or are you related to someone here?" I noticed several other people turning their attention toward me as she spoke. I answered, "Well, no . . . yes, I'm visiting for the day. . . . I'm going to be working as a volunteer."

Rita then repeated what I had stated to the women sitting across from her, and this immediately struck up a conversation about my life. Of course, I was more than willing to answer any of their questions in order to establish a sense of trust and, ultimately, communication. I felt that if I had immediately told them that I was a student and was interested in doing research on the elderly at the center they would have been very suspicious and resistant. Suddenly, I was the object of observation!

Rita: Are you the new nutritionist?

E.F.   No, I'm a student at a university in Berkeley . . . near San Francisco. I'm doing a major research project for school, a thesis, it's called a dissertation . . . and I want to do my work on older Mexican people. So I'm here to learn a little bit about the Center.

Rita: So you're a student, that's good.

Trini: Where are you from?

E.F.:   From the neighborhood, just a couple of miles from here.

Trini: Yes, I have friends out there.

Rita: Are you married?

E.F.:   Yes . . . I've been married for five years.

The question about marriage caught me entirely off guard. The questions continued about my husband, the type of work he did, whether I had children or planned to have any in the near future, and where I currently resided.

I was somewhat unprepared to answer so many questions. I was hesitant because I realized that the first few words I was to speak would be crucial, as they would set the stage for or define the parameters of my acceptance into this community. In other words, I had to be extremely careful how I answered their questions, and I attempted to anticipate the context of the conversation. However, I also recognized that honesty or "coming clean" was equally important. On the one hand, I was concerned with being too honest for fear this might dissuade some of the women from talking with me. On the other hand, being honest was ethically and politically correct. Thus the researcher must be conscious of interdependent dynamics. In attempting to "win over" the community, the researcher must balance the need to be accepted and a sense of professional responsibility to the community being researched.

The receptiveness of these women was largely based on my ability to speak Spanish and my interest in their lives as elderly women. Generally, there is a negative attitude among the elderly toward younger Chicanos who fail to become bilingual. Many stated that either younger people are ashamed to speak Spanish or parents are irresponsible for failing to teach their children the language. They have a tremendous amount of respect for those in the younger generation who are bilingual. Bilingualism for many of these elderly is an indication of cultural pride. The following discussion took place among several seniors:

Rebeca: Mexicans who don't speak Spanish are wasting their time because there are classes now. If they have enough intelligence to learn in their classes at school, they should be intelligent enough to learn Spanish. Even if they speak broken Spanish, the intentions should be there.

Anna: A person who speaks more than one language has a better chance of getting a job. My sons know Spanish perfectly and my grandchildren, it's broken but they know Spanish. Even my great-grandchildren try, because I teach them. Just the other day, my two great-granddaughters said a prayer with me. But parents are at fault too.

Jose: The most beautiful thing is to speak Spanish, that's part of us. I never forgot my language. Parents are responsible for teaching their children but they expect the school to teach them everything. Education comes from parents too.

I also found among these women a genuine appreciation for younger individuals who took an interest in them as individuals—not as grandmothers, mothers, or baby-sitters. Within the context of such relationships, they feel they are expected to express certain ideas, emotions, and feelings, determined by prescribed expectations and notions associated with age. However, interacting with the elderly within the context of a reciprocal relationship provides an opportunity for them to express their ideas concerning politics, health, companionship, sex, and death.[7]

In the process of facilitating my entry into this community, the issue of consent was initially problematic. When observing a large group, consent is difficult to obtain, because constant interaction is taking place among many people. Not only is it physically impossible to inform all parties that they are being observed, it is also damaging to the research itself. As a case in point, an anthropology student from a nearby university informed the Center that she would be observing women who crocheted and did other needlework. The dynamics of the women's interactions and behavior changed tremendously during her observation. Not only did they "perform" for the student, but they interacted and behaved in ways that they thought were expected of them.

As a way of dealing with this issue, I informed the seniors I was there to learn about the Center, and later discussed my observations with all the women during the interview process. Discussing my observations and listening to their feedback served as a validity check.

Establishing rapport requires a tremendous amount of time and energy. The researcher soon learns what is expected of him or her. These expectations are determined by the community itself.[8] Given that I was a volunteer, I was expected to assist the cook, oversee daily attendance sheets, assist in serving the noon meals, and develop activities the seniors found worthwhile. The more I became involved with the Center on this level, the more receptive and appreciative they were of me. This, of course, facilitated my initial conversations with all the women. Gradually, I was able to withdraw from some of these activities and concentrate on establishing personal relationships with the women.

Many times, however, a researcher may not be willing to take part in the interaction and participation determined by the community. This is where researchers must define their own boundaries of interaction in conjunction with those of the community being studied. As an example, the elder who taught crocheting at the Center insisted I learn how to crochet. She even went so far as to bring me a beginner's needle and yarn. She was very offended when I told her that I just did not have the skills to crochet. She felt that this was a great insult and an indication that I did not care to learn this craft. I finally had to convince her that in reality I did not have the time. Consequently, I was challenged to develop our relationship in a different context. Given that she felt crocheting and sewing were worthwhile skills, I brought in and showed her some needlepoint work I had done. In establishing rapport, the researcher is challenged to obtain acceptance and approval based not only on communal standards but on individual standards as well.

Once the process of establishing rapport has begun, maintaining an emotional balance becomes one of the most stressful tasks for the fieldworker. The researcher is constantly "on stage," and must play the role without dropping his or her guard. Further, the role he or she must play may be far from easy and impossible to learn in advance or by instruction.

I attended the Center twice every week. Before I entered the main room of the Center, I would go to the Center director's office to prepare myself to interact with the seniors. I had to put myself in a positive mode of thinking as well as sharpen my awareness so that I would be percep-tive. I would first greet the assistant director, then make the rounds from table to table, greeting and talking with the seniors.

I had to remember to be careful about whom I greeted first, second, or last. My routine was determined according to those who carried the most "power" in the Center. I learned that seniors who sat at tables not considered high in status, visibility, and recognition would not be offended if I greeted them first and saved the most powerful for last. They too understood the pressure I felt from the various groups in the

Center. I, however, was in the vulnerable position, as I was trying to establish a good relationship with all the women so that I could eventually interview them.

As a way to deal with this pressure, I began by greeting the cook, purchasing a cup of coffee, and spending the majority of my time with the assistant director. However, this did not sit well with me personally, as I felt I was setting myself apart from the seniors. On the other hand, I felt I had to establish an independent status. Therefore, I had to figure out a way to interact with all of them without being pressured into identifying myself with one group. I made conscientious efforts to spend equal amounts of time at each table, and changed my greeting routine daily. Additionally, I incorporated some activities in which all the seniors could take part, such as *loteria* (Mexican bingo) and an exercise class.

The preceding discussion focuses on the skills I had to draw upon in this research process. However, it should be noted that these skills were heavily influenced by structural factors. In this case, in the participant observer phase of the research, my age and gender contributed to my building rapport. With respect to age, I was initially referred to as *la señorita,* meaning young, single woman. Once they knew I was married I was recognized by my name, and then eventually affectionately referred to as *mija* or *hija,* implying similar meaning as "my daughter" or simply "daughter." Additionally, both terms imply an age distinction. In essence, I was affectionately recognized as a young married woman, their surrogate daughter, and not a caseworker or social welfare agent.

Being a "young" student worked to my advantage, as many of the women were willing to educate me about old age. If I had been an "older" established professor, they would have expected me to know a great deal more about elderly women based on cultural knowledge. Being young allowed for naïveté that eventually allowed for extensive probing. On the other hand, if I had been much younger I could have been perceived has having a lack of understanding regarding old age.

The underlying dynamic of my communication with the women was one of a traditional age hierarchy. As a younger person, I was expected to recognize this age hierarchy in granting them respect as shown in my behavior and conversation. For example, I addressed all the women as *señora,* and deferred to their authority based simply on age. They, too, recognized this hierarchy in acting as educators. This behavior was not always consistent, but was strongly established as a tradition *in* the Center.

Related to the age issue are the gender dynamics that took place. As mentioned earlier, I was recognized as a volunteer and was expected to perform gender-oriented duties. Posing as a volunteer in a very gender-determined fashion could have been detrimental to the data collection process. Basically, I would have been eventually considered or referred to as *la muchacha,* implying a young single "girl" who performs domestic duties; in other words, a helper. In order to establish a stronger sense of credibility, I began to do simple administrative tasks and was eventually recognized as an assistant to the director. Once I had established this position, my personal interactions began to take on a different context. This became even more apparent when I started conducting exercise classes.

The gender tradition established in the Center influenced not only my behavior but my interactions as well. My interactions were limited to the women. With respect to the men, both gender and age influenced my lack of interaction with them. Given that they were elderly, as a younger person I was expected to greet them, but simply out of respect; I did not have extensive conversations with them. In other words, the age dynamic allowed for my greeting the men, but gender limited the types of conversations between us. On several occasions when I did attempt to "challenge tradition," the women expressed their disapproval. When I asked the women to explain their disapproval, they gave two reasons. First, they said that if a woman approaches a man, her intentions are not considered to be good. Second, they felt that friendships between women and men are all right for younger people, but not for their generation. In other words, these women still operated within very traditional frameworks of male-female relationships. The strategies that I employed were ways of dealing with the age and gender traditions of the Center.

There were many shifting dynamics during the two years I spent at the Center. The above recounts the major dilemmas I encountered as a participant observer. In essence, the researcher has to learn how to finagle his or her way into the life of a group, build up contacts with key actors, and retain emotional balance continually in order not to jeopardize acceptance and also to keep on collecting research material.

There is no question that the participant observer's role is a difficult one. There were many times I felt uncomfortable with the deceit and dissembling that are part of the research role; these occasions raised ethical and political issues for me. Punch (1986) sums up this point, stating that "participant observation, as a form of social interaction, always involves impression management" (p. 70). Additionally, all the tactics a researcher employs are means in continually exercising the "most fundamental technique of all—alleviating suspicion" (p. 71).

Oral Histories/Interviews:
Cuentos de Nuestras Abuelas

Collecting oral histories can be exciting, emotional, and frustrating, as well as time-consuming. My explanations of why I was conducting research and for whom did not initially sit well with the women I eventually interviewed. Many were extremely suspicious of why I was interested in their life histories. Granted, the average educational level of these women was roughly three years. It was difficult for them to understand or appreciate the significance of dissertation research. With the exception of one or two women, they had no idea of what dissertation research even meant, and I knew before I asked for their participation that I would have some difficulty. I do not mean to imply that they had no respect for education, because many of their own children were educated. However, much like people in the general population, they had little understanding about doctoral programs.

Therefore, the first woman I asked to grant me an interview was well respected and had a definite status in the Center, the crochet teacher. My strategy, needless to say, was to establish accessibility to other women by having the crochet teacher condone their granting interviews. Gradually, other women agreed to be interviewed without any hesitation. Many would ask if certain other individuals had already been interviewed. Once the Center members were aware that interviews were being collected, participation increased. There were only one or two women who were very resistant. However, I was able to convince them that their participation was essential for the research.

Participation increased for several reasons. First, a well-respected Center member provided approval for my work and validation of my intentions by agreeing to be interviewed. Second, as interviews were being collected, some women came to feel that their life histories were worth sharing. Others felt they could educate me about old age. Yet others used the interview as a way of establishing a personal friendship. Some may have agreed to grant interviews for all the above-mentioned reasons. How each woman felt about being interviewed definitely influenced the tone and content of the interview itself. Researchers who conduct interviews must take into account the subjects' motivations for granting interviews, and must be aware of how these can affect interview outcomes and thus the data collected.

In conducting interviews to collect data, the researcher's initial concern is whether the interview schedule is a productive instrument. Many times, a researcher will include questions that he or she feels will generate a tremendous amount of enthusiasm or concern. For example, I asked a set of questions concerning life transitions. One area of questioning focused on the transition from marriage to widowhood, a second from "work" to "nonwork," and a third from motherhood to grandmotherhood. I asked about the difficulties involved in these transitions and the types of problems the women encountered. However, the respondents were more interested in telling me how they survived these changes in their lives than in specifically detailing the changes. Many simple stated, "It's hard, but you have to learn to survive." In other words, what is crucial to the researcher may be trivial to the individuals being studied, and vice versa.

Finally, many of the pivotal social skills of fieldwork are difficult to transmit and not always easily applied in specific situations. As mentioned earlier, some women used the interview as a way of establishing a personal relationship. All but three of the interviews were conducted at the homes of the respondents, but these women would intentionally give me gifts in the presence of other women at the Center, rather than give them to me at their homes. Their intentions were to illustrate publicly their ability to establish a friendship with a younger, educated person. More important, however, is that they were displaying their ability to establish a friendship with someone *outside* the Center, whether young or old. And this, many times, created exactly what they intended: jealousy.

Some of the women would ask me to do personal favors for them, which I did not do under any circumstances. Only at the Center would I assist them in reading their mail, writing letters, or preparing meals. In other words, I did what was expected of me as a volunteer and not as a personal friend. When I first began my research, I did personal favors for the seniors. For example, Alicia told me she lived near me and that during one particular week she would have difficulty getting to the Center because of doctor's appointments. She stated she did not want to impose on the Center to make a special trip, so she asked if I would make arrangements with the director to take her to the Center. I agreed to provide transportation for her to the Center on Wednesday and Friday only of that week. However, it turned out to be *every* Wednesday and Friday for a few months. I did not mind giving her a ride to the Center, but the other women certainly minded.

I enjoyed Alicia's company and all the conversations we had about the Center, her life, and her family; we also talked about men and shared recipes. I learned a lot from Alicia as well as from the other women. However, others at the Center did not see my doing favors for various people as favors, but more as favoritism. I learned that it was the *types* of favors I did for the seniors, rather than simply doing personal favors, that stirred up subtle jealousies among the women and subtle tension between myself and other women. Thus taking someone to the post office, dropping her off for a doctor's appointment, or giving her a ride to a hospital to visit a friend or relative was considered admirable and respectable behavior.

There were other equally important issues that surfaced during the interview process. For instance, being interviewed can be a very emotional experience for the respondent. I found myself feeling just as emotional if not more, as I truly cared for these women and felt on one level that I had a better understanding than they did of why they had lived the types of lives they had. During three interviews in particular, I too cried and held the women in my arms to comfort them. Researchers many times may find themselves struggling to maintain emotional neutrality.

It was obvious during the interviews that this was probably one of the few times in these women's lives when they had reflected on their histories in detail with a stranger. The depth of information provided in the interviews varied a great deal. Some women who were very eager to participate actually provided very little information. And then there were those who were resistant, yet provided an abundance of information, only to make me almost beg for more (see Zavella, 1979, pp. 17-29).

In retrospect, I see that it is possible that my questions may have been difficult. More likely, however, is that some of the women had never given serious thought to such questions, or had never been asked such questions. Some women may have felt pressured to answer in ways "appropriate" to their age and gender. Therefore, I had to be sensitive to, as well as critical of, these ongoing dynamics. It is possible that these individuals had not been exposed to the types of interactions conducive to interviews, or to interviews defined by a middle-class orientation. Their interactions and conversations had probably focused for the most part on daily survival, leaving them little time to reflect on such issues or to look back on their lives in such an abstract manner.

Rather than the difficulty with the interview format being caused by the content of the questions, it may be that these women simply narrated their stories in a form not recognized in the social sciences. How Chicana elderly provide information may be not only influenced by age and gender but culturally determined as well. I would argue that the manner in which Chicana elderly provide information is key to understanding the interview process among this population.

In essence, the researcher must be aware that social science research dictates that individuals provide data, but many times providing these data calls for abstract thinking. Even what is defined as abstract in the social sciences carries a "scientific bias," a middle-class orientation. Thus the challenge is to recognize these biases in methodologies in order to facilitate and increase the reliability of the data collection process. To extract as much information as possible, the researcher may have to construct feasible approaches determined by the community's norms, values, and standards.

A final important issue is the researcher's exit from the community being studied. How does one lessen rapport once it is established? The continuous struggle to establish rapport, alleviate suspicion, and remain emotionally detached must suddenly come to an abrupt end at the conclusion of the research. How this process is completed when the researcher finds the study personally, politically, and emotionally significant is no doubt complicated.

Once a researcher comes to this stage, class, race, and gender become tangibles that contribute to the significance of the study. The meaning of the study becomes more than simply an analysis of how these dynamics influence subjects' lives. These are the realistic dimensions of their lives that touch the researcher emotionally and personally. How does the researcher ultimately speak to this experience, and how does it actually influence the study outcome? Is social science too confining in addressing this dynamic of the research? Is it the very language that speaks to this aspect of our research that we find limiting?[9]

A related issue is how the community itself reacts to the researcher's departure. Some reactions can be totally unexpected. The women who participated in this study all had very different responses to my departure. Mrs. Garcia, for example, was very sad. She looked at me as though I were deserting her and stated, "Well, I guess I won't ever see you again." After all my struggles with the crochet teacher, she too looked at me as though I were deserting her. She felt betrayed; she simply dropped her head and went on with her crocheting. Others, such as Juanita, sincerely wished me good luck and happiness. She stated, "I *really* do hope you finish school." I had never heard this tone of voice from Juanita. I knew and felt she was very sincere in her wishes. Concepción was very supportive and encouraging, and showed almost as much enthusiasm for my work as I did. Celia wished me luck with school and stated, "I feel like crying." I told her, "Don't cry Celia, I'll see you again, I promise." And finally, Maria commented on how important my work was for my own personal benefit. She stated, "A lot of people probably don't appreciate what you do, but all that matters is that it's important for you. I know that this work is important for your future. It doesn't matter what people say or think, because for you this work means something."

Many times the researcher may feel compelled to promise future contacts, to establish friendships, and so on. Naturally, the researcher feels obligated to reciprocate to the community under study for the invaluable material gained and ultimately the personal goals he or she has met at the cost of the community members' exposing their most personal feelings, attitudes, and behaviors. However, the researcher somehow has to deal with the reality of conducting research that asks for so much and gives so little in return. We can rationalize or intellec-tualize these feelings by convincing ourselves that our work contributes to the political struggles of our community and takes issue with ideol-ogies of the academy, yet there is an emotional aspect to the research that is difficult to accept on an intellectual level. Consequently, as with entrance to a community, departure must be honest and ethical. The researcher must "leave clean."

Notes

1. See Elsasser, MacKenzie, and Tixier y Vigil (1989); this book provides a rich source of information through interviews with Hispanic women ranging in age from their early 30s to late 80s. See also Cuellar (1978) and Sotomayor (1973).

2. Aged Chicanos would probably refrain from using the term *Chicano* as a means of self-identity. Rather, they seem to prefer *Mexicano* or *Mexican*. Other acceptable terms are *Mexican American* or *Spanish speaking* (Maldonado, 1979, p. 175). The elderly who choose other self-identifying terms do not mean to disassociate themselves from those who call themselves Chicanos. Rather, their choices reflect a relatively high rate of foreign birth, strong identification with Mexican culture, and the relative newness of *Chicano* as a general term of identification. For purposes of this study, the terms *Chicano elderly woman* and *Chicana elderly/aged* will be used interchangeably.

3. Accessibility of a potential sample leads to a researcher's making valid judgment choices. I would argue that a criticism of bias in selecting a sample cannot be directed at those researchers studying individuals or groups who are not available in traditional settings for research investigation or toward those individuals conducting ethnographic studies.

4. Tobias (1986) notes that social and health service agencies proved generally unwilling and unable to locate Mexican American widows. Mexican American widows were not likely to respond to impersonal advertisements or letters. Most of the Mexican American widows in Tobias's study were located primarily through churches.

5. Marital status (1980) among the aged indicates that more than 75% of elderly men are married and living with their wives, whereas only 38% of elderly women are married and living with their husbands. Half of elderly women are widows, while one out of eight elderly men is a widower. Elderly widowers remarry at a rate seven times higher than that of widows.

6. For a more detailed list of references concerning this discussion, see Punch (1986).

7. Unidirectional relationships of grandchild to grandparent and child to parent, characteristic of age-graded societies, limits the direction as well as the content of communication. Here the concept of age grading becomes quite appropriate as age becomes a determining factor influencing the elderly's access to particular roles. Thus they are expected to partake in activities that they may not be entirely willing to perform. In the reciprocal relationship, as suggested by Benedict (1983), areas of companionship and sex are not regarded as "inappropriate" or "taboo" issues of concern.

8. Some argue that the researcher's presence necessarily alters the informants' world, and of course that is often true. But sometimes the researcher's presence can be overrated. After a period of time, one becomes, sometimes, part of the woodwork. Becker (1970) argues that group members live within well-established traditions that constrain their actions. The presence of an ethnographer is a new constraint, but it is in competition with many others that have the weight of tradition behind them.

9. Agar (1986) proposes that ethnographers need to create their own language to describe the way their research actually works. Garfinkel (1976) attempts to build much of ethnomethodology to address the gap between the received view, a view that centers on the systematic test of explicit hypotheses, and the study of how people accomplish their everyday lives. Geertz's *The Interpretation of Cultures* (1973) and Goffman's *Frame Analysis* (1974) also set forth well-written perspectives on the study of social life that set out to do the same. But none of these quite works. Each is too partial, too narrow in focus, and too detached from ethnographic practice.

$\longrightarrow$ p 233

6

Analyzing Racism
Through Discourse Analysis

Some Methodological Reflections

TEUN A. VAN DIJK

This chapter draws some methodological conclusions from a research program on the reproduction of racism through discourse and communication. At the same time, it is my hope that these reflections allow other scholars engaged in the study of racism to assess the theoretical and methodological relevance of discourse analysis for our understanding of ethnic and racial inequality.

In a multidisciplinary research program on discourse and racism, carried out since 1980 at the University of Amsterdam, I have studied the ways majority group members write and talk about minorities, for example, in everyday conversations, textbooks, news reports, parliamentary debates, and academic and corporate discourse. These analyses have focused on the following major questions, among others (for details, see van Dijk, 1984, 1987a, 1987c, 1991):

1. How exactly do members or institutions of dominant white groups talk and write about ethnic or racial minorities?
2. What do such structures and strategies of discourse tell us about underlying ethnic or racial prejudices, ideologies, or other social cognitions about minorities?

3. What are the social, political, and cultural contexts and functions of such discourse about minorities? In particular, what role does this discourse play in the development, reinforcement, legitimation, and hence reproduction of white group dominance?

Although these questions focus on "texts" and their cognitive and sociocultural "contexts," study of the issues raised requires a multidisciplinary approach that involves several disciplines in the humanities and the social sciences. One of the attractive roles of discourse analysis is that it is able to integrate such a multidisciplinary approach, also in the equally multidisciplinary study of ethnic or racial prejudice, discrimination, and racism. The major contribution of discourse analysis, however, takes place at the micro level of social practices involved in the enactment and reproduction of racism.

The Relevance of Discourse Analysis

To spell out the broad multidisciplinary relevance of discourse analysis for our understanding of racism, I will very briefly summarize some of the relations between discourse and racism in several disciplines of the humanities and social sciences. For the new discipline of *discourse studies* itself, the study of the discursive reproduction of racism through text and talk provides not only a highly relevant field of application, but also more insight into the relations between various structures of text and talk on minorities on the one hand, and the mental, sociocultural, and political conditions, effects, or functions—that is, various "contexts" of the reproduction of racism on the other hand. Overlapping with its sister discipline of *linguistics,* the study of racism and discourse shows how various grammatical structures, to be discussed below, may express or signal the perspectives and ethnic biases of white group speakers. The study of *history* is largely based on the many types of discourses (stories, documents) from and about the past, including those about race and ethnic events and relations. A detailed discourse analysis of such historical texts allows us to make inferences about otherwise inaccessible attitudes and sociocultural contexts of racism in the past.

The social *psychology* of intergroup relations, and especially that of prejudice and ethnic stereotyping, focuses on, for example, the social cognitions, interpretations, and attribution processes of white dominant group members. In both laboratory and field experiments and survey research, the data for this research are largely discursive: question-naires, experimental responses, think-aloud and recall protocols, stories or argumentation and accounts, among many others. Discourse analysis allows us to make explicit the inferences about social cognitions of majority group members about minorities from the properties of their text and talk.

Political science and the study of *law* are also largely based on discourse, such as government deliberations in decision making, par-liamentary debates, laws, regulations, and so on, also with respect to ethnic affairs. Detailed study of these many forms of political discourse reveals underlying sociopolitical and in particular ethnic attitudes of politicians, and the strategies of agenda setting and the manufacture of the ethnic consensus, among many other processes of the politics of ethnic affairs and immigration.

In *sociology* and *anthropology* (ethnography) discourse analysis plays a primary role in accounting for the structures of everyday interaction, for instance, in conversations in culturally variable sociocultural contexts. In both intercultural communication and talk and texts about ethnic minorities or non-Western peoples, thus, majority group speakers, or more generally people in the West, may engage in the local production and reproduction of white, Western group dominance, in communicat-ing stereotypes and more generally in the reproduction of social, cul-tural, or political hegemony. Such studies thus are not limited to the micro level of everyday interaction in sociocultural contexts, but also involve macro notions such as groups, social formations, or institutions, such as schools, business corporations, and especially the mass media. Such processes involved in the reproduction of racism are more specif-ically also studied in various subdomains of *communication studies.*

We see that discourse plays a central role not only in the "text" studies of the humanities, but also in the social sciences, and virtually all dimensions of the study of prejudice, discrimination, and racism also have an important discursive dimension. This is primarily the case for all the basic *data* studied in these disciplines, namely, text and talk of white group members. Second, discourse itself may be the *object* of research when it is seen to express, signal, confirm, describe, legiti-mate, or enact ethnic dominance, as in communication *with* or *about* ethnic minorities. This is true, third, both for the micro level of every-day interaction and for broader societal structures and processes involving groups, group power and dominance, ideologies, and institutions. One of the aims of this chapter is to urge social scientists engaged in the study of racism to take (more) seriously the many discourse data or discursive aspects of their object of study: Both theoretically and methodologically, they allow fine-grained and well-founded insights into the often subtle structures and processes of modern racism.

In sum, ethnic and racial inequality in all social, political, and cultural domains is multiply expressed, described, planned, legislated, regulated, executed, legitimated, and opposed in myriad genres of discourse and communicative events. Such discourse is not "mere text and talk," and hence of marginal relevance. On the contrary, especially in contemporary information and communication societies, such text and talk are at the heart of the polity, society, and culture, and hence also in their mechanisms of continuity and reproduction, including those of racism.

The Study of Discourse

Not only in the humanities but also in the social sciences, this prominent role of discourse is increasingly becoming recognized and subjected to systematic study—so much so, however, that confusion about the theories, goals, and methods of discourse analysis has become as widespread as their application in various disciplines. Indeed, the now often fashionable "postmodern" uses of the concept of "discourse" have not always contributed to our understanding of the complex structures, strategies, mechanisms, or processes of text and talk in their sociocultural or political contexts. Therefore, we also need to summarize some of the backgrounds, goals, and approaches of what we see as the more explicit, critical, and relevant discourse-analytic approach to racism.

Although discourse studies historically go back to classical rhetoric, most contemporary approaches find their roots between 1965 and 1975, in the new structuralist or formalist approaches to myths, folktales, stories, and everyday conversations in anthropology, ethnography, semiotics, literary studies, and microsociology. Much of this work was influenced by the sophisticated methods and concepts of linguistics, which itself also went beyond the self-imposed boundary of isolated sentences in order to explore the more complex grammatical and other structures of whole texts, and especially those of naturally occurring talk. Similar developments took place, as from the early 1970s, in the new cognitive psychological approaches to the mental processes of text comprehension. Other disciplines, such as social psychology and media and communication studies, followed suit in the 1980s, which also brought increasing multidisciplinary overlaps, influences, and integration. Thus dialogic interaction or other "texts" in courtrooms, classrooms, parliaments, or doctors' offices, among many other contexts, came to be studied by sociolinguists, ethnographers, sociologists, communication scholars, psychologists, legal scholars, and political scientists alike (for an introduction to and survey of the different methods, fields, and applications of discourse analysis, see the contributions in van Dijk, 1985b).

Text in Context

Unfortunately, while focusing on the detailed structures of text and talk, many of these earlier approaches tended to neglect the relevant relationships with the historical, sociocultural, and political contexts of discourse. Only in later developments do we find increasing attention to such notions as power, dominance, ideology, and institutional constraints, and to the roles of class, gender, and race in the production, comprehension, and functions of text and talk in society (see, e.g., Chilton, 1985; Fowler, Hodge, Kress, & Trew, 1979; Kedar, 1987; Kramarae, Schulz, & O'Barr, 1984; Seidel, 1988; Wodak, 1989). Obviously, a discourse-analytic account of racism needs to tie in with these later, more critical, sociopolitical and cultural approaches to discourse.

That is to say, in my view, discourse analysis has a double aim: a systematic theoretical and descriptive account of (a) the structures and strategies, at various levels, of written and spoken discourse, seen both as a textual "object" and as a form of sociocultural practice and interaction, and (b) the relationships of these properties of text and talk with the relevant structures of their cognitive, social, cultural, and historical "contexts." In sum, discourse analysis studies "text in context." The critical momentum of such an approach lies in the special focus on relevant sociopolitical issues, and especially makes explicit the ways power abuse of dominant groups and its resulting inequality are enacted, expressed, legitimated, or challenged in or by discourse. This critical orientation in discourse analysis also allows us to make a significant contribution to the study of racism.

Discourse and Racism

It is within this complex framework of the study of discourse that we need to examine, more specifically, the role of text and talk in the social, political, and cultural structures and processes that define the system of ethnic and racial dominance of white groups over minorities. The logic of these relationships is relatively straightforward; the argumentation features the following steps:

1. The white dominant group is able to reproduce its abuse of power only through an integrated system of discriminatory practices and sustaining ideologies and other social cognitions.

2. Part of the discriminatory practices are directly enacted by text and talk directed against minority groups, for example, by derogation, intimidation, inferiorization, and exclusion in everyday conversations, institutional dialogues, letters, evaluative reports, laws, and many other forms of institutional text and talk directed to minority groups and their members. Given the official norm against discrimination and racism, whites will not normally admit such discriminatory practices to other whites, at least not in official contexts of inquiry. This means, methodologically, that such practices should primarily be accessed through the accounts of everyday discrimination experiences of minorities themselves (Essed, 1991).

3. At the same time, however, the social cognitions of white group members about minorities are developed, changed, or confirmed so as to maintain the overall social cognitive framework that supports discriminatory actions in the first place. Whereas discriminatory acts may be verbal or nonverbal, influencing the social minds of white group members is mainly discursive: Majority group members often speak and write *about* minorities, and thus persuasively formulate and communicate personal and socially shared opinions, attitudes, and ideologies. This chapter focuses on this kind of "majority discourse about ethnic affairs."

These three "modes" of the discursive enactment and reproduction of racism should be understood within the framework of a broader theory of social group dominance based on discourse. That is, if (social) dominance is simply defined as the abuse of power with the goal of maintaining self-serving inequality, such as unequal access to socially valued resources, we need to know how power and power abuse may be implemented by discourse. Theoretically, my approach to the discursive reproduction of racism analyzes discourse as an interface between both macro and micro levels of racism (that is, between racism as a system of ethnic group dominance and racism as everyday discriminatory practice), and between social actions and cognitions (again at the micro and macro levels, namely, as actions and ideologies of groups or institutions, and as actions and attitudes of social members). Obviously, such insights should contribute to a broader, multidisciplinary study of contemporary racism, which will not be further detailed in this chapter (see, e.g., Dovidio & Gaertner, 1986; Essed, 1991; Katz & Taylor, 1988; Marable, 1984; Miles, 1989; Omi & Winant, 1986; Wellman, 1977; see also the other chapters in this volume).

Mental Models and Social Cognition

Social and political analyses of power and dominance usually focus on groups, social formations, classes, or institutions. Occasionally, more cognitive notions, such as "consciousness" or "ideology," may also be involved, but the sociopsychological dimensions of these rather vague notions tend to be neglected. In order to link discourse with the social situations and structures of ethnic and racial inequality, the theoretical framework employed here features a powerful and crucial *sociocognitive interface* of both personal mental models and socially shared mental representations.

Such social representations include (a) general knowledge about the rules of language, discourse, and communication; (b) other "world knowledge," such as "scripts" of stereotypical episodes (e.g., "going to the movies" or "participating in a demonstration"); (c) general opinion schemata or attitudes (e.g., about "immigration" or "affirmative action"); and (d) more fundamental ideological systems that construe and organize these attitudes, such as in terms of basic norms, values, interests, or goals of groups (e.g., sexism, xenophobia). That is, the "prejudice" component in a theory of racism is accounted for in terms of such social cognitions, and especially in terms of its "evaluative" parts, namely, attitudes and ideologies. Note, however, that this approach to social cognition has a less individualistic orientation than in much contemporary social psychology (see, e.g., Fiske & Taylor, 1984), and focuses especially also on the social context (acquisition, uses, institutional embeddings) of social representations of people as group members (van Dijk, 1990).

Another cognitive notion needed in our account of discursive dominance and influence is that of a mental *model* (Johnson-Laird, 1983; van Dijk & Kintsch, 1983). A model is a personal, ad hoc, and unique mental representation of an event or situation, such as one personally experienced or heard/read about. Such a model is a subjective representation of the relevant structures of the event (setting, participants, actions, and so on), but it may also include a personal evaluation (opinion) about the event. Each time we read a text—for instance, a news report in the press—we either recall and update a relevant old model on the same event (e.g., "Skinheads attacked refugees in Germany in the fall of 1991") or build a new model about a new event we now witness or hear or read about (van Dijk, 1985a, 1987b).

Such models are not built from scratch: Not only may they embody fragments of old models, they also feature particular instantiations of more general social beliefs (scripts, attitudes). That is, even personal, unique models of an event may have a strong social dimension: In my personal model about the German skinhead attacks, gradually construed from my reading of many newspaper and television news reports, I share with others some knowledge about Germany, skinheads, refugees, and so on, and maybe also personal versions of more general opinions about skinheads, racial attacks, or the reactions against these attacks by German politicians. Conversely, scripts and attitudes are developed by generalizing and abstracting from those model fragments we share with others.

One special type of mental model is the kind built by speech participants of the present communicative situation. This *context model* features self- and other representations of the speech participants; of their goals; of ongoing action and interaction; of the type of communicative event; of time, location, or setting; and so on. This context model monitors which information or opinions language users will take from their models of events as relevant input for discourse production. Indeed, the context model may "warn" speakers not to voice their personal opinions about minorities in some situations, or at least to mitigate them with such well-known disclaimers as "I have nothing against refugees, but . . . ." Hence context models feature particular instantiations of general attitudes and norms about appropriate communication, about the own group, and so on. That is, context models monitor the well-known processes of face keeping and positive self-presentation in talk and text. In sum, each text or talk is monitored by underlying (a) (event) models, (b) context models, and—often indirectly, that is, through models—(c) social cognitions (knowledge, attitudes, ideologies).

With these few cognitive notions at hand, which also explain part of the crucial "context" of text and talk, we now have a more sophisticated instrument to use in detailing further the issues of discursive and communicative power and dominance.

Discourse and Dominance

Basically, the enactment of social power entails (more or less legitimate or illegitimate) social control over others (for details about the very complex notion of power, see Lukes, 1986). This control applies to the range of possible actions and cognitions of others: More powerful actors have the means and resources to influence the actions or the minds of the less powerful. However, because actions are also cognitively based (on intentions, that is, on mental models of future activities), we may assume that, with the exception of the exercise of bodily force, most forms of power enactment first of all control the minds of people. Since mind control is typically one of the goals and consequences of text and talk, systematic discourse analysis also allows us to examine the detailed enactment of power and power abuse, and hence dominance, ethnic dominance, and racism (van Dijk, 1989).

To take a first example from the realm of discourse to illustrate this form of control, consider the use of directive speech acts. Even in direct commands, orders, or threats, in which more powerful social actors tell others to (not) do something, these others have the freedom to refuse, although various sanctions may in practice limit such freedom considerably: People may in that case prefer to comply rather than to incur the physical, social, or economic sanctions implied by the directive speech acts. Thus the police or immigration officers may abuse their power by threatening "illegal" immigrants with expulsion if they do not comply with specific police demands. Discursive power here consists of directly limiting the freedom (to act) of less powerful others by making the others know about possible sanctions.

In the same way, judges, professors, politicians, and employers are able to control minority group members directly by more or less (il)legitimately constraining their freedom to act or their participation in socially desired social values—that is, with physical, social, or economic sanctions (such as prison sentences, low grades, or harsh legislation) or by firing or not hiring minorities, respectively. Discourse power in this case is a direct function of social power: Outside their own power domain these social actors may, almost literally, have nothing or little "to say" over others. Note, however, that direct discursive racism is involved when majority actors feel entitled to thus control minorities with directive speech acts only because of their dominant group membership.

Most power in contemporary society, however, is less directly coercive. Often, in interaction, it may be subtly negotiated. People may be controlled to act more or less voluntarily according to the interests or wishes of the more powerful. That is, it may be much more effective to control the minds of others through persuasion—by making them comply out of their own free will. Even more than in coercive forms of power abuse, such persuasive dominance is typically enacted by discourse.

This more subtle mental control through discourse can take many forms. Thus actions often presuppose knowledge about specific events or situations (that is, mental models). This means that actions may be indirectly controlled through influence on the models that monitor them. This typically may be the result of providing wrong, biased, or self-interested information, or by withholding relevant information about such events and situations, as may be the case in scholarly reports or news reports. Through repeated exposure to such biased models (for instance, about "black crime" or "economic refugees"), recipients of such discourse may—without alternative sources of information—generalize from such models and form equally biased, socially shared attitudes, such as ethnic prejudices. Prejudices need not be formed, however, through generalization and abstraction from biased models. Racist discourse may also directly express and convey general ethnic attitudes, for instance, in racial slurs and in well-known over-generalizations (e.g., "Turks are . . . ").

Once these ethnic prejudices are firmly established, they will in turn control new models, and hence the future perceptions and actions of dominant group members. These negative social attitudes may further be generalized toward even more embracing and fundamental, and hence monitoring, ideologies. Although the mental representations, strategies, and processes involved here are vastly complex, and also require a detailed account of their sociocultural contexts, we may conclude that discourse dominance may be defined as the communicative control of knowledge, beliefs, and opinions of those who have few (re)sources to oppose such influence. This also means that the discursive control of ethnic attitudes—and, indirectly, of discrimination—is a prominent component in the overall system of the enactment and reproduction of racism.

Elite Discourse and Racism

Not all whites participate equally in the discursive reproduction of racism. Elites, by definition, have more power and hence more control over and access to the means of public communication, such as official propaganda, information campaigns, the mass media, advertising, scholarly publications, textbooks, and many other forms of public and potentially influential discourse about ethnic affairs. This implies that the ethnic consensus is largely preformulated and persuasively conveyed, top-down, by various (symbolic) elites, such as politicians, bureaucrats, scholars, journalists, writers, and columnists, as well as corporate managers. Despite conflicting interests between elites in other domains, their interests in the domain of ethnic affairs are largely similar; that is, they are those of the white dominant group. This also becomes clear in the many interactions and mutual influences of elite discourses on ethnic affairs: Scholarly reports are being read by politicians and journalists, politicians in turn are being heard and quoted by journalists, and the media are being read by all other elites. Instead of an elite conspiracy, however, we have routine communicative cooperation, coordination, and the joint production of the contents and the boundaries of an ethnic consensus, with the usual variation between liberal and conservative tenets, of course. Ignoring many other dimensions of the sociocultural and political backgrounds of the reproduction of racism, this will be the major context for the study of the "texts" of these reproduction and communication processes below (for details on elite racism, see van Dijk, 1993).

Text Analysis

In this complex theoretical framework, then, I shall now focus on some properties of this elite discourse, and again highlight the methodological implications of such an inquiry. Although discourse analyses may be very technical and sophisticated, depending on the aims of an inquiry, I will remain as informal as possible here and limit a potentially large number of references to a minimum (for details, see, e.g., Brown

& Yule, 1983; van Dijk, 1985b). My point here is not to give an introduction to discourse analysis, but to highlight some of the links (and their problems) between discourse structures and the sociocultural and political dimensions of racism (see also Wodak et al., 1989). Given the theoretical remarks made above, this means that I will focus on those aspects of text and talk that are particularly suitable for use by elites in controlling the minds of others. It is methodologically very important to stress, however, that such structures are not "racist," as such: Their functions in the reproduction of racism also depend on the sociocultural and political context, for instance, on the speech participants, their social cognitions, and the group(s) of which they are members.

Surface Structures

Discourse structures are often informally divided into *surface* structures and *deep* or *underlying* structures. Although all (abstract) structures are of course invisible, while mental or theoretical constructs, surface structures are usually associated with the forms of language use one can see or hear, such as sounds, intonations, gestures, letters, graphic displays, words, and the order of words in a sentence. These surface structures are typically accounted for in such linguistic or semiotic subdisciplines as phonology, morphology, and syntax, or in the—still unnamed—discipline of written or graphical structures of discourse. Underlying structures are usually associated with meaning, or (inter)action, and sometimes with cognitive phenomena, such as mental representations or strategies of understanding and production.

With this scholarly metaphor of surface versus underlying structures, common in many disciplines, we assume that the underlying structures, such as meaning or action, are being "expressed" or "realized" in surface structures. I shall be brief about surface structures, but it should be recalled that meaning structures require surface structure expressions or "coding," and these surface structures again are crucial in the comprehension of discourse. The reason I focus on meaning structures is that they have a more direct and explicit link with ethnic knowledge, opinions, attitudes, and ideologies that we assume to be controlled in discursive dominance.

One good reason, however, to account also for surface structures in the analysis of discursive dominance is that they are less and less easily controlled by speakers than "content" or meaning. In spontaneous conversations, speakers may make pauses, hesitate, correct themselves, or otherwise show less "fluency." This may signal lack of knowledge or confidence but also, as I have seen in my own work on conversations about minorities, functional hesitations about the "correct" way to speak about delicate issues such as ethnic affairs (van Dijk, 1987a). This suggests that self-monitoring, based on the present context model, may be particularly strong in talk about ethnic affairs. That is, detailed analysis of seemingly incidental properties of everyday talk may reveal much about the underlying mental strategies and representations of majority group members, such as whether or not their opinions about minorities are in line with the general formal norm (of tolerance) or those of the recipient.

Similarly, a boss, judge, or professor may seemingly make a "friendly request," but the "tone" of the request, featuring intonation, pitch, loudness, gestures, and face work, may still convey the implication of an unfriendly command (for a survey, see, e.g., Berger, 1985). If such a command violates norms of interaction, such a violation may be characteristic of many forms of everyday racism directed against minority group members (for instance, if it has no acceptable excuse, and if it is only because the recipient does not belong to the majority group) (Essed, 1991). In sum, although usually dependent on meaning, surface structures may more or less directly signal such psychological dimensions of discourse and interaction as speech production processes, opinions, emotions, and "true intentions." This is the case not only in dialogical interaction *with* minorities, but also when dominant group members speak *about* minorities. In this case, negative opinions about minority groups may be expressed and conveyed by intonation or gestures that may be inconsistent with seemingly "tolerant" meanings.

Somewhat closer to underlying meanings are the *syntactic structures* of sentences, for instance, word order or the use of active or passive constructions. Thus, among other things, word order may express the role and the prominence of underlying meanings. In the description of action, for instance, the responsible agent of an action is usually referred to with the expression that is a syntactic subject of the sentence, and that occurs in first position. Other roles, such as patient, experiencer, object, or location, are usually expressed later in the sentence. Thus order may signal how speakers interpret events, that is, what their mental models of such events look like.

Thus if majority speakers want to mitigate negative actions of their own group members, they may tend to make their agency less prominent, for instance, by expressing the agent role later in the sentence, as in the passive sentence "A group of black youths was harassed by police officers," or by wholly omitting such an agent, for instance, in headlines: "Black youths harassed." Similarly, agents may also be concealed through the use of nominalizations instead of full clauses, as in "The harassment of black youths was a major cause of the riots in Brixton." The converse may be true if speakers or writers want to emphasize the negative actions of out-group members. Thus when black youths engage in deviant actions, we may expect that they will be prominently mentioned, as semantic agents and syntactic subjects, early in the sentence (Fowler, 1991; Fowler et al., 1979; van Dijk, 1991). Here is one example from the British press that combines both tendencies: There is no doubt about the identity and the qualifications of the Asians, but *who* attacked the Asians is not mentioned:

[Four Asians acquitted] They were among a mob of 50 Asians who smashed up an East London pub after a series of hammer attacks on other Asians. (*Sun,* August 14)

This may also be the case for the order of the text as a whole, for instance, in a news report, in which information that is found to be important will be highlighted by its placement early in the report, as in the headline or in the lead (van Dijk, 1988a). Hence textual order may express or signal prominence, relevance, importance, or interestingness, according to the mental models, and hence the possibly biased opinions, of the author. As the overall strategy of much majority discourse about minorities is to emphasize the positive properties of *us* and the negative ones of *them*, we may generally expect discourse to code such a strategy also at the level of its surface structures, that is, in intonation, gestures, face work, and the order of words and sentences in the text, as in the following characteristic headline:

WEST INDIAN GANG INVADED PUB IN REVENGE RIOT (*Telegraph,* August 23)

This may even be the case for graphic or visual expressions such as the position of news reports (front page versus inside pages, top or bottom of page), size and fonts of headlines and leads, and the use of photographs (Hodge & Kress, 1988). If pictures of police actions or of "drug scenes" often feature Blacks as suspects (and not as police officers), such visual information may be a compelling means for the interpretation of texts, and hence for the formation of (biased) models of the events the texts are about. Indeed, such visuals may "racialize" or "ethnicize" models that would otherwise simply be about "crime" or "drugs."

Surface structures not only code for underlying models of speakers. Given more or less the same meaning, stylistic variations of expressions, they may also be a function of the sociocultural context. Thus, depending on who is speaking to whom, or about whom, we may expect stylistic differences that may "mark" class, gender, ethnicity, social position, and, more generally, relations of dominance (Scherer & Giles, 1979). Familiarity, formality, (im)politeness, deference, respect, and many other social attitudes or properties of social situations and actions may thus be subtly expressed through variable surface structures (Giles & Coupland, 1991). This also characterizes ethnic encounters, as well as talk about minorities, and may therefore be used to enact, emphasize, or confirm dominance and inequality between "us" and "them." Lack of the usual markers of respect or politeness, for instance, may be a typical way of subtly derogating or inferiorizing minority participants in or referents of discourse.

Lexical Style

At the boundary of surface structure "forms" and underlying meanings, studies of "political language" often focus on lexical style, that is, on the context-dependent use of "words" (Edelman, 1977; Geis, 1987). Even more than sounds, graphics, and syntax, such variations in the very choice of words may signal vast underlying complexes of contextual significance. The wornout example of "freedom fighters" versus "terrorists" is a case in point. In the lexical description of the properties and actions of majority versus minority groups, we find the major surface manifestations of underlying mental models of ethnic events, and hence of ethnic prejudices. Whereas in modern public discourse about ethnic affairs overt racist abuse has become rare or marginalized, signaling of negative associations may occur rather subtly. The very changes during the past few decades in the descriptions and names of various minority groups (e.g., coloreds, Negroes, Blacks, Afro-Americans, African Americans) show how closely lexical style may follow changing attitudes, and this is even more the case for the large register of words of racist abuse of minority groups.

In recent conservative political and media discourse about refugees in Germany, the term *Asylanten* (asylees) is often used instead of *Asylbewerber* (applicants for asylum, asylum seekers), which, however, recalls many other negative words in German ending in *anten,* such as *Simulanten* (simulators, frauds) (Link, 1990). Similarly, in several European countries, the term *economic refugees* has received wide currency for denoting all those who, according to authorities, are not true or bona fide political refugees. That is, a seemingly respectable bureaucratic term is used to conceal a negative political-legal judgment: They are only "fake" refugees (van Dijk, 1988b).

Whereas minorities allegedly engaging in crime, riots, or drug trafficking may routinely be described in negative terms, there are some limits to the overt forms of lexical derogation in contemporary public discourse. However, white or unspecified group dissidents or ideological and political opponents, such as leftist antiracists, may safely be described by a panoply of harshly negative words taken from the registers of animals, mental illness, or oppression, as are the following words used in the British press (see van Dijk, 1991):

snoopers (*Daily Telegraph,* August 1, editorial)

a noisy mob of activist demonstrators (*Daily Telegraph,* September 23)

these dismal fanatics, monstrous creatures (*Daily Telegraph,* September 26)

unscrupulous or feather-brained observers (*Daily Telegraph,* September 30)

the British race relations pundits (*Daily Telegraph,* October 1)

Trotzkyites, socialist extremists, Revolutionary Communists, Marxists and Black militants (*Daily Telegraph,* October 9)

race conflict "high priests" (*Daily Telegraph,* October 11)

bone-brained Left-fascism (*Daily Telegraph,* November 30, editorial)

the multi-nonsense brigade (*Daily Telegraph,* January 11)

mob of left-wing crazies (*Mail,* September 24)

THE RENT-A-RIOT AGITATORS (*Mail,* September 30)

what a goon [said about Bernie Grant] (*Mail,* October 10, Frank Chapple)

he and his henchmen . . . this obnoxious man, left-wing inquisitor [about Grant] (*Mail,* October 18)

SNOOPERS, untiring busibodies (*Sun,* August 2, editorial)

blinkered tyrants (*Sun,* September 6)

left-wing crackpots (*Sun,* September 7)

a pack trying to hound Ray Honeyford (*Sun,* September 25)

unleashing packs of Government snoopers (*Sun,* October 16)

the hysterical "anti-racist" brigade. . . . the Ayatolahs of Bradford, the left-wing anti-racist mob (*Sun,* October 23)

Meaning

Although surface structures are the more"visible" part of discourse, language users are mainly oriented toward meaning. Depending on the meanings of words, sentences, and whole texts, the surface structures may also take on different associations. The variable meanings of words have already been described above. The same is true for the syntactic expression of variable roles (agents, patients) of participants described in sentences. In the more complex semantic structures of whole sentences and texts, however, there are other means to convey or signal speaker perspective, underlying opinions, or contextual structures. Of this vast number of semantic properties of discourse we examine only a few that are particularly relevant for the issues discussed in this chapter.

Perspective. Events are usually described from a specific perspective. This may literally be the point of view from which events are seen, or more generally the social or political "position" of the speaker. Thus "race riots" are often described in the media from the perspective of the police, or from that of (white) officials or "experts," as is also often true for camera positions in news film (Wilson & Gutiérrez, 1985). Perspective may be expressed or more indirectly signaled in many ways, for example, by the choice of specific verbs (as in *buying* versus *selling,* or *coming* versus *going*), but also more generally appears in lexical items, sentence structure, and the overall meaning of propositions. Thus, from the point of view of victims or that of an antidiscrimination organization, it may be true that "Blacks were discriminated against during the recruitment procedure," whereas this claim may be represented by the press as "Blacks were *allegedly* discriminated against" or "Blacks *claimed* they were "discriminated" against." In the same way, acts of racism are rather differently described by victims and perpetrators, or more generally from the perspective of majority group members or that of minority group members. As soon as descriptions of ethnic events may imply negative properties of the majority, and especially of white elites, they may be seen as "controversial," and such a controversial interpretation is usually marked with quotation marks or expressions of distance or doubt. In other words, what is knowledge of minorities, based on experience and socioculturally transmitted expertise about ethnic relations, may count only as "opinion" from a white perspective

(Essed, 1991). Similarly, the right-wing press may describe accusations of racism as "branding" someone a racist, an expression that is not used in self-description: One does not say, "I branded him a racist." Similarly, the use of context-dependent pronouns (called *deictics*) may signal perspective, as is most obvious in the well-known opposition between *us* and *them*. Who belongs to "our" people or lives in "our" country depends very much on who is speaking, and with whom the speaker identifies (J. Wilson, 1990). In sum, descriptions of ethnic events should be carefully examined for the various perspectives that are signaled by the words used in the description.

Implications. Discourse may be seen as a semantic iceberg, of which only a few meanings are expressed "on the surface" of text and talk, whereas others' meanings remain "implicit" knowledge stored in mental models. With our knowledge of the world, however, we are usually able to infer such implicit meanings from the meanings that are actually expressed. When we read in the newspaper that "ten Tamil refugees were yesterday expelled," we may infer, among other things, that Tamil refugees were in the country, that they are now outside of the country, that the police or other officials were involved in putting them across the border, and so on (for details about this Tamil example, see van Dijk, 1988b). That is, from our social scripts we know how expulsions usually take place and such knowledge allows us to spell out a number of implications of the text in the news report. Implications play an important role in discourse and communication, also because they allow us to convey meanings that are not actually (literally) expressed in the text, for example, because such implications may be inferred anyway, or because they are irrelevant for the present communicative event, or because the speaker or writer prefers to conceal such implicit information.

In discourse about ethnic minorities, implications may specifically play a role in the strategies of positive self-presentation of white group speakers, or in the negative other presentation of minority groups. Thus when the newspaper reports that many immigrant youths have "contacts with the police," it may thereby imply that immigrant youths are particularly criminal without actually saying so. That is, given the norm of nondiscrimination it may be too blunt to express the latter, implied, proposition. On the other hand, if we read that police officers of the city are taking lessons in Turkish, we may infer that "our" officials are doing their best to improve race relations through better contacts with Turkish immigrants. In the following example from the London *Times* the description of a policeman as someone "who lost his temper" because of someone else shouting at him may be read to imply not only momentary lack of control and hence less responsibility, but also an excuse for his loss of temper, an excuse we never find for the actions of the Blacks in Brixton, despite the fact that their "rioting" was occasioned by the shooting of an innocent Black women:

> [Brixton] A policeman at the head of one detachment lost his temper with a man who had been shouting at him and hit him in the face with his shield. (*Times,* September 30, 1985)

That such implied "excuses" for white reactions are not exceptional may be seen in the following example:

> [Discrimination] A club manager banned a coloured singer after he had been mugged three times by blacks, an industrial tribunal heard yesterday. (*Mail,* August 16, 1985)

Presuppositions. A specific type of implication is presupposition. Presuppositions may be signaled in many ways in a discourse and represent the knowledge speech participants must share in order for a specific sentence to be meaningful. Again, meanings may thus be conveyed without being explicitly stated. For instance, when a corporate manager says that "lacking qualifications of minority applicants need to be eliminated by additional educational programs," it is presupposed that such applicants *do* in fact have lacking qualifications. Such a presupposition may be induced by a negative corporate attitude about minority hiring, or by an implicit strategy to conceal other reasons for minority unemployment, such as discrimination (R. Jenkins, 1986). In the following typical example from the British press, the journalist presupposes that Britain is in fact a tolerant country:

> [Racial attacks and policing] If the ordinary British taste for decency and tolerance is to come through, it will need positive and unmistakable action. (*Daily Telegraph,* August 13, 1985, editorial)

Coherence. Text and talk typically consist of sequences of sentences that express sequences of propositions. The propositions of such sequences are multiply related among each other. That is, discourses are usually more or less (made or interpreted as) "coherent." Coherence between subsequent propositions, that is, so-called local coherence, is first of all based on their relations with (our interpretations of) the events a discourse is about: Proposition P may be coherent with proposition Q for instance if P refers to a fact F(P) that is a condition (e.g., a cause) of the fact F(Q) denoted by proposition Q, as in "Minority unemployment was again on the increase last year. Therefore, the government persuaded employers to hire more minorities." Similarly, propositions may also be coherent if their meanings fulfill specific functions relative to other propositions, for instance, the functions of explanation, generalization, specification, example, and contrast, as in "Minority unemployment worsened again last year. More than 40% of Dutch minority groups are now out of a job," in which the second sentence/proposition is related to the first through the function of a specification. In other words, such meaning coherence that (partly) defines the unity of text and talk is based on our knowledge of the structures of the world: We know that unemployment of minorities is an important social issue, that improving minority employment is a government policy, and that more employment depends on employers, and that hence asking employers to employ more minorities is one of the ways to reduce minority unemployment. It is such knowledge about minorities, employers, and work that provides the structure of the situation the text is about, that is, the mental model of the speaker, and that allows specific sentences to be connected into coherent sequences.

As elsewhere in the study of discourse meaning, we see that coherence is relative, it depends on the knowledge as well as the attitudes of the speaker. Speakers may presuppose knowledge that is at least controversial, or even patently false, and thus signal coherence between sentences that is void. For instance, if a cabinet minister intimates that immigration should be reduced *because* of increasing resentment of majority group members against (further) immigrants, the use of "because" suggests that xenophobia is caused by immigration, that is, by immigrants and not by majority group members (or elites, such as the media) themselves (Reeves, 1983). Examples of such spurious "explanations" of ethnic relations abound in parliamentary discourse, as in the following example taken from a debate on immigration in the British House of Commons:

If we are to work seriously for harmony, non-discrimination and equality of opportunity in our cities, that has to be accompanied by firm and fair immigration control. (c. 380)

In the same way, a critical analysis of discourse about ethnic relations may uncover many of the assumed beliefs of speakers or writers that subjectively define the coherence of their discourse. As is the case for implications and presuppositions, these forms of quasi-coherence thus assume a possibly biased view of ethnic affairs, and spelling out all implications and (other) presuppositions reveals what the contents and structures are of these "ethnic beliefs."

Relations between propositions may also take the functional role of moves in an overall strategy. Thus I have already noted the role of disclaimers such as *apparent denials,* as in "I have nothing against Turks, but . . . " and *apparent concessions,* such as "There are also intelligent Blacks, but . . . ," in which the first part plays a role in the overall strategy of positive self-presentation, and the second part contributes to the overall negative other-presentation characterizing much discourse about minorities (van Dijk, 1987b).

Level of description and degree of completeness. Events may be described at various levels of generality and specificity (as in headlines versus the later details in a news report), and each level may again be described more or less completely. Generally, more important or newsworthy aspects of an episode tend to be described with more details. However, the relevance of such details may depend on the mental models and the ethnic attitudes of the speaker or writer. Thus in the press we may find many details about the negative acts of minorities (e.g., Black youths) and many fewer details about equally negative police actions. Indeed, the very mention of the ethnic backgrounds of news actors in crime news may itself be irrelevant for the comprehension of news reports, but such information may nevertheless be given as if it were an explanation of the actors' actions. Similarly, why would the information about the background of Mr. Ajeeb, mayor of Bradford, in the following example be relevant?

[Comments of Mayor Ajeeb on CRE and Race Relations Act] Mr. Ajeeb, former peasant farmer from Pakistan, was speaking to . . . (*Daily Telegraph,* October 16)

Global coherence and topics. Discourse is not coherent merely at the level of subsequent sentences. It also displays overall, global coherence, for instance, by the topics that are defined for longer parts of a text or talk, or for discourse as a whole. The topics, or semantic macrostructures, define what the text "is about," globally speaking—

for instance, a whole event—and play a fundamental role in the production and comprehension of discourse. Thus the topic is the information that is best recalled of a text, and hence also plays a primary role in influencing the audience. Discourse about ethnic affairs may thus feature specific topics such as "Minority unemployment rises to 42%," or "Los Angeles police bludgeoned Black motorist."

The highest topics of a news report are typically expressed in the headline and in the lead of the report. As suggested above, this also allows manipulation: Some important topics may be "downgraded" and not be expressed in the headline, whereas more detailed information of a news report may nevertheless be expressed in the headline. Thus in the coverage of two "riots" in 1985 in the British press, the occasion of these riots—the shooting death of a Black woman resulting from a police raid—was less prominently topicalized than the ensuing violence of Black youths (van Dijk, 1991).

More generally, then, it is important in the analysis of any discourse about ethnic affairs to establish what its overall coherence and major topics are, and how such topics are expressed, signaled, or otherwise given more or less prominence in the text. In analyses of news reports about ethnic affairs, of parliamentary debates, of scholarly publications, or of textbooks, we thus need to establish which topics, or more general topic classes (such as immigration or the arts), are characteristically found relevant or interesting by white elites. Much research, as well as my own, has shown, for instance, that negative topic classes such as immigration problems, crime, violence, deviance, and (unacceptable) cultural differences are among the most frequently covered in the press (Hartmann & Husband, 1974; van Dijk, 1991). More neutral or positive topics, such as the everyday lives of minorities or their contributions to the economy or culture (with the exception of popular music), tend to be covered much less than for majority group members (C. Martindale, 1986). As is also the case in everyday conversations, topics in many types of elite discourse about ethnic affairs typically focus on problematic differences, deviance, or threats of minorities, while at the same time downplaying or fully ignoring the topics that show the negative actions or cognitions of white group members, such as prejudice, discrimination, and racism.

Schemata

Much in the same way as the meanings of sentences are expressed and ordered in/by syntactic structures, the overall meaning or topics of a discourse may be organized by more or less conventional forms or *schemata* (also called *superstructures*). Thus an argument may be globally organized by traditional schematic categories, such as premise and conclusion; everyday conversations usually begin with greetings and often end with leave-taking; scholarly articles often begin with titles, abstracts, introductions, statements of aims, and the like, and close with conclusions; and newspaper reports typically feature such categories as summary (consisting of headline + lead), recent events, context, background, verbal reactions, and evaluation.

As we have seen for many of the other structures of discourse mentioned above, such overall schematic forms may be modified in several ways, and such changes may signal elements of meaning or context that may be sociopolitically relevant. We have already seen that some lower-level topical information may thus appear in the headline, or vice versa, and that such up- or downgrading may be related to what kind of information the speaker may find more or less relevant or important. In ethnic affairs reporting, for instance, this is typically the case for positive or negative actions of minorities and majorities: Negative minority actions and positive majority actions are usually emphasized, for instance, by putting them in an early and prominent category of a text—in the headline, in the lead, in the summary, or in the conclusion. The reverse is true for positive actions of minorities and negative ones of majority group members.

Similarly, in news reports the verbal reaction category normally features quotes and hence opinions of prominent news actors or politicians. This is less so, however, when prominent minority leaders are involved or could give reactions. Instead, what we often find is the "expert" opinion of a white elite group member, especially when the topic is rather "delicate," such as discrimination or prejudice (Downing, 1980; van Dijk, 1991).

Sometimes, categories may also be missing. For instance, in an analysis of a large number of everyday stories about minorities in various Amsterdam neighborhoods, I found that the customary resolution category following the complication category in narrative structure was often absent (about 50% of the time; van Dijk, 1987a). That is, only the problem or the predicament may be expressed and thus may highlight the fact that minorities are seen to "cause" problems, and solutions are not attempted or focused upon. Thus the structures of such stories also express the ways the events of a story are being perceived and evaluated in speaker models. Other research shows that besides the "apparent" story of an incident (e.g., a car accident) there is usually the "real" story (e.g., about minority incompetence or threat; van Dijk, 1992).

Among the major schematic structures organizing various types of discourse, I finally should also mention argumentation. Errors and abuse in this field are specifically known as such, that is, as fallacies, and it is clear that critical argumentation analysis of discourse about minorities is of primary importance (Windisch, 1978). Tacit assumptions, once made explicit, may indicate general ethnic opinions or prejudices of speakers or writers. Consider, for instance, the following fragment from an editorial in the British tabloid the *Sun* (August 14) about recent racial attacks against Asians:

> Britain's record for absorbing people from different backgrounds, peacefully and with tolerance, is second to none. The descendants of Irish and Jewish immigrants will testify to that. It would be tragic to see that splendid reputation tarnished now.

Instead of focusing on the racist nature and the causes of racial attacks, the *Sun* argues for another perspective, namely, that this attack should be seen an incident, as a regrettable spot on an otherwise unblemished past of racial tolerance in the United Kingdom. That is, the main point of the editorial is first supported by presuppositions and claims about British tolerance, which are in turn supported by the example of the position of the Jews and the Irish in Britain. Both "arguments" are controversial at best, but they are posited as facts that must support the (implicit) conclusion: Racial attacks are incidents and "un-British."

Sometimes argumentation and storytelling are combined, as when a negative story about immigrants is told to support an overall negative conclusion about such immigrants. Indeed, such "foreigner stories" are seldom told with the usual communicative function of amusing the audience, but as an element in a broader argument, as support for a complaint or accusation, and generally in order to persuade the audience of the negative character of minorities.

Action, Interaction, and Speech Acts

I have stressed that discourse is not merely meaning plus expression, but also a form of social practice, action, or interaction. It is what language users "do," "engage in," or indeed "participate in," most clearly so in spoken dialogue, but also in written communication such as letters, news reports, textbooks, and e-mail messages. Similarly, with specific utterances in specific contexts, we may accomplish so-called speech acts, such as assertions, questions, requests, accusations, and promises—that is, social acts that are typically performed through verbal utterances. Thus dialogues may consist of more or less orderly exchanges of turns, which are regulated by specific rules of allocating, distributing, or appropriating next turns, or by sequences of moves in effective storytelling or argumentation. The execution of such verbal interaction may be subject to the usual properties of spontaneous speech: pauses, hesitations, self-corrections, restarts, and incomplete sentences (for details about conversational interaction, see, e.g., Atkinson & Heritage, 1984; Boden & Zimmerman, 1991).

Speech acts. As is the case for other forms of action and interaction, discourse may be used and abused to enact, express, and legitimate power and dominance, as we have seen in many examples above for the expression or representation of ethnic relations. In action analysis, this becomes particularly relevant in the account of direct power abuse, for instance, in speech acts such as commands, orders, or threats when—inappropriately—used against minority group members by white group members who are not their formal superiors (Levinson, 1983). Similarly, also other "offensive" speech acts may be addressed to minorities and thus contribute to their delegitimation, exclusion, and marginalization, for instance, in accusations. Even sequences of assertions about minorities may thus indirectly function as derogation, defamation, or other verbal acts that present minorities in a negative light, as we have seen for the other levels of discourse.

Turn taking. The same is true for other aspects of action and interaction involved in the use of discourse. Thus in conversations and other dialogues speakers in principle change turns, and thereby follow strategies for the allocation and appropriation of turns. Power differences, as well as institutional rules, however, may influence such turn taking: Some speakers may refuse to let others speak, or a next speaker may continually interrupt at inappropriate places. In ethnically mixed conversations, it may happen that minority group speakers may thus be marginalized in conversations—for example, when they literally cannot get a word in edgewise. Similarly, in more formal dialogues, institutionally more powerful speakers (chairpersons, judges in courtrooms, professors in classrooms) may subtly or overtly refuse to allow minority members to speak—by not addressing them, by prohibiting their interruptions, or by curtailing the length of their speech turns (Atkinson & Drew, 1979).

Impression formation. Among the many overall strategies that may be accomplished in discursive interaction, impression management plays an important role (Goffman, 1967; Tedeschi, 1981). Speakers thus go through the moves of "saving face" and of positive self-presentation, so as to avoid making a bad impression or simply to convey a positive impression to the audience. As noted above, semantic moves such as the apparent denial "I have nothing against Blacks, but . . . " may serve as part of overall strategies of positive self-presentation. What follows after the "but" in such cases will usually be a move in the complementary strategy of racist talk, that is, negative other presentation. More generally, we have found in many types of discourse (conversations, news reports, textbooks, parliamentary debates) about ethnic affairs that positive presentation of *us* and negative presentation of *them* is a major strategy in the discursive reproduction of racism. This finding is consistent with familiar observations in social psychology about in-group versus out-group perception and presentation (D. L. Hamilton, 1981).

Politeness and deference. In a similar way, spoken discourse especially multiply signals the social distances and hierarchies between speakers and hearers. Many expressions in talk thus express politeness or deference toward the addressee, such as when the addressee is socially more powerful, has more status, or is older (Brown & Levinson, 1987). These rules may vary for different cultures. In general, we may say that ethnic dominance may also manifest itself by lack of respect, and hence lack of "normal" politeness or deference for minority speakers, as in the notorious example of the white policeman addressing famous African American psychiatrist Dr. Poussaint on the street with "What's your name, boy?"

In sum, in discursive action and interaction there are many complex rules and strategies for effective, socially constrained communication. Ethnic dominance, like other forms of abuse of power, may thus enact or change the normal rules of appropriate dialogues, for instance, by derogating, marginalizing, or inferiorizing minority participants. Both theoretically and methodologically the upshot of this brief overview is that, given the rules and strategies of appropriate action, interaction, or discourse in specific sociocultural contexts, deviation from such rules (as when compared with those applied for majority speakers) may have the following social implications if the participants are minority group members:

1. Minorities may be virtually excluded from the communication context, through censorship or limited access, for instance, in the mass media

(e.g., as journalists, or in quotations, letters, or opinion articles of readers or experts), at scholarly conferences, in journals or other publications, at formal meetings or sessions, or in informal conversations.

2. Minorities may be admitted, but their actual rights of speaking are seriously curtailed, as in limiting or interrupting turns at speaking, or limiting the relative and context-dependent freedom of topic choice and stylistic variations.

3. Minorities may be addressed in many ways that express or signal social superiority of dominant group members, such as inappropriate directives (commands, demands, threats), impoliteness, lack of required deference, or presuppositions of inferiority (such as lack of knowledge or expertise).

4. Besides these contexts of "mixed" interaction and discourse, minorities may also be more or less subtly inferiorized, problematized, falsely accused, threatened, marginalized, or derogated in majority discourse *about* them, for instance, by expressing and persuasively conveying at all levels of discourse models that feature lack of respect, the misattribution of negative properties, and general instantiations of ethnic stereotypes and prejudices.

Context Analysis

In the previous sections I have repeatedly referred to elements of the "contexts" of text and talk: social cognitions, communicative situations, relations between in-groups and out-groups, institutions, and many other properties of social structure and culture that need no further analysis here. The theoretical and methodological point, however, is that critical or sociopolitical analyses of discourse as a form, expression, or means in the enactment or legitimation of ethnic inequality always need to make explicit specific discourse structures in relation to their various "contexts." Thus meanings of discourse may be related to mental models and (through models or directly) with underlying ethnic stereotypes or prejudices, which are in turn related to the goals, interests, privileges, and sociopolitical dominance of the group to which the speakers/writers belong. Surface structures may code for hierarchical relations that are enacted, negotiated, imposed, or legitimated by discourse, for instance, by intonation, gestures, face work, or syntax. Style generally signals contextual constraints such as group membership, social distance, formality, or friendliness, among others, or positive or negative opinions about "others" talked to, or talked about. That is, given a body of text or talk, we may infer properties of the social context, such as an unequal relation between speech participants or people talked about.

Conversely, we may also, as would be most obvious in a sociopolitical approach to racism, analyze the various patterns of ethnic inequality, and then proceed to find evidence in various types of discourse for the ways such inequality is enacted, expressed, signaled, coded, referred to, presupposed, confirmed, described, defended, legitimated, or persuasively conveyed among majority group members. For instance, immigration in Europe may involve selective exclusion of non-European people of color, and we may want to know exactly how such exclusion is prepared, discussed, decided upon, executed, defended, or otherwise legitimated in various types of political, legal, or media discourse, such as in cabinet meetings, parliamentary debates, police interrogations, court trials, or sessions of special legal bodies. Once such a specific "domain corpus" is established, a more detailed analysis may be made of the discourse structures mentioned above: How are refugees or immigrants actually addressed and talked about?

The critical and practical relevance of such analyses is that in situations where tolerance, equal rights, and the rule of law are officially respected, discourse may subtly signal that this is not the case. Even moderate feelings of superiority, stereotypes, prejudice, and de facto relations of social inequality defining "modern" racism (Dovidio & Gaertner, 1986) may be involuntarily presupposed, expressed, or signaled in text and talk. That is, critical discourse analysis may literally reveal processes of racism that otherwise would be difficult to establish, or that would be formally denied by the majority participants. In this respect discourse analysis may yield an instrument that may provide insights that contribute to the establishment or confirmation of counter ideologies that in turn support dissent and counterpower.

A Sample Analysis

In order to illustrate further the various principles and notions discussed above, I will now finally give a somewhat more detailed (although still very succinct) analysis of a longer example. This is also necessary for a more structured insight into the many relationships in discourse: Discourse properties must always be examined in their mutual relations and relative to their specific sociocultural contexts.

The example is a fragment of a debate held on April 16, 1985, in the British House of Commons about the well-known Honeyford affair in 1985. Honeyford was a headmaster of a school with a large majority of Asian children in Bradford, England. He was first suspended, then reinstated after a court decision in his favor, but finally dismissed with a golden handshake, because of his writings against multicultural education. Many of his opponents, including the parents of his students, considered these writings to be racist. British conservatives and especially the right-wing press supported Honeyford as their "hero," who was being harassed, as also our speaker claims, by "anti-racist busibodies" for telling the "truth" about multicultural education.

The speaker in this fragment is Mr. Marcus Fox, Conservative MP and representative of Shipley.

Mr. Marcus Fox (Shipley):   This Adjournment debate is concerned with Mr. Ray Honeyford, the headmaster of Drummond Road Middle School, Bradford. This matter has become a national issue—not from Mr. Honeyford's choice. Its consequences go beyond the issue of race relations or, indeed, of education. They strike at the very root of our democracy and what we cherish in this House above all—the freedom of speech.

One man writing an article in a small-circulation publication has brought down a holocaust on his head. To my mind, this was a breath of fresh air in the polluted area of race relations. . . .

Who are Mr. Honeyford's detractors? Who are the people who have persecuted him? They have one thing in common—they are all on the Left of British politics. The Marxists and the Trots are here in full force. We only have to look at their tactics, and all the signs are there. Without a thread of evidence, Mr. Honeyford has been vilified as a racist. Innuendoes and lies have been the order of the day. He has been criticised continuously through the media, yet most of the time he has been barred from defending himself and denied the right to answer those allegations by order of the education authority. The mob has taken to the streets to harass him out of his job. . . .

The race relations bullies may have got their way so far, but the silent majority of decent people have had enough. . . . The withdrawal of the right to free speech from this one man could have enormous consequences and the totalitarian forces ranged against him will have succeeded. . . .

... He [Honeyford] dared to suggest that in a classroom dominated by coloured children white children suffer educationally. Mr. Honeyford should know, because in his school 92 percent of the children are of Asian origin. If he had commented the other way round, that in a school with 92 percent white children the 8 percent coloured children were at a disadvantage, he would have been praised by his present detractors, not vilified.

Mr. Michael Meadowcroft (Leeds, West):   Not so.

Mr. Fox: It is all right the hon. Gentleman saying "Not so." Let him just listen to what I have to say.

Mr. Meadowcroft: I have listened.

Mr. Fox: The hon. Gentleman has not heard half yet. In practice Mr. Honeyford is trying to rectify the situation in his school by emphasising that all his children are British—I see that the hon. Gentleman agrees; that is hopeful—and that English should be their mother tongue. (*Hansard,* April 16, 1985, cols. 233-236)

Unlike the theoretical approach taken above, which began with the analysis of the surface structures of text and talk, and then proceeded to the "underlying" structures, my analysis of this sample begins with some remarks about the various contextual properties of the debate, then moves to action and interaction structures, and finally to the semantic, schematic, and surface structures of this fragment. Most steps in the analysis correspond to the notions introduced above, which will not be further explained here.

Context

Access. Mr. Fox is allowed to speak, in this context, because he has permission of the Speaker of the House, and more generally is entitled to speak because he is an elected MP. In other words, access may be "layered" at several levels: It may be constrained contextually, here and now, or it may be constrained generally, or generically, for specific types of communicative events, contexts, and speech participants. For the overall sociopolitical structure of the reproduction of racism in the United Kingdom, such access is crucial: It means that those who oppose a multicultural society, write in extremist right-wing publications, and are considered racists by minority groups may be symbolically "represented" at the highest level of political decision making and thus even influence legislation on multicultural education.

Setting, medium, and audience. Mr. Fox, speaking in the House of Commons, shares in the power of all MPs as it is also symbolized by the setting of his talk. Since television has recently entered the House of Commons, such symbols are also relevant for the public "overhearers" of parliamentary debate. That is, through the media, the setting of this fragment extends beyond Parliament, which has British society as a whole as its indirect scope (as is also clear from the meaning, to be addressed below). Whatever MPs say in their powerful function of elected legislators is thus further enhanced by the formal setting of their speech and the presence of an audience of other MPs. Locally, Mr. Fox's power and influence coincides with his having the floor, marked not only by his speaking, but also by his standing up while the other MPs are seated. However, besides his power as an MP, Mr. Fox, in the broader setting of his speech, has even more power, as a spokesman of the Conservative Right and all those opposing multiculturalism in the United Kingdom (see below).

Genre. One other important element of context constraining the properties of text and talk is the type or genre of text and talk involved, here a parliamentary speech. Particularly, the lexical style, formal topic announcement ("This debate is about . . . "), and forms of address in this fragment signal this genre. For our analysis of the elite reproduction of racism, we may simply observe that the discursive processes involved in this reproduction process are operating at the highest genre levels in the legislature.

Social action and social relations. This speech fragment expresses or signals various social meanings and categories of social interaction. At the interaction level itself, politeness is signaled by the formal modes of address ("the honorable Gentleman"), whereas political closeness may be marked by "my friend . . . ." Since the politeness markers are mutual here, social power relations seem to be equal, although it should be recalled that Mr. Fox is member of a government party that is able to control much of the parliamentary agenda and that therefore is able to hold a parliamentary debate on Honeyford in the first place. That is, the very speech of Mr. Fox signals social and political dominance.

At another level of social relations, however, that is, relative to the social situation and events talked about by Mr. Fox, there is no question of formal equality. By defending Mr. Honeyford, Mr. Fox also attacks their common, leftist, antiracist opponents, and because of his powerful position as an MP he adds considerable weight to the balance of power of this conflict between Honeyford and the parents of his students, as is also the case for the right-wing media supporting Honeyford. We see how the conservative elites, who may otherwise be little interested in "ordinary" teachers, may take part in the struggle between racism and antiracism, between "British values" and the values of multiculturalism scorned by Mr. Honeyford.

Indeed, rather surprisingly, Mr. Honeyford was even personally received by Prime Minister Margaret Thatcher at 10 Downing Street, which again signals the highest support for his case. Similarly, that a conflict of a headmaster became a topic of a parliamentary debate by itself already suggests the importance accorded to the conflict, and to the sociopolitical positions to be defended at all costs. Finally, the association of Honeyford's opponents (mostly Asian parents) with Marxists and "Trots" not only means that the case of these opponents is discredited against the backdrop of largely anticommunist consensus in the United Kingdom, but also, more politically, that the Labour opposition to which Mr. Fox's speech is primarily addressed is thus attacked and discredited. Below, we shall see how such attacks, marginalization, discrediting, and other sociopolitical acts are enacted by properties of discourse. Here, it should be emphasized that the ultimate functions of such a speech are not merely linguistic or communicative (expressing or conveying meaning), but political.

Participant positions and roles. We have seen that Mr. Fox obviously speaks in his role as MP, and as a member of the Conservative party, among several other social identities, such as being a politician, white, and male. This position institutionally entitles him to put the Honeyford case on the parliamentary agenda if he and his party deem the issue to be of national interest. Obviously, however, it is not only his role of conservative MP that influences the structures and strategies of his speech, but also his identity as a member of the white dominant group, and especially his identity as a member of the white elites. Thus his party-political position explains why he attacks Labour, and the Left in general, his being an MP influences his alleged concern for democracy and the freedom of speech, and his being white explains his collusion with racist practices and his aggression against Indian parents and their supporters.

Interaction

Turn taking. It should first be noted that in this *Hansard* transcript it appears that the change of turns follows the rules of appropriate dialogical interruptions: there is no overlap, and speakers are even able to finish whole clauses or sentences. Note also that since most parliamentary speeches are read, speakers may often ignore interruptions and continue reading their discourse. They literally "have the floor" as long as the House Speaker allows it, and interruptions need not be attended or replied to, even when they are heard in the first place. In this example, however, the speaker does react to an interruption, which suggests that the point of the interruption is too important to leave unattended or the criticism too serious to remain unchallenged, or, possibly, the opponent too well known, prominent, or powerful to ignore. Thus ignoring or not ignoring interruptions in formal dialogues may have many reasons and functions, one of which is the (relative) power of the speech participants involved (for a further analysis of the political role of interruptions in Parliament, see Carbó, 1992).

Apparently, what is taking place here is a small conflict about speaking and listening between two MPs. That is, they momentarily do not speak about the topic of debate, the Honeyford affair, but about the ongoing discourse and interaction itself. Mr. Meadowcroft begins this exchange by interrupting Mr. Fox, and by denying Mr. Fox's last statement. Mr. Fox then first seems to accept the interruption, but then invites his opponent to listen, which presupposes that he thinks Mr. Meadowcroft did not listen, a presupposition that the latter challenges in a next turn.

The request by Mr. Fox ("Let him just listen") is, however, more than a request that Mr. Meadowcroft listen. It is also a reproach, first because Mr. Meadowcroft has interrupted the speaker in an early stage of his speech, but also, as he claims, that Mr. Meadowcroft has violated another norm of appropriate interaction, namely, that conversational participants are supposed to listen, so that the reproach may also be interpreted as an accusation and hence as an attack on the opponent. Indeed, from our knowledge about parliamentary rules, we may, even without considering the actual content of the dispute—whether or not Honeyford has acted in a racist way—infer from this exchange that Mr. Meadowcroft is part of the opposition, and not a member of Mr. Fox's party. Thus conversational conflict here also signals and symbolizes political conflict on ethnic affairs.

Interestingly, the interaction even goes beyond a rejection of interruption, a reproach of not listening, and an attack on an opponent. Mr. Fox knows very well that Mr. Meadowcroft has listened, simply because the latter's interruption, "Not so," is a relevant continuation, to the point, and an appropriate denial of the preceding assertion of Mr. Fox. The reproach of "not listening," thus, is rather a rhetorical strategy, namely, to translate into a "metacomment" (about the interaction itself) a rejection of what takes place at the level of the interaction and the flow of discourse, namely, that Mr. Meadowcroft explicitly denies the last statement, and hence explicitly signals that Mr. Fox is wrong.

When Mr. Fox takes his turn again, he reacts to the previous interruption and the further reaction of his opponent, by emphasizing again that Mr. Meadowcroft was "speaking out of turn," simply because, as Fox claims, he *"hasn't heard half yet."* In other words, Mr. Meadowcroft is accused of speaking too early. Note that in the middle of the next sentence, Mr. Fox seems to react to a nonverbal (nontranscribed) signal of Mr. Meadowcroft that Fox interprets as an agreement, and hence welcomes (*"hopeful"*) as a small victory in an argumentive debate.

Address. Although there are many other interactional strands and layers that may be analyzed in this small fragment, I close this brief analysis of the interactional dimension of this fragment by noting the formality of the exchange: The speakers do not address each other by the pronoun *you,* or even by first or last name, but by using the third-person deictic *he* and the standard address phrase here transcribed with an abbreviation, *hon. Gentleman.* Apart from their purely ritual nature as defined by the rules of address in Parliament, such forms of address are of course also signals of politeness, deference, and formality, if not of collective institutional "face work," by which the "real" conflicts, oppositions, and power plays may be masked. I shall come back to this power play below.

Speech acts. Most of Mr. Fox's speech consists of assertions, and also at the global level of macro speech acts, he primarily accomplishes an assertion. However, we have observed that, indirectly, he also accuses Honeyford's "detractors" of vilification, lying, and intimidation. At the same time, he thereby accuses and attacks his Labour opponents, whom he sees as supporters of Honeyford. Again, within Parliament his accusations and allegations may be met by appropriate defense by his sociopolitical equals. Not so, however, beyond the boundaries of Parliament, where his accusations may be heard (literally, over the radio) or read (when quoted in the press) by millions, who may thus be exposed to biased information about Honeyford's opponents (most of whom are not Marxists or Trotzkyites at all). For other discussion on the role of elites in the reproduction of racism, this means that the function and the scope of speech participants may largely define the effectiveness and "authority" of their speech acts. Indeed, other supporters of Honeyford may legitimate their support by referring to such accusations in Parliament. We shall see below how the accusation is actually carried out and supported by (semantic) "evidence."

Schemata

Argumentation. One major form of text schema is argumentation. Also in Mr. Fox's speech, as in parliamentary debates in general, argumentation plays a prominent role. As we have seen above, his main political point coincides with his argument's "position," which consists of his opinion that an attack against Honeyford is an attack against democracy and the freedom of speech. How does he support such a position? His first argument is a negative description of the facts: One man who writes in a "small-circulation" publication has brought a "holocaust" on his head. In other words: Whatever Honeyford has written, it was insignificant (published in a "small-circulation" publication), and the reaction was massively destructive (a "holocaust"). Moreover, what he wrote was also a "breath of fresh air in the polluted area of race relations" and hence not only not reprehensible, but laudable. For Mr. Fox it follows that a massive attack against laudable critique is a threat to the freedom of speech, and hence against democracy. We see that we need several steps to "make sense" of Mr. Fox's argument, and that such a reconstruction needs to be based on the subjective arguments and attitudes of the arguer. After all, Mr. Honeyford was able to speak his mind, so that the freedom of speech was not in danger. To equate criticism or even attacks against him with a threat against the freedom of speech and against democracy is, therefore, from another point of view, hardly a valid argument, but hyperbole, a rhetorical figure we also find in the rather inappropriate, while trivializing, use of the term *holocaust.* To understand this argument fully, however, we need more than to reconstruct Mr. Fox's attitudes. We need to know, for instance, that antiracist critique in the United Kingdom is more generally discredited by right-wing politicians and media as a limitation of free speech because it does not allow people to "tell the truth" about ethnic relations in general, or about multicultural education in particular—hence the reference to the "polluted area of race relations."

The second sequence of arguments focuses on Honeyford's "detractors," by whom Honeyford allegedly has been "vilified as a racist." By categorizing such opponents as "Marxists and Trots," and by claiming they have been engaged in lies and innuendo and even "harassed [Honeyford] out of his job," Mr. Fox details how, in his opinion, free speech is constrained, while at the same time discrediting Honeyford's opponents as communists and as "totalitarian forces," that is, in his view, as the enemies of freedom and democracy. A third component in his argumentation is the claim that Honeyford is helpless and is not allowed to defend himself. He even ranges the media among the opponents of Honeyford, although most of the vastly dominant conservative press supported him.

In sum, the argument schema features the following steps (propositions or macropropositions), of which the implicit arguments are marked with square brackets:

Arguments

1. Honeyford wrote an original and deserved critique of multicultural education.
2. His opponents attacked and harassed him massively.
2.1. [Massive attack and harassment of critics constitute an attack against free speech.]
2.2. His opponents are totalitarian communists.
2.2.1. [Totalitarian communists are against freedom and democracy.]

Conclusion

3. By attacking Honeyford, his opponents are totalitarian and limit the freedom of speech and attack democracy itself.

Interestingly, the argument, if valid, would also apply to Mr. Fox's argument itself, because by thus attacking from his powerful position as an MP, and given the massive attacks against Honeyford's opponents in the right-wing press, the freedom to criticize racist publications is delegitimated, if not constrained. That is, Honeyford's opponents hardly had the access to the mass media that Honeyford and his supporters had. Indeed, their arguments, if heard at all, were usually ignored or presented negatively in much of the press. On the other hand, Honeyford got the most unusual privilege of explaining his opinions in several long articles he was invited to write for the *Daily Mail*.

The validity of Mr. Fox's argument itself, however, hinges upon his definition of the situation, which is not only biased, but unfounded: Honeyford's critics are not Marxists and Trotzkyites (at least, not all or even most of them are), they did not prevent him from writing what he wanted to write, and, apart from protests, demonstrations, and picketing of his school, they did not harass him. Moreover, the majority of the press did not attack him, but supported him. What happened, however, was that he was suspended because he had publicly derogated his Asian students and their parents, and thus, for the Education Authority, he had failed as a headmaster.

The point of this brief analysis of the argument schema of (part of) Mr. Fox's speech for the discussion in this chapter is that a powerful and influential speaker, an MP, whose arguments may be quoted in the media, may misrepresent the facts, discredit antiracists as being un-democratic and against free speech, and at the same time support and legitimate racist publications. Unless his audience knows the facts, and unless it knows the opponents of Mr. Honeyford and their arguments, it may thus be manipulated into believing that Mr. Fox's argument is valid, and thereby associates those who oppose racism with "totalitar-ian" methods. This indeed is very common in the press, not only on the Right, and Mr. Fox reinforces such a negative evaluation of the struggle against racism. Ultimately, thus, Mr. Fox legitimates racism and enacts the dominance of the white group, not only by marginalizing antiracism, but also by discrediting multicultural policies in education. His political power as an MP is thus paired with his symbolic, discursive power, consisting of controlling the minds of his (secondary) audience, the media, other elites, and finally the public at large.

Meaning

Topics. The topic of the debate in the British House of Commons, as signaled by Mr. Fox himself ("The debate is concerned with . . ."), is clearly "the Honeyford case." Propositionally, however, the topic may be defined in various ways, for instance, as "Honeyford wrote dispar-aging articles about his Asian students and about multicultural educa-tion more generally," "Honeyford has been accused of racism," or "Honeyford is being vilified by antiracist detractors." It is the last of these topics that is being construed by Mr. Fox. At the same time, however, topics have sociopolitical implications, and these implica-tions also are made explicit by Mr. Fox: The debate is not only about Honeyford, or even about race relations and education, but about the "very root of our democracy," namely, free speech. This example nicely shows how events, including discourse about such events, are represented, at the macro level, as a function of underlying norms and values, that is, within the framework of dominant ideologies. That is, Mr. Fox and other supporters of Honeyford, also in the conservative media, interpret Honeyford's racist articles and his attack on multicultural education as a "breath of fresh air," and hence as an example of justified criticism, whereas his opponents are categorized as restricting free speech, and hence as being intolerant and undemocratic. This reversal of the application of values is well known in anti-antiracist rhetoric, where those who combat ethnic and racial intolerance are themselves accused of intolerance—that is, of the "freedom" to "tell the truth" about ethnic relations.

Relevant for this discussion is that Mr. Fox as an MP has the power to define and redefine not only the topics of debate, but also the situation. That is, the point is no longer whether or not Honeyford has insulted his students and their parents, or whether or not a teacher of a school with many minority students is competent when he attacks the principles of multiculturalism, but rather whether the critique leveled against him is legitimate in the first place. By generalizing the topic even beyond race relations and education to a debate about democracy and free speech, Mr. Fox at the same time defines both his and Mr. Honeyford's opponents—including Labour—as being against free speech and democracy, and hence as enemies of the British state and its fundamental values. By thus redefining the topic at issue, Mr. Fox no longer merely defends Mr. Honeyford, but reverses and generalizes the charges, and attacks the Left. He thereby conceals the fundamentally undemocratic implications of racism in education, and manipulates his secondary audience, the public at large, into believing that Mr. Honeyford is merely a champion of free speech, and his opponents as attacking British values if not democracy in general. As we shall see below, most of his speech tries to support that topical "point" persuasively.

Degree of completeness. One of the most conspicuous forms of overcompleteness in discourse is the irrelevant negative categorization of participants in order to delegitimate or marginalize their opinions or actions. This also happens in Mr. Fox's speech, where he irrelevantly and untruthfully categorizes Honeyford's critics as Marxists and Trotzkyites, which for him and much of his anticommunist audience implies association of the political-ideological enemy (the communists) with his moral-social enemy (the antiracists).

At the same time, Mr. Fox's argument, as we have seen, is also seriously incomplete, because it says little (in the rest of his speech, not reproduced here) about the nature of what Mr. Honeyford has written. It does, however, detail the many alleged negative actions of his opponents. He does not summarize their actions by saying that Honeyford was "criticized" or even "attacked," but mentions lies, vilification, harassment, and so on. In this case, thus, incompleteness is a semantic property of argumentation, but also a more general move of concealment and positive self-presentation: Honeyford's racist articles are not discussed, but only positively described, at a higher level of specificity, as "a breath of fresh air."

Perspective. Little analysis is necessary to identify the perspective and point of view displayed in Mr. Fox's speech: He defends Honeyford openly, supports his view explicitly, and severely attacks and marginalizes Honeyford's opponents. However, Mr. Fox also speaks as an MP—he refers to "this House"—and as a defender of democracy. Using the politically crucial pronoun "our" in "our democracy," he also speaks from the perspective of a staunch defender of democracy. This identification is of course crucial for a right-wing MP and for someone who openly supports someone who has written racist articles. Finally, he claims to be the voice of the "silent majority of decent people," a well-known populist ploy in conservative rhetoric. This also implies, rather significantly, that the parents of the Asian children in Bradford do not belong to this majority of "decent people." On the contrary, they have been categorized as, or with, the enemy on the Left.

Implications and presuppositions. Spelling out the full presuppositions and other implications of Mr. Fox's speech would amount to specifying the complex set of specific knowledge about the Honeyford case (the Honeyford model of Mr. Fox, and those of his audience and critics), as well as the general opinions on which his evaluations and arguments are based, as we have seen above. Hence I will mention a few examples: If the matter has become a national issue "not from Mr. Honeyford's choice," this strongly implies that others, his opponents, have made a national issue of it, whereas it also (weakly) implies that Mr. Honeyford's publications in a widely read national newspaper (e.g., the *Times Literary Supplement*) and later the *Daily Mail* did nothing to contribute to the national issue. The use of "small-circulation" as a modifier of "publication" implies that, given the small audience of the publication (he probably refers to the extremist right-wing *Salisbury Review*), the publication is "insignificant" and hence "not worth all the fuss" and certainly not a "holocaust." The major presupposition of this speech, however, is embodied in Mr. Fox's rhetorical question, "Who are the people who have persecuted him?" which presupposes that there actually *were* people who "persecuted" him. Finally, important for the political power play in Parliament, note the implications of his categorization of Honeyford's opponents as being "all on the Left of British politics," which immediately addresses Mr. Fox's opponents in the House of Commons: Labour. By vilifying Honeyford's opponents, and antiracists generally, as communists, as undemocratic, and as enemies of free speech, he implies that such is also the case for Labour.

Local coherence. There is one interesting coherence feature in Mr. Fox's speech, when he begins a new sentence with the definite noun phrase "the mob." Since no mob has been mentioned before in his text, we must assume either that this phrase generically refers to an (unspecified) mob or that the phrase corefers, as is clearly his intention, with the previously mentioned discourse referents (Honeyford's detractors and so on). Such coreference is permissible only if it is presupposed that the qualification indeed holds of previous identified participants. In other words, Mr. Fox, in line with right-wing news reports about Honeyford's critics, implicitly qualifies Honeyford's opponents as a "mob" and presupposes this qualification in a next sentence. This is one of Mr. Fox's discursive means to derogate his opponents.

Lexical style. Mr. Fox's lexical style is characteristic not only of parliamentary speeches, featuring technical political terms such as "adjournment debate," or of "educated" talk in general, as we see in "intellectual" words such as "innuendo," "detractors," "totalitarian forces," and "vilified," but at the same time he uses the well-known aggressive populist register of the tabloids when he characterizes his and Honeyford's opponents as "Trots," "the mob," and especially "race relations bullies." That is, Mr. Fox's lexicalization multiply signals his power, his political and moral position, and his persuasive strategies in influencing his (secondary) audience, the British public.

Surface Structures

Syntax. The syntax of Mr. Fox's speech shows a few examples of semantically controlled topicalization and other forms of highlighting information. Thus, in the fourth sentence, the object of the predicate "to strike at, namely, "the freedom of speech," is placed at the end of the sentence, after its qualifying clause ("what we cherish in this House above all"), in order to emphasize it—a well-known strategy of syntactic and rhetorical "suspense." Conversely, "without a thread of evidence" is fronted somewhat later in his speech so as to specify in a prominent position in the sentence that Honeyford's vilification was without grounds. Note also the agentless passives: By whom, indeed, was Honeyford continuously criticized in the media? Surely not by Marxists and Trotzkyites, who have no access to mainstream publications in Britain.

Pronouns. In the discussion of the perspective and point of view in Mr. Fox's speech I have already suggested his multiple political and social "positions" and with whom Mr. Fox identifies. Position and identification also determine the use of pronouns and deictic expressions (such as "this" in "this adjournment debate," which signals Mr. Fox's participation in the debate). Most significant in this fragment, however, is the use of "our" in "our democracy," a well-known political possessive phrase in much conservative rhetoric. Obviously, Mr. Fox signals himself as participating in "our democracy," which may refer to British democracy, or Western democracy, or the kind of democracy as it is interpreted by Mr. Fox. The rest of his argument, however, clearly shows that the Left, and especially Marxists, Trotzkyites, and the supporters of Mr. Honeyford, are excluded from this definition of democracy, because they allegedly violate the freedom of speech.

Rhetoric

Several of the other properties of Mr. Fox's speech discussed above also have rhetorical structures and functions. Besides being argumentative, his speech is largely rhetorical. He glorifies Honeyford and derogates, accuses, and marginalizes Honeyford's opponents. In the beginning of this fragment, which opens the debate, Fox immediately extends the topic from the Honeyford case to much more provocative and politically relevant topics of the freedom of speech and democracy, and he does so by using an enumerative climax, culminating in a traditional metaphor ("the root of our democracy") that emphasizes free speech as the "foundation" of democracy while at the same time making Mr. Fox's speech more important, as it addresses such "fundamental" issues. The insensitive metaphor of the "holocaust" has been discussed above, and interpreted as hyperbole for a "massive destruction." Apart from the fact that not a single person died or was even bodily hurt in the Honeyford conflict, the hyperbolic metaphor also has a number of vicious implications not mentioned above, namely, that Honeyford's opponents are associated with Nazis or mass murderers, an association that is also explicitly made in the right-wing press for antiracists.

Similarly, within the ecological domain, Mr. Fox finds both a contrastive comparison and two metaphors to identify Honeyford's original ideas ("breath of fresh air" and the "polluted" atmosphere of race relations). Again, after associating Honeyford's opponents with Nazis, he now associates them with polluters, a new officially certified enemy. Interestingly, as shown earlier, we may interpret such qualifications also as reversals, since it is precisely the extreme Right that is politically closer to fascism, and to industrial pollution, and not the radical Left that Mr. Fox is speaking about. That is, in attacking the Left, right-wing speakers often make use of classical accusations leveled by the Left, simply by "inverting" them, and as if to deny their own lack of democratic zeal, for instance in supporting someone who writes racist articles.

Also, the rest of the speech makes full use of the usual tricks from the rhetorical bag: Rhetorical questions (e.g., "Who are Honeyford's detractors?"), parallelisms (the repeated questions), alliterations ("full force"), and especially contrasts between *us* and *them* (as in "race relations bullies" and "the majority of decent people") and between the lone hero and the irrational and threatening mass ("One man . . .") and his opponents (Marxists, Trots, totalitarian forcers, mob, vilification, lies). These rhetorical features emphasize what has been expressed and formulated already at the semantic, syntactic, and lexical (stylistic) levels of his speech, namely, the positive presentation of Honeyford (us, conservatives, and so on) on the one hand, and especially the negative presentation of the Others (them, the Left, antiracists, Asian parents).

Conclusion

The dominance expressed, signaled, and legitimated in this speech does not reside merely in the political realm of the House of Commons, for instance, in Mr. Fox's role as MP and as representative of a government party who is allowed to provoke a debate about the Honeyford affair in Parliament. Similarly, by attacking the Left he does not attack only Labour, as may be expected from a Tory speaker. Rather, the dominance involved here extends beyond Parliament to the media and especially the public at large, when Mr. Fox uses his political influence to support publicly a teacher of students whose parents think he writes racist things, and especially in order to discredit and marginalize both these parents and their supporters. Indeed, the rest of this speech, not analyzed here, sketches in more detail what Mr. Fox sees as a wonderful teacher, while at the same time denying, as is common in much elite discourse, the racist nature of Honeyford's writings. That is, Mr. Fox's power, authority, and dominance are not even those that come with being an influential MP. Rather, his authority, in establishing what racism is, is that of a member of the white elite. It is in this way that such a speech indirectly supports the system of ethnic-racial dominance, that is, racism.

7

Urban Ethnography

Another Look

MELVIN D. WILLIAMS

Ethnography in America is flawed by hegemony (see Rose, 1990). It is culture bound. We have Third World regions in the United States (e.g., Black inner cities) where imperialism and colonialism are international. We sell finished industrial products there and increasingly deny the people who reside there the opportunities to participate in the rewards of production. The dilemmas of race and ethnic relations know few boundaries (Willis, 1974).

The frequent themes of ethnography in cities—sexism, racism, classism, colonialism, and imperialism—are human adaptive strategies that have come about during cultural evolution (e.g., the Agricultural and Industrial Revolutions and the impending Ecological Revolution). These strategies will become obsolete after the Ecological Revolution. The new ethnography will consider these social transformations and eschew its traditional participation in the reproduction of social inequality. The new ethnography will compensate for the old, which documented the "traditional" lives of the people as they and their ways of life were being systematically destroyed.

A new theoretical approach to urban ethnography is one that ceases to treat oppression and discrimination as abnormal human behavior. It is one that takes a realistic look at the needs and possibilities of behavior modification in this area. It is one that discusses the prospects and possibilities based on this new perspective.

Social scientists examining the cities of the world and the racial relations therein have failed to discover the common denominators that underlie the oppression and discrimination they have found. I suggest that there are basic panhuman characteristics responsible for these practices.

I begin this chapter by outlining the basic characteristics of humans that underlie racial, ethnic, religious, and class oppression and discrimination, treating the problem as a worldwide phenomenon. I then proceed to describe some of the dilemmas and predicaments of urban oppression and discrimination, and present some of the contributions of African Americans, notwithstanding their lack of access to many institutional resources. Finally, I address avenues for ending poverty, oppression, and discrimination throughout the world. The discussion includes brief examinations of the Black middle class, the Black underclass, women, and the power elite who oppress all of them.

Humans and Oppression

In this new examination of race relations, I will analyze them as another human design for the reproduction of social inequality. I will abandon the Marxist model for an evolutionary one that focuses particular attention on the development of human culture. This paradigm is broad, simple, and general. It attempts a metatheory that organizes the reproduction of social inequality, including artificially defined human populations, as another abuse of the earth and its resources. I attempt to offer a hypothesis for this abuse and its ravages and use race relations as a simple test of that hypothesis. The test, if successful, promises a different human relationship with and perception of the poisoned planet and all of its resources, including its people and other forms of life. The history and the study of race relationships demonstrate how difficult the problems are to ameliorate, but this situation must be transformed if humans are to survive into and through the next century.

In my earlier examinations of Black people and their relationships, I have followed them into their institutional arrangements and questioned both the values and the attitudes that constitute the ideology of racial superiority and the people who sacrifice so much to reach for racial supremacy and attempt to maintain it (Williams, 1981a, 1981b, 1984, 1989, 1992a, 1992b). I am convinced that such examinations and the insights that derive from them can tell us far more about human behavior than we can learn from the drive and tenacity in racial supremacy. The drive to separate ourselves into artificial groups and populations for invidious comparisons, discrimination, oppression, and genocide (e.g., of African Americans, Native Americans, Jews, Armenians, Kurds, Iraqis, Kuwaitis) is closely related to what is compelling us to indiscriminately destroy the earth's ecosystems. That human inferiority complex (after Austrian psychiatrist Alfred Adler, 1964) cannot be assuaged by achievements wrought in our cultural evolution—the Agricultural and Industrial Revolutions. It must be socialized out of us in the Ecological Revolution. Otherwise it is like pouring ocean water over a man dying of thirst—it may give the illusion of helping, but it does not treat the malady.

With this new theoretical approach to urban ethnography, we must also train ethnographers who resist the traditional research path of studying the victims, their social contexts and social networks. Instead, we must study the perpetrators and the collaborators. Most oppressed racial and ethnic groups have members who collaborate with the oppressing group (see the discussion below). Who are they and why and how do they function? We must abandon the dead-end research pathways that focus on the symptoms and behaviors of oppression and discrimination. Many researchers themselves enjoy privileges of status, prestige, income, and class that are structurally supported by the racial and ethnic relations that they continue to study and fail to transform. Such privilege creates vested interest in the current structure and influences the nature and conduct of researchers. Ethnography has its problems (recall the Margaret Mead controversy and the reflexive ethnography debate), as does any research design that studies human behavior, but an able ethnographer can identify and communicate the values and attitudes of his or her "own people." He or she must be accepted as a member of the population. Thus we need to train members of the "power elite" to study, understand, and explain the needs, designs, and ramifications of the oppressors' behavior. This will be possible once we convince ourselves of the bases for racial oppression and the present maladaptive nature of the behavior.

Contrasts of Oppression

Almost a century ago, W. E. B. Du Bois (1903/1961) said, "We feel and know that there are many delicate differences in race psychology, numberless changes that our crude social measurements are not yet able to follow minutely, which explain much of history and social development" (p. 123). Du Bois was expressing a sentiment that still exists today. That sentiment is that African people from sub-Saharan Africa have a distinctive psychological temperament. Leopold S. Senghor described it as Negritude. Asante (1987) has described it as Afrocentric. And recently, Leonard Jeffries at the City College of the City University of New York has called it humanistic, communal, and caring. Of course, Michael Levin at the same university persists in claiming that the difference is lower intelligence for African Americans (Blum, 1990).

My own suggestions about DDDAK (the denial, defiance, and defilement of our animal kinship, pronounced did-did-did-dac) are motivated by the resistance to modernity in sub-Saharan Africa. We can yet find hunters and gatherers among the Bushman, Pygmy, Sandawe, Hatsa, and Dorobo. The African American endurance during slavery, the Civil War, and Reconstruction are noted. My explanation is that the quality and intensity of the human inferiority complex may vary among human populations. These variations determine the extent to which people perceive themselves as part of the web of life, as components of the biosphere rather than as separate species designed to control the planet and other species. Certain populations, such as those in sub-Saharan Africa and women generally, may have less drive to manipulate, control, and exploit the environment. A popular American perspective on some individual ramifications that may result from the intense human inferiority complex are discussed by Kinder (1990) in his book *Going Nowhere Fast* as well as by Baritz (1988) in his volume *The Good Life*. Thorstein Veblen (1927) discussed some of these same behavioral dynamics more than 65 years ago.

If my suggestions have some validity, humans will have some exemplary selective populations to examine when it finally becomes evident that we can no longer survive with the quality and intensity of inferiority complexes that have created modern society.

I have observed oppressive human environments among the Straits Salish Indians of Vancouver Island, British Columbia (Williams, 1979, 1989), and among the Black ghettos of Pittsburgh, Pennsylvania (Williams, 1984, 1992a, 1992b). The contrasts are noteworthy. African Americans are often robust, ribald, and vividly expressive in their poverty and economic oppression. Such responses have often created the mythology that they are "happy" by nature. But the Native Canadians seem desolate, despairing, abandoned, and hopeless. Even when in groups, drinking to become intoxicated and to forget life for a while, my Indian informants were sullen and forlorn. Both populations are oppressed and the recipients of social and economic discrimination, but the African Americans appear to endure these conditions so well that the myth of the poor, happy Black has been perpetuated for centuries. No such myth exists on the Canadian Indian reserves.

This phenomenon was also recorded on the American slave plantations. The Native Americans were decimated in slavery and ultimately rejected as not suitable. Meanwhile, African Americans survived and propagated, to make slavery in the New World a profitable enterprise. Blacks adopted the master's religion. It is often described as a "slave religion" for Blacks because it preaches that slaves should love their masters, notwithstanding their state of servitude. African Americans not only adopted the master's religion, they adopted it with a passion. They may be the most religious population in the United States. I argue that this adoption of Christianity is the result of a lack of intensity of DDDAK. Such a constitution allows them to endure hardship in the hegemony of America. Such a constitution is an African survival. It has prompted those more endowed with DDDAK to call Africans and African Americans lazy, shiftless, happy, and irresponsible for 400 years.

It would seem that the oppressed African American would have high levels and more intense qualities of inferior feelings as a result of the socialization in this society. But that logic is at a lower level of abstraction. DDDAK is a constitutional emotion that determines the relational identity with life forms within ecosystems. Such identity tends to control inferior feelings generally. So in spite of oppression in America this suspected lower level of DDDAK in the general population of African Americans may allow them to constitutionally endure and to tolerate better the hardships of living. This tolerance level may be a factor in the global discrimination against dark-skinned people. In any case, a technique to measure and calculate the intensity of DDDAK will further clarify the usefulness of the concept. And further, we need to study the landlords of Blacks, the Black middle class, the merchants in African American neighborhoods, and the power elite to understand why they tolerate, perpetuate, and collaborate in these conditions for the Black and the poor.

An Anthropological Approach

The study of the Black and the poor requires a new theoretical approach that considers cultural and evolutionary parameters. Racism is a distinctively human behavior. It persists in spite of wars, laws, and education to prevent it. It resists analysis, notwithstanding centuries of efforts to understand and explain it. It is pervasive even though those who practice it deny it. To understand it one must come to terms with some basic characteristics of human behavior. Such an understanding allows us to comprehend not only racism but also many other social problems that find their genesis in the nature of man/woman—classism, sexism, imperialism, and religious intolerance. My approach to the study of race and ethnic relations will show the relationships among culture, society, human nature, and race and ethnic groups. It will enable students of race and ethnic relations to understand, identify, and explain the institutions, values, attitudes, and human characteristics that continue to allow humans to label, legitimate, license, and lobby the inferiority of other humans.

This anthropological approach to race and ethnic relations will provide a new and heuristic meaning to the concepts of race and ethnicity. It may provide the integrative catalyst for the diverging fields of anthropology. Much of the biological basis for the concept of race and ethnicity has lost its credibility, especially after the racial determinism scholarship of Stewart Houston Chamberlain, Joseph Arthur, comte de Gobineau, and Friedrich Nietzsche. But race and ethnicity continue to have social, historical, political, and economic impacts on those populations that are distinguishable by phenotypical, political, geographic, and historical characteristics. Ethnic groups have cycles of prominence that display fission and fusion relative to the strength and intensity of nationalism or larger political bonds. They persist with social, historical, political, and geographic significance into contemporary societies. The transformations in the former Soviet Union and Yugoslavia give a dramatic contemporary view of the dynamics of ethnicity. Racism is a result of the acceptance of race as a standard of identifying separate human populations, the development of cultural values, and the nature of the evolutionary human experience. My approach will bring unity to these disparate vectors.

Racial and ethnic intolerance is global. Examining this intolerance from a holistic, evolutionary, and global perspective will give us new insights into the history and the future of humankind. Such an examination requires a review of the possible origins of culture so that we may better understand the unique behavioral and historical development of *Homo sapiens*. The discussion below will review the theories of Freud, Jung, Lévi-Strauss, and others who have attempted to comprehend that origin and development. It will trace the salient features of human history and contemporary modernity to explain the nature of humans, with their pervasive racial and ethnic perspectives. It will allow us to compare and contrast discrimination based on race, ethnicity, religion, social class, and gender. In this approach the comparisons will be generic because the genesis of the discriminations is the same— culture and human nature. The understanding of human nature and its development will enable us to comprehend, explain, and resolve racism, classism, sexism, imperialism, and religious intolerance. Are these discriminations fundamental to the character of human culture? Are they, like modernity and its other social problems, characteristic of civilization? These are some of the questions with which my approach will wrestle.

This examination of human culture will require us to return to the discussions of Leslie White (1949, 1973; culture is autonomous) and Alfred Kroeber (1917; culture is superorganic) to determine the possible social transformations that contemporary society may require to ban these forms of human distinctions, discriminations, and intraspecies hostilities. Can we eliminate them and other social problems that threaten human survival, or are the seeds of human extinction incorporated within the essence and creation of human culture? These are some of the issues that this approach will demand that we explore. Perhaps the dinosaurs had the seeds of their extinction incorporated within the essence and creation of their adaptive success. But humans have culture, which is malleable. If we learn quickly enough, we can transform the nature of humans.

Research Problems

Inner-city ethnography must focus on the sources of inner-city problems, not on the symptoms of those problems. Like the slaves throughout recorded history, the serfs of Europe, the peasants of the world, the workers in early industrial England, and the Soviet proletariat, members of the underclass in American cities are not the source of the problems there. So why do we continue to study them? Perhaps it is to avoid identifying the source of the problems. Black scholars, particularly, must make the difficult transition from their historically limited roles in scholarship to the study of the white, rich, power elite who determine life in the inner cities. There are critical needs for welfare reform, education reform, housing programs, employment training, child care, child support, medical access, and equal opportunity. Studying the Black and the poor will never provide these.

As Hylan Lewis (1971) has advised, we need to study the rich and the oppressors:

> My own view is that the most important research into this area now should focus not on the culture of poverty but on the culture of affluence—the culture that matters more and that is far more dangerous than the culture of poverty. Jean Mayer has put the thrust and the focus succinctly:
>
> "There is a strong case to be made for a stringent population policy on exactly the reverse of the basis Malthus expounded. Malthus was concerned with the steadily more widespread poverty that indefinite population growth would inevitably create. I am concerned about the areas of the globe where people are rapidly becoming richer. For rich people occupy much more space, consume more of each natural resource, disturb the ecology more, and create more land, air, water, chemical, thermal and radioactive pollution than poor people. So it can be argued that from many viewpoints it is even more urgent to control the numbers of the rich than it is to control the numbers of the poor." (p. 358)

In the postindustrial age, when service employment supersedes industrial employment, we must learn to understand the values and attitudes that abandon the people who operated the industrial plants after the closings of the factories of the Rust Belt. Just as we should not abandon the retired elderly, we should not abandon the closed-mill unemployed. We must study the human processes that allow such abandonment and resocialize our children to prevent them. This is the task of the new research in urban ethnography. Arbitrarily defined and identified populations must be included within the human community, not only rhetorically and ideally but also in terms of social policy and human values. I argue that these are values and attitudes that are not only desirable but obligatory in the twenty-first century. Our research must show us the pivotal institutions that have created this cultural lag in our social and political skills in an era when our technological sophistication is threatening life on earth.

Hegemonic groups expend great efforts and resources to maintain their hegemony. What are the pervasive natures and resources of these efforts and how are they executed, operationalized, and perpetuated in cities? What drives people to maintain exclusive power from generation to generation even at considerable human cost to themselves, their families, and those they exploit? How can we examine these discourses in power?

The poor do not suffer in silence. They rob, kidnap, and assassinate their oppressors. They deprive their oppressors of privacy. The poor support the media that expose them and their families to lies and distortions. The oppressed punish the power elite again and again, but their actions are often not recorded. Like the "great man" histories of the past, our ethnographies have not escaped their colonial and historical origins. The new urban ethnography must break with these old conceptual models and examine the nature and character of the oppressors. It must fully explore how racial groups and their perpetuation serve the purposes of the oppressors. We must study the nature and character of a social system that constructs "racial relations" and then directs all the attention of the problems created by such concepts onto the victims. Such traditional ethnographic research is not designed to ameliorate the plight of these victims, for we know that as long as these social systems persist, "the poor will always be with us"; it is analogous to studying pornography and vividly describing the artifacts and the illustrations, a process that reinforces the abuse of women and children and pornography's other victims.

Ethnographic Distortions

I have returned to Belmar, a neighborhood in Pittsburgh, several months every year for the past decade to observe the social and physical transformations in this neighborhood. The economic decline in Belmar that I described in 1981 continues 10 years later. It will not reverse itself until values change, both in the United States in general and in Belmar. Black "leaders," poverty programs, public policy agents, government intervention, private investment, housing code enforcement, school desegregation, and political realignments in Belmar and Homewood (the larger region containing Belmar) are cosmetic factors that do little to address the problems of the neighborhood. Houses continue to decay and be replaced by lots full of debris. Pool halls are replaced by drug streets, street corners, and houses (crack houses), while activities elsewhere—the library, taverns, street corner groups, wino groups, street-mechanic groups, street and schoolyard game groups, Huffy bicycle groups, and the swimming pool—seem to wane in the face of major economic enterprise in street drug traffic. Even the vandalism, burglary, and robbery activities appear to have decreased as money seems more available in the drug traffic. The rubbish and garbage that the residents remove from their property in the early mornings after busy nights of transactions reveal the new and more expensive eating and drinking habits of those who work and litter there.

The alterations in family, church, and neighborhood life have had a major impact on educational goals, single-parent families, teenage pregnancy, and the unemployable. The spirit and the activities seem dominated by the young men and women who ply their trade and participate in drugs. The children are surrounded by and sometimes inducted into these drug activities. They see and know the dealers and their cars. They admire the clothes, shoes, money, cars, loud car stereo systems, and business acumen of the dealers. One 21-year-old male dealer called to a 9-year-old neighbor as he stored his drugs in the trunk of his parked-car business location, "Milton, watch my stuff. Don't let anybody mess with it. If you see anybody messing with it, let me know who it is."

The neighborhood continues to lose its "core members" (those who invest in their community without expectation of immediate returns). Even Deacon Griffin (Williams, 1981b, p. 55), who was "mainstream" and resigned to "live out my days" in Belmar, has moved. If he could see the traffic in front of his former house today, he would have no regrets. The neighborhood seems alive with young adults, and many older residents appear overwhelmed by the drug networks, activities, control, and noise, and their dominating impact on them and their children.

This process of blaming and debating about the victims diverts attention from the problem—"inferior" people created by those who require "inferior" people to sustain their own mythical superiority. That problem has reached gigantic proportions—infant mortality, the AIDS epidemic, the homeless, the "underclass," the health care debacle, environmental disaster, and irrational economic greed—that can no longer be ignored. There are no superior people or other less important forms of life. We are all in this web together. And together we must begin the Ecological Revolution.

The human inferiority complex created by DDDAK has forced us into a mythical superior status and role on Earth. But we humans are animals that perspire, and perspiration has its odor. We secrete mucous from the eyes, lungs, bronchial tubes, skin, sexual organs, and colon. We salivate, masticate, expectorate, regurgitate, urinate, defecate, masturbate, fornicate, gestate, exudate, suppurate, lacrimate, lactate, fight, kill, sleep, hemorrhage, die, and decay. Yet we reject our animal kinship and even subordinate other arbitrarily defined humans to prove our superiority. This is the problem, and it has become so severe that it threatens not only Belmar and other places like it, but the very Earth. Shakespeare illustrates the problem:

> What a piece of work is a man! How noble in reason! how infinite in faculty! in form, in moving, how express and admirable! in action how like an angel! in apprehension how like a god! the beauty of the world! the paragon of animals! (*Hamlet,* act II, scene ii)

As long as humans use artificial categories to conceptualize arbitrarily identified human populations and place other forms of nonhuman life outside of the human community and inferior to humans, there is little to prevent circumstances that allow human populations to be shifted about in terms of significance and even to be regarded as nonhuman (e.g., Jews in Nazi Germany) and thus outside of the concentric circles of the human community. This "concentric circle" conception of the human community is an abiding threat to all humans. At any time, genocide, homelessness, war, or some other human circumstance may place any of us on the margins or outside the human community, along with other "lower" forms of life.

It is not easy to communicate the values of one population to another population with different values. Attempts at translation are distorted despite precautions. My approach here is to illustrate through the analogy of an invading army; this analogy is intended only to be suggestive.

It is difficult to occupy a people's territory for long without their complicity and corruption. Approximately 30 million African Americans experience discrimination as a result of American values that posit all African Americans as inferior and deprive many of them economically.

The "genuine" (some lower-class) African Americans can be depicted as cultural resistance fighters who attempt to demoralize the occupying army. In carrying out their sabotage, they have many casualties, take great risks, and are the objects of the enemy's relentless roundups, hostage taking, firing squads, and other persecutions. But these "freedom fighters" never allow the enemy to forget that they are occupying another people's territory. The sufferings of the "genuine" keep the truth before us and benefit all African Americans when the propaganda of the enemy would have us believe that his rule and control will create a better world for African Americans. The enemy teaches us that his values are best for everybody, notwithstanding that those values create the perception that African Americans are inferior. The enemy selects only the cultural traitors as his collaborators and gives them limited economic opportunities. But he does not share power with them. The enemy "props up" these collaborators as "leaders," role models, scholars, businesspeople, and politicians. He gives them dubious status and the illusion of power, and pretends that they are important, allowing them limited association among the enemy as long as they provide useful information and perform activities vital in the control of their own people. Like the accused "Vichy French," these collaborators court power. They have sex, friendships, and conspiracies with their enemy, the occupying army. They do the enemy's bidding in scholarship, business, education, and politics. In this analogy the "spurious" (those with "white" values) and mainstream (most middle-class) Blacks are the collaborators. Every occupying army depends upon collaborators to oppress and control the conquered peoples. The collaborators rationalize that if you have no power or courage, then you must live by the myths of those who do. The resistance fighters say that the will and courage to resist is power. We have heard the stories of the enemy burning the books of the conquered people, but there is no need to burn books that have never been allowed to be published, or, if published, are not distributed, promoted, and utilized in the schools. You do not have to be concerned with the truth if you control most of the means of communication.

The freedom fighters would rather die in the resistance movement than acquiesce to perpetual "inferiority" and servitude. Like Harriet Tubman, they come from a long line of African American resistance fighters. They are being labeled "gang members," "crack dealers," "roving packs" (note the animal imagery), and "the underclass." They are not only victims but "inferior" devils as well. But perhaps many of them are just members of the resistance movement who are saying in their own subcultural way, "Give me liberty or give me death."

We must cease to discover diversionary devils in the inner city and instead attempt to locate the evils that rob these neighborhoods of community, family, education, and churches. Proposing idealistic social and economic policies without the value and attitude transformations that must accompany them is mere ivory-tower "scholarship." It is economic mythmaking. It will require a revolution—the Ecological Revolution—to halt this reproduction of social inequality.

I argue that this revolution, an aftermath of the Agricultural and Industrial Revolutions, will come as a result of a series of ecological disasters (e.g., the Persian Gulf oil spills, the desertification of California, and nuclear accidents) that will force global transformations for human survival. These transformations will require that we have appropriate ethnographies of cities (where most people live) so that we can understand the policies and procedures that will allow humans to endure and manage such changes.

Academic disciplines and other modes of organizing knowledge continue to restrict the views of students and scholars about the relationships of human behavior. Anthropology's four field approach was once a concerted effort to combat such restrictions but the informational deluge of modernity, the technological prestige of assembling it, the misuse and misunderstanding of ethnography, and the scholarly supremacy of restricted access to narrow and highly specialized "knowledge" threatens all forms of interdisciplinary efforts. After the Ecological Revolution anthropologists will cease to project and displace their own social problems on to "others." There is nothing wrong with ethnography as a social science method. Reflexivity and "other voices" treat the symptoms of the researchers. The problems are with the readers and writers of ethnography. They read and write about "different" people—"primitives, savages, simple societies, classes, races, ethnic groups, genders, sects, ages, nations and others." They exploit "others" to reinforce their own fragile selves. After the Ecological Revolution, anthropologists will write about and readers will read about humans in order to find themselves. The new social scientists will study humans so that readers and writers can look into the "mirror for man" and see themselves, not "others."

Cultural Evolution

As the brain in the nonhuman primate developed into the Rubicon of self-reflection, the ability to objectify oneself, to stand apart from oneself, and to consider the kind of being one is and "what it is that" one "wants to do and to become" (Bidney, 1964, p. 3), humankind began to separate itself from the "lower" animals. This panhuman characteristic or universal cultural pattern is coterminous with the human mind that is conscious of awareness, experiences the self as an object, and conceptualizes changes in that object. That mind compared other species of

animals with itself and created "consciousness of kind." It conceptualized that the other animals were "lower" animals and began an unconscious process of creating inferiority complexes in human groups,
complexes that have influenced human behavior ever since.

In the beginning, the conceptualization of other species as "lower"
animals facilitated the creation and development of culture. Culture
allowed humans to adapt successfully throughout the world. This success has now reached a point where humans dominate and manipulate
the world without the necessary respect for the delicate web of life that
includes humans themselves. This success has also resulted in the
conceptualization of artificially distinct human populations as "lower"
or "inferior" people. Collective inferiority complexes have been exacerbated by this process.

In a book that remains one of the definitive statements on collective
inferiority complexes, E. Franklin Frazier (1957/1968) describes the
behavior of middle-class African Americans who are socialized to be
"inferior" and are desperately attempting to legitimate their upward
mobility. Frazier's critics assert that the behavior that he describes and
discusses can be observed among middle-class Jews in particular and
among all middle-class populations in general. Frazier agrees with his
critics and explains that he merely limited his account to middle-class
African Americans. He concludes: "Some of my Jewish friends, including
some young sociologists, went so far as to say that the book was the best
account that they had ever read concerning middle-class Jews" (p. 13).

Much of Frazier's work has not been well received because it strikes
at the heart of human nature and human mythology. Not only all
middle-class groups, but all human beings, regardless of race, class, and
ethnicity, are victims of a collective inferiority complex. That is my
thesis. I explain this complex on the basis of a theory called DDDAK.

As Rogers (1988) states:

> Most social scientists would agree that the capacity for human culture was
> probably fashioned by natural selection, but they disagree on the implications
> of this supposition. Some scientists believe that natural selection imposes
> important constraints on the ways in which culture can vary, while others
> believe that any such constraints must be negligible. (p. 819)

At a certain period in human evolution, increased brain capacity,
self-consciousness, and fear caused humans to distinguish and to divorce themselves psychologically from "lower" animals. The fear was

created by the unknown, the unknowable, and the meaninglessness of the animal cycle of birth, struggle, and death. This transition to a unique pattern of human social learning constrained the ways in which culture can vary. The extent of those constraints I leave, for now, to the sociobiologists and their critics. My efforts in this chapter are to examine, describe, and explore the constraints themselves and some of their effects on human behavior.

Freud (1949), Jung (1933), other psychologists, and Lévi-Strauss (1963, 1967, 1969, 1979) have attempted to give us some insights into the psychology of human origins and evolution. The transition to human social learning or culture must have occurred with severe traumas, as the biblical story of Eden demonstrates. The response of humans was to perceive themselves as superior to the other animals and to select companions on the basis of this perception. The perception of qualitative distinction and superiority had severe impacts on the psyche of humans forced to survive in similar ecological niches with the "lower" animals, especially given that these other animals possessed so many physical characteristics that were similar to those of humans. The response of human beings was an ever stronger effort to distinguish themselves from animals, a strength that I characterize as a denying, defying, and defiling of their animal kinship (DDDAK). This effort may help to explain the development of primate traits that biological anthropologists cannot adequately trace, such as upright posture, language, skin color, and bipedalism.

DDDAK was critical in the origin of humankind, in the formation of a permanent component of humans' constitutional character. That character, as we shall see, helps to explain certain behaviors in human societies. Humans' 3 million years as hunters and gatherers, in competition with "lower" animals and each other, reinforced DDDAK in human character and transferred it by psychological displacement into an important component of human perception, a perceptual dichotomy and deep-structure binary opposition: inferior/superior. During this entire period and in the present, "lower" animals are vivid perceptual images and models for humans' codified standard of the "inferior."

During the 3 million years humans roamed the earth as hunters and gatherers, they stood upright to stretch as tall above the "lower" animals as possible, with hands free to make tools and weapons. With these weapons, humans killed animals for food and for their habitats. This was a further expression of DDDAK for these omnivores. It was manifested by ranking human populations (even fossil remains of humans once were described in terms of the hunted, *Zinjanthropus*, and the hunter, *Homo habilis*). Status was conferred on the basis of knowledge of ritual, tradition, game movements, terrain, healing, articulate speech, and other critical aspects of social life. But power continued to elude humans. DDDAK took the form of elaborate kinship relationships among humans themselves and their intricate regulations against indiscriminate sexuality. It encouraged cooperation for hunting, for protection from "lower" animals, for social solidarity that contrasted with its perceived absence among the "lower" animals, and for survival as a "higher" form of animal life that maintained relationships with the supernatural.

Approximately 15,000 years ago, hunters and gatherers began to domesticate plants and "lower" animals. On the fertile banks of certain rivers more food was grown than the populations growing it could consume. The nonhuman primate that stood and freed his hands perhaps had increased his brain capacity by using them. That brain capacity had created culture that continued to increase brain capacity. All of this culminated in the Agricultural Revolution, which brought humans economic surplus. The convergence of economic surplus and DDDAK created the equivalent of an explosion in culture, and humankind's brief history after this period has been dominated by DDDAK-inspired attempts to utilize the economic surplus to prove human superiority. The human inferiority complex has dominated our efforts to distribute and utilize the economic surplus. Thus the surplus changed the character of human societies, which became marked by social stratification, slavery, human exploitation, oppression, warfare, tyranny, and that human satisfaction described by Thackeray as the true pleasure of life—associating with one's inferiors. The events of the next 15,000 years were dominated by questions of who gets the surplus and how to control the "inferiors" who are deprived of it.

Another major event in human cultural history, the Industrial Revolution, occurred about 200 years ago with the scientific discoveries that led to modern machine technology, which in turn created surplus even more rapidly. For 200 years, human populations have waged war and indulged in economic intrigue to determine who will control the vast surplus created by modern science and machine technology. Ingenious distinctions have been created in the world's populations to rationalize the distribution of that surplus. Some of these distinctions are region, race, religion, ethnicity, nation, and class specific; some are a combination. All of these distinctions are manipulated by humankind's DDDAK and the resulting human inferiority complex. Humans have used the surpluses from the Agricultural Revolution and the Industrial Revolution to surround and clothe themselves with elaborate wealth, sophisticated technology, meaningless leisure (see Veblen, 1927), a complexity of titles, and systems of social stratification to document their superiority over "lower" animals and fellow humans.

This brings us to the present era of modern society. Technology, communication, and the military-industrial complex of the present have created a global society that is completely interdependent. The competitive race for human superiority has raped the planet's resources, polluted the planet's elements, eliminated many of the planet's species, threatened the existence of all forms of life, and reduced the lives of many humans and "lower" animal populations to despair and desperation. Ironically, however, our human solution to all of this is to become even more "superior." With our superior intellects we propose to solve the problems that the intellect has created. We propose to save our "endangered Earth" (see "Planet of the Year," 1989).

Humans evaluate their own activities as intricate, complex, and modern. We create and validate our own "progress" and its resulting "civilization." But as Lowie (1922) said years ago:

> *Voila! L'ennemi!* In the insidious influence of group opinions, whether countenanced by Church, State or a scientific hierarchy, lies the basic peril. The philosophic habit of unremitting criticism of one's basic assumptions is naturally repugnant to a young and naive culture, and it cannot be expected to spring up spontaneously and flower luxuriantly in science while other departments of life fail to yield it nurture. Every phase of our civilization must be saturated with that spirit of positive skepticism which Goethe and Huxley taught before science can reap a full harvest in her field. (p. 161)

My thesis is a simple effort to reexamine a basic assumption—that humans are the "highest" form of animal and that this preconception exalts our existence. My position suggests several propositions:

1. The denial, defiance, and defilement of animal kinship is an important component of contemporary human behavior.
2. The culture is designed to disguise and destroy the animal character of humans.
3. Humans, the animals, are unique but no "higher" or "lower" than other animals, and the cultural design for this hierarchy permeates our social

systems and creates, supports, and reinforces racial, religious, ecological, and nationalistic prejudices.

4. Much of the world population is disdained because it lacks the resources to pretend that it is "higher" than the other animals or its fellow humans.

5. All of the above propositions have impeded the scientific study of primates, and of prehistoric and "primitive" humans.

6. Considerable confusion can be avoided if we substitute the word *animal* for the word *nature* in the discussion of "nature, culture, and gender" (see Ortner, 1974).

7. We are the primate animal with the big brains, "and we are not saved."

The analysis is in the tradition of structural thought. The unconscious component of it began with Boas's (1920) distinction between the conscious and the unconscious. As Lévi-Strauss (1967) states, Boas was the first to argue that a structural interpretation is easier when the population has not attempted to explain a category of facts. Lévi-Strauss says that conscious structural models are usually known as "norms" and are "very poor ones, since they are not intended to explain the phenomena but perpetuate them" (p. 273). So it is with humans' hierarchical position in the animal kingdom.

The discussion presented here does not follow that aspect of structural anthropology that examines the relationships of items as contrasted to the content of items. Rather, in this work I attempt to discover the structural character of social phenomena. Like Lévi-Strauss, I look for universals, the basic social and mental processes of which cultural institutions are the concrete external projections or manifestations. If anthropology is a science of general principles, the ones that I adopt here are general and purposefully simple. They are applicable to all societies and valid for all possible observers. They underlie the various manifestations of social life cross-culturally.

Genesis (1:26) states that God decided to make man in the image of God, in His "likeness." And then God (1:28) gave man "dominion" over all of the animals of the earth. God created Eve as Adam's companion "and they were both naked, the man and his wife, and were not ashamed" (2:25). But when they ate the forbidden fruit, "the eyes of them both were opened, and they knew that they were naked; and they sewed fig leaves together, and made themselves aprons" (3:7). In this account we have an early written record of humans' obsession with and concern for their animal appearance and character. An ecological anthropologist has observed:

An enormous amount of intellectual effort and not a little emotion has been expended by men on distinguishing themselves from the other creatures with which they share the earth, and it may be that some fundamental characteristic of human psychology lies beneath this enterprise, for it seems to manifest itself in both science and religion as well as in everyday thought. Be this as it may, the notion that through culture man has transcended nature is perhaps reminiscent of certain religious notions. It can be argued that in its attempt to view man naturalistically, anthropology unwittingly produced a conceptualization of man's position in nature not unlike that of the theology with which it took issue. (Rappaport, 1971, p. 248)

As long as humans were not self-conscious, they, like other animals, were not ashamed of their anatomy. But when the human brain developed the capacity for self-consciousness, humankind began the long trek to disguise itself, re-create itself, and create a world in which humans controlled the other animals. These efforts manifested themselves in culture.

Sexual "inferiority" is only a small component of the human inferiority complex that is created by DDDAK. Race is another. Human beings compensate for perceived animal deficiencies by releasing aggression on suitable scapegoats. DDDAK and our ever-present animal bodies create an appropriate framework for legitimating the practice of racial discrimination. As we struggle to prove that we are not "lower" animals, we are constantly made aware that we cannot escape our own animal-based feelings of inferiority by projecting and displacing that "inferiority" onto others. These projections and displacements are a part of the human condition, but they do not resolve the human dilemma. We have the mark of the beast (an animal body) and a mind that contemplates God.

Such a powerful obsession with our animal kin requires a reevaluation and reanalysis of human behavior to consider the overarching effects of this obsession and our exaltation of the human position in the animal kingdom. Humans may have acquired language and upright posture in distinguishing themselves from the other animals, but they heralded these as characteristics of "higher" beings. Race, class, gender, and poverty must be reexamined in terms of the stresses and tensions of DDDAK and of the use of available resources by humans to behave and appear different from the "lower" animals. Some of the earlier examinations are confused by the use of the general term *nature* where the specific term *animal* would be better. Darwin, Freud, Jung, and Rousseau struggled with these ideas, but all were reluctant to treat humans as the animals they are. These theorists lacked the key insight—DDDAK.

The inferiority complex of humans has motivated them to achieve and to be "superior." That motivation has provided us with 3 million years of survival and dominion over most of the animals of the Earth. But that motivation has also been very costly in terms of racism, classism, sexism, and warfare.

The human inferiority complex urges us constantly to provide things and people that will allow us to evaluate ourselves up from the "lower" animals and the "lower" people. To reinforce that end, we have allocated privileges and surplus resources to the "elites." But sustaining the concept and the working categories of "elite" people requires "inferior" people for conceptualization. The "elites" spend countless hours and fortunes surrounding themselves with expensive things and wealthy people in their constant efforts to reinforce the myth of superiority.

We have created human categories and multiplied them since the Agricultural Revolution. For instance, one of the unique inventions in the New World was the creation of the category of race. Race, which is almost meaningless outside of political designs, has become pregnant with political interpretations and beliefs (see Ashley Montagu, 1952). We attempt to assign all humans to races, to give all races rankings, and to deny the depravity of this process. Notwithstanding the denial of their existence, racial classification and ranking persist, and most nations of the world reflect this persistence in their respective minority problems. The Ibo of Nigeria; the Luo of Kenya; the Blacks (note the bellicose situation between the Xhosa and the Zulu), Coloureds, Boers, British, and Hindus of South Africa; the Tamil of Sri Lanka; the Hutu of Ruanda; the Kurds of Iraq; the Ukranians of the former Soviet Union; the Armenians of Turkey and the Soviet Union; the Jews of Nazi Germany; the Eta and Ainu of Japan; the Indians of the Americas; the barbarians in China; the Catholic Irish in Britain; and the African Americans and Hispanics in the United States are all examples of the use of race (or similar categories) by people to separate other people, often for oppressive ends (see Berreman, 1972).

Conclusion

I have attempted to discuss an approach to race relations that ceases to treat discrimination as abnormal human behavior. To discriminate, to rank, and to identify "inferior" people is part of the nature of humankind. If we choose to transform this modern malady, with all of its technological threats to life on earth, then we must alter the socialization of our children. Fortunately, these changes—the Ecological Revolution—must come if humans are to survive our modern ecological crises.

The future focus of urban ethnography must be on the structures and the people within them that create and perpetuate "inferior" people and neighbors. For example, city police departments are very effective in identifying, creating, and maintaining "inferior" neighborhoods. They are among the first to know when political patronage is distributed in the form of permissive illegal commerce in designated districts. This permissiveness in one crime area attracts other criminal elements. It is similar to legal gambling and the criminal elements that are attracted by it. Such criminal trade sets the stage for the deterioration of communities in utility services, zoning, housing, street and sewer maintenance, refuse collection, code enforcement, and building condemnations and demolitions. Other city agencies follow the lead of the police in their benign neglect, and then real estate interests conform as well. These are the processes we must study, not the Black and the poor.

I have attempted to point out that the basic characteristics of humans create racial, ethnic, religious, class, and gender discrimination and oppression, which are worldwide phenomena. What follows from these practices are social systems in which the power elite and their collaborators systematically socialize the poor and the oppressed to be "inferior" societal "failures." This allows the oppressors to enforce the myths of superiority and to distribute the limited resources unequally. It allows, in hegemonic fashion, some of the wretched lives of the rich to be perceived as "happiness" because of prevailing values and attitudes. I have described some of the dilemmas and predicaments of urban discrimination and oppression. Some of the contributions of African Americans to American culture and society have been crucial (see Williams, 1990, p. 144), notwithstanding the denial to African Americans of access to many of the institutional resources and opportunities considered necessary elements of success. And I have suggested the mechanism—the Ecological Revolution—for ending racial strife, poverty, oppression, and discrimination throughout the world. The new cooperation between the United States and Russia in the United Nations Security Council may facilitate the Ecological Revolution—the real "new world order."

The Earth has become analogous to a closed system. We cannot transform racism in an artificially isolated culture and society. The brief discussion offered here of the Black middle class, the Black underclass, women, and the power elite who oppress them all puts in bold relief the urgent need for major transformations in human social and political skills. Such changes will compensate for the cultural lag relative to human technological expertise. That cultural lag renders humans impotent to control the massive destruction of the Earth, its resources, its people, and its life forms in their ecosystems. Race and ethnic relations cannot be divorced from these phenomena.

Finally, race and ethnic relations are only one component of a massive problem, and we cannot control racism in isolation from the total transformation—the Ecological Revolution—that will end social inequality and its reproduction. Humans must be able to look into that mirror (urban ethnography) and see themselves, not others.

PART III

Quantitative Methods

8

Demography and Race

CAROLE C. MARKS

The wisdom of Mark Twain that there are three kinds of lies, "lies, damn lies, and statistics," seems a predictable beginning for a nondemographic examination of knowledge production in the demography of racial and ethnic groups. Cries of "numbers crunching" from without and "journalism" from within have historically marked the aged combatants who occasionally square off against each other, but more typically tend either to talk past one another or to talk not at all.

In this chapter I attempt to begin a dialogue by raising concerns from an outsider's point of view. As it is not feasible in a few pages to comment upon all research done even within the past few years, I concentrate on the topic of race, and within that area I selectively survey recent literature. My intent is not to condemn but to challenge. I have a suspicion, in fact, that some demographers have eschewed the study of race for precisely the thrust and content of the critique that follows. A cursory examination of the journal *Demography* from January 1980 to November 1985 lends some support to this notion. There appeared, during that time, fewer than a dozen articles concerned with race, averaging out to a rate of only slightly better than one per year. This is, arguably, not the sum total of demographic research on racial and ethnic groups, but does nonetheless reflect the cutting edge. There is by no means a proliferation of race research in the field.

AUTHOR'S NOTE: This chapter appeared previously as an article in the March/April 1987 issue of the *American Behavioral Scientist*.

In studying subgroups, I do not insist that some ascribed "insider's doctrine" is mandatory. Obviously, non-Blacks have made a number of important contributions to research on the Black community. My intent, in any case, is not to gauge the relative merits of the past contributions of Black and white scholars. My purpose may best be summarized by Pettigrew's "urgent" call in the 1985 *Annual Review of Sociology* for "integrative work across 'theories' and across the micro- and macrolevels." This work, Pettigrew insists, "is easier to call for than to conduct, for it requires innovative approaches and data collection strategies." "Without them," he argues, "little progress will be made toward understanding the newly emerging racial pattern" (p. 344). At the 1983 Population meetings, a similar call for "accommodating macro and micro approaches to each other" was made by then President Stolnitz (1983, p. 415).

In surveying what "passes for knowledge" in the field of the demography of racial and ethnic groups, one finds that what is problematic is not so much the methodology of the research as some of its underlying assumptions. In the past, the frequent use of census data in such work was questioned because of the acknowledged undercounting of Black males. But at least part of the criticism represents an exercise in overkill. Many researchers are keenly aware of such biases and state them at the outset. Daniel Price, for example, in his 1969 *Changing Characteristics of the Negro Population,* makes continual reference to the problems of "the changing levels of underenumeration at different levels and from one census to the next" (p. 223). Others extol the virtues of the data that outweigh the acknowledged flaws. Reynolds Farley (1984), who in *Blacks and Whites: Narrowing the Gap?* makes extensive use of census information, states:

> The data used in this investigation are the most comprehensive available. . . . Most of the questions and procedures used to gather information about educational attainment, employment status, occupational achievement, and earnings have been used repeatedly over the years. This continuity facilitates the study of time trends as well as the comparison of blacks and whites. (p. 11)

Demographers, on the whole, are particularly sensitive to the limitations of their research. Farley readily admits that there are two important areas of study that the demographic approach is ill equipped to handle. First, "an issue that cannot be fully explored in a demographic study is racial discrimination." It is impossible to "prove," suggests

Farley, "the presence or absence of discrimination." Hirschman and Wong (1984) further explore this shortcoming by indicating, "Discrimination is not measured directly but is the residual (or net) difference between majority-minority attainment after other factors are held constant" (p. 585). It is an unhappy resolution to the extent that attainments are themselves a product of discrimination, but it is nonetheless a problem over which demographers express concern.

Second, Farley (1984) argues, "Another limitation of a demographic study is that it can provide only partial answers to questions about the underlying causes of racial change" (p. 13). Although this assessment is an honest one, it often produces very tentative and, to the novice reader, frustrating conclusions, such as a recent comment on fertility and marital dissolution that ended, "The results indicate that additional studies need to be undertaken in order to reach any definitive conclusions" (Koo & Janowitz, 1983, p. 142).

Acknowledging that demography cannot prove whether or not discrimination exists, or show its connection to racial change, suggests ultimately either that such issues are irrelevant or that something of equal importance, or at least major significance, may be understood apart from them. It is this point that leads first to more serious charges of triviality and second to ones of collusion. Stanfield (1985), for example, writes:

> The use of "empirical data" to explain the causes and consequences of racial differences in income, educational attainment, intelligence, mobility patterns, family structures, and residence perpetuates the myth that race is relevant in defining human differences and therefore confirms the stratified racial order. (p. 18)

Although it is not possible to ignore these endemic concerns, it is valuable to explore the demographic contribution to our knowledge of the groups under study apart from them. This represents an important focus of this inquiry.

According to Bean and Frisbee (1978), "To be meaningful, research into the determinants of demographic variation by race, ethnicity, or minority group status must involve, at a minimum, some reasonable determination of the universe of variables that may be expected to afford some degree of explanatory power." Such a starting point immediately brings to mind an endless list of variables limited only by the capacity of the data analyzer. However, Bean and Frisbee add, "Inevitably, it would seem, the decision as to where to look for explanations will be premised on some notion, however vague, of the nature of the subpopulations to be studied" (p. 2). Vague notions of the nature of subpopulations to be studied are, I submit, the real sticking point of much demographic research for the nondemographer.

I shall begin with the study of marital instability, an area of "interest that has long attracted social scientists" (Frisbee, Bean, & Eberstein, 1978, p. 143). Most of the work done in this area attempts to discover why Blacks and certain other "disadvantaged" minorities have much higher rates of marital instability than the general population. Frisbee et al. (1978) argue that there are in the literature three "alternative hypotheses" to explain "differential levels of racial-ethnic group marital instability" (p. 146). The first they call "the self-perpetuating and fragmented structure of black families." The major thrust of this well-known hypothesis centers on the relatively weak position of the Black male vis-à-vis the Black female, "originating in the effects of slavery and of historical socioeconomic deprivation" and continuing in a pattern that is "self-perpetuating" (p. 146). These authors also cite an alternative hypothesis based on socioeconomic factors that, they are careful to point out, rejects the "cultural or ethnic factors" of the first explanation. A third explanation, which involves concepts of "familism" and "Catholicism," suggests that cultural factors relating to kin support networks and religion may also support marital stability. Data used in the research were "obtained from the 1970 (5%) Public Use Samples for five southwestern states." Only women were included in the samples. Using sophisticated methods of data analyses, the authors conclude that "neither ethnicity-specific nor socioeconomic factors alone are adequate explanations of these differentials but that these two sets of variables interact in the determination of racial-ethnic differences in family solidarity" (p. 148).

In the context of the careful manner in which the research was constructed and carried out, Frisbee et al.'s conclusions appear both sensible and logical. But the underlying assumptions of the "ethnicity-specific" approaches, the foundation of the analysis, are handled in a very casual, even offhand, manner. The three hypotheses are offered as reasonable and fairly exhaustive explanations about marital stability. Therefore, it must be assumed that (a) if Blacks, regardless of education/income, have higher rates of marital instability than the others, then the first alternative (self-perpetuating, fragmented Black families) is supported; (b) if the data show that differences in marital instability disappear with increasing education/income, then the second alternative (the socioeconomic) is supported; and (c) if Mexicans, regardless of education/income, have lower rates of marital instability, then the third alternative (Latino familism) is supported.

The research affords no opportunity to bring under scrutiny the underlying assumptions. Indeed, limitations of space make it necessary that these important areas of concern are merely taken as givens. Presumably, for the careful reader, reference may be made to the sources cited as supportive of each position. For the first alternative, the major source is Moynihan (1965), with Frazier (1939) and Blood and Wolfe (1960) also cited. Frazier's contribution to the "fragmented Black family" literature is found in his observations in *The Negro Family in the United States* (1939). In that work, he argues strongly for the existence of a matriarchy in slavery and contends that "in the urban sections of the South" in the 1940s (the rates were considerably lower in rural areas), as many as one-third "of the Negro families were without male heads" (p. 200).

Frazier was writing in 1939. Since that time, there has been a wealth of scholarship debating the pros and cons of his position. While not thoroughly discredited, Lieberson's (1980) assessment that "explanations based on the heritage of slavery" are "becoming increasingly doubtful" represents a position too widely held to be ignored (p. 173). In addition, a pattern generously found to exist in only a small segment of a racial group seems hardly sufficient to be designated, ipso facto, as an "ethnicity-specific" pattern. Wilson (1978), for example, found that in 1974 "only 18 percent of the children in black families with incomes of less than $4,000 lived with both parents, while 90 percent [of the children] of families with incomes of $15,000 or more lived with both parents" (p. 132).

Frazier (1939), moreover, does not ignore the importance of economic factors in contributing to his theory of matriarchy, as he states, "Their [Negro families'] success or failure depends largely upon their cultural as well as economic resources" (p. 280). Moynihan, in his 1965 government report, produced a more statistical analysis than Frazier and estimated a rate of female-headed households of about 25%. The question remains, Can one, with any confidence, suggest that differences found between populations are related to this presumed cultural factor unlinked to other forces? Stack, for example, writing in 1974, argued that "the instability of employment among black men was a critical factor hampering the formation and maintenance of a stable husband-and-wife family" (cited in Hogan & Kitagawa, 1985, p. 829; see also Wilson, 1987). Others have made similar claims about related dependent variables. As early as 1970, Duncan and Duncan concluded that "the disproportionate number of Negro men reared in broken families contribute to, but by no means account for, the racial difference in occupational success" (p. 169). In the face of so much countervailing evidence, it seems unlikely that the nonutility of this theory would need still another proof. Yet the fragmented family as an independent variable is tested and retested.

Further, why apply a theory of male behavior to data from which males, a key ingredient in the explanation, are excluded? This assessment is reinforced in the more recent findings of Michael and Tuma (1985). In their article on marriage and parenthood, they suggest, "Our work differs from most studies of fertility in one important way: while most demographic analyses focus on the fertility patterns of females only, we analyze data on males as well as females" (p. 517). Moreover, in drawing conclusions from their research, Michael and Tuma state:

> We are struck by our lack of success in identifying reasons for black-white differences in teenage entry into marriage or in teenage males' entry into parenthood, despite the large number of family background variables included in our study. We resist calling our ignorance about the factors influencing marriage of black youths "discrimination" or "cultural differences." Still, the long-standing challenge of explaining marital patterns of young black Americans remains. (p. 540)

The addition of males, it would appear, makes conclusions much less obvious.

"Familism" in the third alternative explanation relies on the work of Bean et al. (1977) and Farris and Glenn (1976), and "Catholicism" on Alvirez (1973). Two of these works address patterns assumed to exist within the Mexican American community, and the third represents a comparative analysis between Mexican Americans and Anglos. Yet, given the way in which the hypotheses are set up, it seems problematic to conclude that Mexican Americans have stronger (or weaker) kin networks and religiosity than Blacks. The authors, however, suggest, "To illustrate, if Mexican American families caught in untenable economic positions are more able than are Anglo or Black families to call upon and receive support from kin, the impact of socioeconomic variables on family stability may be mitigated." But again, without independent confirmation, we must take it on faith that differences found within the two populations are indeed attributable to differences in kin support. This is particularly so in light of the finding, cited by Yancey and Erikson among others, that "sociological studies of the Negro family have demonstrated the existence of an extended kinship system of mothers, grandmothers, aunts and other relatives that is surprisingly stable" (quoted in Duncan & Duncan, 1970, p. 451), and of the more recent statement by Taylor (1986), "While there are only a few quantitative studies of the informal social support networks of blacks, ethnographic literature provides a rich source of information on the transfer of assistance in black families" (p. 67). Is it not reasonable to ask that the authors show some evidence to the contrary?

Another related field of study is differential fertility. Those wishing to add to our understanding of the area would do well to heed the warning of Zimmer (1981) that "the search to find factors that account for fertility differentials among subgroups of the population appears to be almost without limits. Yet the evidence to date, even in the United States, is inconsistent as well as confusing and often contradictory" (p. 120). Many, it would seem, prefer instead to add to this confusion.

In "Differential Fertility and the Minority Group Status Hypothesis," Bean and Marcum (1978) attempt to understand "the forces underlying racial and ethnic fertility." Among the "numerous efforts to interpret the magnitude and persistence of fertility differences among racial and ethnic groups," Bean and Marcum cite two principal explanations. The first they label "social characteristics," an explanation that relates differential fertility to "differences in socioeconomic composition between racial-ethnic and majority populations." The second, labeled "minority-group status," relates differential fertility "to aspects of minority life besides those associated with socioeconomic status" such as religion and sociopsychological and sociocultural processes (p. 193).

Much of the early research in this area supported the "social characteristics" explanation. Typical was the conclusion that "Negroes have no cultural trait that affects natality independently of their occupation or education. Race is not a cause of family size but an index of social class" (Petersen, 1961, p. 226; quoted in Bean & Marcum, 1978, p. 193). However, later research has suggested that acceptance of the social characteristics model would suggest "there must be no statistical interaction between racial and ethnic group membership and economic factors in their effects on fertility" (Bean & Marcum, 1978, p. 201). In the case of Blacks, for example, it is found that those of low socioeconomic status have higher fertility levels than their white counterparts, and those of high socioeconomic status "have lower fertility than their white counterparts" (p. 201). That is, the persistence of differences after controlling for socioeconomic status suggests support for a "minority status group" hypothesis.

As in the case of marital instability, it is at the very point at which interest is piqued as to the origin of differences that the research ends, usually with a call for further research. Farley and Allen (1989) suggest:

> Since racial differences in fertility appear at all economic levels, the minority group hypothesis seems to be the more plausible of the two explanations. However, we cannot confidently endorse this theory because blacks have been in the fertility-control stage of their demographic transition for only one quarter of a century, and it is impossible to tell if the higher fertility of blacks is the result of cultural values and preference. (p. 102)

We are back to square one.

In the example of the low fertility of high-status Blacks, Goldscheider and Uhlenberg (1969) suggest that "higher status members of minority groups resort to exaggeratedly low fertility in order to overcome the insecurities of minority group status and to sustain progress toward the achievement of socio-economic goals acquired in the process of acculturation" (quoted in Bean & Marcum, 1978, p. 203). Although this may be a perfectly logical explanation of events, Bean and Marcum, curiously, provide no supportive evidence. Further, use of such value-laden expressions as "exaggeratedly low fertility" suggests deviance that requires much greater explanation. Could it be that Black women, depending on their economic status, are at once blamed for having too many and too few children? Finally, the phrase "to sustain progress toward the achievement of socio-economic goals" seems a convoluted way of saying that they cannot afford it, a finding that makes the debate between "social characteristics" on the one hand and "minority group status" on the other seem like a sophisticated exercise in hairsplitting.

The last point raises still another dilemma in the comparison of high-status Blacks and their white counterparts. Drawing comparable populations is never easily done, as Black populations have consistently been shown to be more likely to have family incomes based on the dual wages of spouses and to have fewer savings and lower assets—in short, to be more vulnerable to economic insecurity and reversals even though, by conventional measures, they may appear to be similar to other populations. Use of SES variables alone rarely reflects these elements of incompatibility. Unfortunately, the "nature of the subpopulation" is given little attention in Bean and Marcum's study, and, consequently, what is measured neglects a significant aspect of what is sought.

Of all the SES variables, demographers have been most "hopeful" about the declining gaps in educational attainment levels. The differences between Blacks and whites found in the 1940s significantly narrowed in the 1980s and, among the youngest age cohort in particular, differences nearly disappeared. Gaps, however, still exist, and any optimistic assessment must of necessity end with the caveat that there is still a long way to go. The assumption is made in much of the educational attainment literature that changes in educational attainment will be reflected over time in the two variables that have shown less decline, income and occupation. The logic of this assessment rests on the wisdom that past disparities between Blacks and whites in income and occupation were mainly based on the lack of skill and training of Black workers and, importantly, on the historic belief of employers that such workers were inefficient or nonproductive. These attempts to put the best face on such findings may well be self-deluding. As Stanfield (1985) points out, "Race continues to be a central determinant of life chances, but its impact has been ignored or explained away by theories and ideologies centered on assimilation and integration that view the U.S. as a melting pot" (p. 346).

In his discussion of educational gaps, Farley (1984) indicates that Black students in college have lower employment levels than comparable white students and that one explanation for this, cautiously advanced, is that "young white men who attend school may find it easier to get part time jobs than do black men" (p. 45). The persistence of discrimination even among those who are educationally most similar implies that discrimination, at least as a residual measure, cannot be ignored (or declared overestimated) and may have historically been as central to explanations of SES gaps as education itself. Hirschman and Wong, in a 1984 *American Journal of Sociology* article on the socio economic gains of Asian Americans, Blacks, and Hispanics, hint at this when they report a "contrasting role of education as an intervening variable in minority group achievement" (p. 602).

Relatedly, Farley and Allen (1989) make an effort to point out John Ogbu's discovery of "diametrically opposed explanations for minority educational problems" in majority group and minority group literature

(p. 191). Ogbu cites explanations of "social, cultural, familial or bio-logical inadequacies" in the one, and "legal-extralegal discriminatory policies" in the other (Farley & Allen, 1989, p. 191). Still, Farley and Allen conclude, "American society had historically discriminated against blacks [in education], and blacks have over time come to expect such discrim-ination as normative" (p. 208).

Even this halfhearted admission is discarded out of hand in most other research: Historically there were gaps in educational attainment levels; there is a connection between education and occupation and income level; therefore, "social, cultural, familial, or biological inadequacies" explain the differences. It is rather like the old joke about looking for lost keys under a streetlight rather than in the dark, where they were lost.

The dilemma of discounting current discrimination is most apparent when one studies the relationship between education and employment. Robert Hill (1981), for example, found that "black college graduates have jobless rates three to four times higher than white college gradu-ates, and that white high school dropouts have lower jobless rates than blacks who have attended college" (p. 52). According to Farley and Allen (1989), "If a black man in 1980 had the characteristics of the typical white man and worked as many hours, he could expect to earn $2,900 less than the white man; in 1985, $3,200 less" (p. 355).

The literature on women and labor force participation takes on similarly myopic vision. Over the years, the gaps have been narrowing both among white women and white men and between Black and white women. Yet the cause for optimism in these findings is misleading. Black women have apparently narrowed the gap by working longer hours, in hazardous and remote locations, under, by societal standards, unfavorable conditions (Farley, 1984, p. 124). In so doing, they have achieved in some instances virtual parity with white women, who are themselves severely discriminated against in the marketplace.

What is confusing is the basis for the optimism, for surely the fact that Black women have "caught up" under these circumstances does not of itself suggest that gaps will continue to be narrowed in the future. This is particularly questionable given that white women, in Farley's (1984) words, "have fared poorly" during the same period (p. 120). It makes even less sense to claim that there is "an advantage to being a black woman in the contemporary labor market" (p. 128) when Black women have consistently high unemployment and long hours of work.

Some of the most interesting work is done in the field of urban-suburban racial composition. For example, William Frey, in a 1985 article in the *American Sociological Review,* presents an excellent analysis of age-related metropolitan migration patterns. Frey hypothesizes that a narrowing of residential segregation may occur because of one of two possibilities: (a) Through a process of "gentrification," metropolitan areas will become whiter, or (b) through a combination of greater opportunities and lesser discrimination, suburban areas will increase their Black populations, particularly among younger age cohorts. In combination, metropoliswide residential segregation may be reduced. Frey's research involves data from six large SMSAs: Detroit, Chicago, New York, Boston, Philadelphia and Washington, D.C., with Detroit representing the most segregated, "worst-case" setting and Washington the best. Frey concludes that generally the first hypothesis is not supported, with only Washington seeming to experience a "gentrification" process, a finding he attributes not to future societywide patterns but to the unique combination of political and economic forces within the district itself. For the second hypothesis, on the other hand, he finds at least limited support for all SMSAs, with Detroit, the worst-case example, experiencing the lowest rate. Frey concludes that the optimistic assumptions of urban analysts that over time disparities will narrow must be viewed in the context of slow change—change that may indeed not be noticeable until the turn of the century.

Unlike previous analyses that produce questionable underlying assumptions in the study of racial and ethnic groups, Frey's research is distinguished by its failure to step back from the data at all. Missing are any attempts to assess the importance of the findings for public or social policy. This hesitancy to go beyond the data is the root of much unhappiness among many nondemographic researchers, who argue that when you strip away the sophisticated methodology what you are left with is, at best, a restatement of the obvious or readily observable. But the problem is more deeply rooted than a mere cataloging of elements neglected and relates to fundamental differences in perspective.

Failure to go beyond the data, with the exception of a few well-chosen final sentences that recommend such activity for future work, limits the applicability of the study. There exists a philosophical unwillingness to engage in speculation, or even in the discipline's honored activity of prediction. Frey, in the last paragraphs of his article, states in characteristic fashion:

> Finally, the reader is reminded that the projections shown in this analysis are not to be taken as literal predictions of the future. They merely provide a

vehicle for demonstrating the redistribution implications of recent white and black lifecourse destination selection patterns when "reasonable" values for other demographic components of change were held constant. (p. 824)

It is as if these "lifecourse destination selection patterns" exist in a vacuum. Neglected is the important assessment made by Long (1980), that "federal open-housing legislation may be opening up the suburbs to black families" (p. 72), a suggestion that would have important implications for both the pace and duration of the phenomenon of Black suburbanization itself. It also ignores the finding of Berry and Kasarda (1977) and Taeuber and Taeuber (1965) that Blacks moving into suburban areas often enter segregated communities. And finally, Taeuber's (1975) finding that "the relatively poorer circumstances of blacks are only a small part of the explanation for black concentrations in central cities" suggests a dynamic of "lifecourse decisions" that has little to do with individuals. The last is most unsatisfying, for it is as if some paragraphs were left at the printer's or were accidentally removed by an electrical surge.

It would be remiss to ignore some of the research that has already begun to resolve conflicts and bridge gaps. Using the 1900 U.S. Census, Stewart Tolnay (1981) has attempted to address troubling historical issues on Black fertility by testing whether physiological or sociological factors lowered rates in the 1890s and the economic impact of tenancy on problems of family formation. The research takes a fresh perspective on these issues and destroys some of the more unlikely claims of previous research about Blacks and venereal disease. Tienda and Glass (1985), in viewing labor force participation and fertility, address issues that have troubled ethnographic writers for some time and back up commonsense speculations with hard data and not a single reference to fragmented family structure. Hogan and Kitagawa (1985), in their examination of Black adolescents, consciously attempt to integrate ethnographic with demographic data and produce a result that seems to advance the theoretical and methodological concerns of both sides. Hirschman and Wong (1984) manage, in their comparative analysis of socioeconomic gains, to merge concerns of demography with more structural literature. And finally Farley (1984) makes an important contribution to testing future patterns of race relations from a variety of competing perspectives.

Berger and Luckmann (1967) have characterized "the social stock of knowledge" as something differentiated "by degrees of familiarity." They indicate, "It provides complex and detailed information concerning those sectors of everyday life with which I must frequently deal. It provides much more general and imprecise information on remoter sections" (p. 43). In the study of race, sociology itself has only begun to add to the stock. There are vast and uncharted fields of inquiry. Still from all sides of the discipline, small pieces of the puzzle come into focus, gain entry into the intellect, and become reified. Others come and go. But one cannot become expert on a subpopulation with only vague notions of its internal dynamics. It is not possible to discover all that is relevant to the concept of race by reading *Tally's Corner* (Liebow, 1967), *The Declining Significance of Race* (Wilson, 1978), and *The Truly Disadvantaged* (Wilson, 1987) no matter how great their individual contributions. Of course, reasonable people may disagree about the meaning of findings, but disagreement is one thing—operating as if the other does not exist is quite another.

From an approach that has developed sophisticated techniques of data analysis, there is much that could contribute to our understanding. As Hirschman has observed, "The accumulation of systematic knowledge can be very useful to those of us with political concerns about the state of society. We can argue (in our role as citizens), armed with the 'objective' analyses of 'science' " (personal communication, 1986).

The first step toward innovative and informed research is the striking of just this kind of balance. I do not insist that demographers spend all their time reading novels, diaries, biographies, and the like, although a little instruction of that sort would not hurt. Nor should one necessarily condone, on the other side, scholarship that seems to germinate full blown out of the vivid imagination of the scholar, with little attempt at confirmation or detachment. But there is a lot of published information, some of it even demographic, that would inform the demographic study of racial groups. Before judging exaggeratedly high or low fertility, fatherless homes, the overestimation of discrimination, or the advantageous position of Black women, it is essential that "the validity of knowledge taken for granted" be always and continually exposed, examined, and brought into question. There is an expediency in the production of a new level of professional research. Ralph Ellison (1967), a novelist, strikes at the heart of the matter:

> Prefabricated Negroes are sketched on sheets of paper and superimposed upon the Negro community; then when someone thrusts his head through the pages and yells, "Watch out there, Jack, there's people living under here," they are all shocked and indignant. (p. 76)

9

Measuring and Detecting Discrimination in the Post-Civil Rights Era

SAMUEL L. MYERS, Jr.

In *City of Richmond v. Croson* (1989), the U.S. Supreme Court ruled in a 6-3 decision that a city ordinance that set aside 30% of public works funds for minority-owned construction companies was unconstitutional. Justice Sandra Day O'Connor wrote in the majority opinion that such set-aside programs could be justified only if they served a "compelling state interest" in redressing "identified discrimination" (*City of Richmond v. Croson*, 1989, p. 505). Analysts have concluded that this ruling affirms the Court's recent move toward a "strict scrutiny" interpretation of the Equal Protection Clause of the Fourteenth Amendment. This means that any government action that fosters preference of one race over another is suspect, requiring both a very demanding set of evidence in support of charges of previous injustice and a compelling state's objective to justify the preferential treatment. Instead of permitting governmental remedial efforts to reverse centuries-old discrimination patterns by preferential treatment of minority group members, in the *Richmond* decision, the Court demanded a "strict scrutiny" of this and other suspect racial classifications. Justice O'Connor wrote, "The standard of review under the Equal Protection Clause is not dependent on the race of those burdened or benefitted by a particular classification" (p. 494). The Court did not embrace Thurgood Marshall's dissenting opinion that a lesser standard should be applied, one that admits "race-conscious classifications designed to further remedial goals [that] serve important governmental objectives . . . [and that are] substantially related to achievement of those objectives" (p. 535). Since minority business set-aside programs exist in more than 200 local governments and in 36 states, this case has been viewed by some as the death blow to government affirmative action programs designed to enhance minority economic well-being.

In *Wards Cove Packing v. Atonio* (1989) the ground rules for litigating discrimination cases were redrawn. The case involved a salmon cannery firm with two types of jobs: low-wage, low-skilled "cannery jobs," held mostly by Filipinos and Native Alaskans, and "noncannery jobs" held largely by white workers hired from Washington and Oregon. The plaintiffs in the case attempted to demonstrate a disparate impact of the firm's hiring policies by showing the large disparities between the two job segments in the proportions of nonwhites. Justice White, writing for the majority, stated that these statistical disparities did not make for a *prima facie* case of disparate impact. Beyond that, the majority shifted the traditional emphasis of who must prove or disprove the employer's assertion that the adverse employment action was based solely on legitimate business considerations. The burden of proof in demonstrating that an alleged discriminator had no "objective, business-related justification for the challenged practices" was now placed squarely on the shoulders of the plaintiff rather than the defendant, as had been the case for nearly 20 years of civil rights litigation. Moreover, the Court wrote in a 5-4 split decision that it was not enough to demonstrate that racial disparities existed; evidence must be marshaled by plaintiffs showing that specific employment practices caused these disparities (reported in the *New York Times,* June 6 and June 18, 1989). These and other recent decisions have virtually erased established statistical standards for proving discrimination.

As one *New York Times* columnist noted:

> The . . . 5-4 conservative majority that now dominates the Court on civil rights issues rewrote long-settled ground rules of proof and procedure in employment discrimination cases. The decisions . . . make discrimination suits harder to bring, harder to win, and more vulnerable to attack if successfully concluded. (Greenhouse, 1989) (Copyright © 1989 by The New York Times Company. Reprinted by permission.)

Many view these reversals as the culmination of a decade of retrench-
ment from activist legislative and judicial support for civil rights. For
example, a congressional study group on affirmative action reports:

> Despite their gains in a widening range of occupations during the past decade,
> many minorities and women believe discrimination still limits their labor
> market opportunities. . . . There is a perception that senior executives of
> major corporations have downgraded the importance of affirmative action,
> and that minorities and women have borne the brunt of company work force
> adjustments necessitated by efforts to reduce production costs. (Anderson,
> 1986, p. 14)

That group concludes:

> What seems apparent is that in the wake of increased criticism of goals and
> timetables by senior officials of the federal government, including the Attor-
> ney General, the Chairman of the U.S. Commission on Civil Rights, and others,
> some business firms have abandoned their focus on numerical measures of
> compliance with anti-discrimination policies since 1981. . . . the result is a wide-
> spread perception that affirmative action is less important today than before—a
> perception reinforced by the virtual silence of senior corporate executives on the
> importance of equal opportunity and affirmative action. (p. 40)

Concerns about the demise of affirmative action follow in part from
often legitimate fears that when legal remedies to discrimination are
discarded, enforcement efforts on behalf of victims of discrimination
become impotent. The remedies—including in many instances not only
corrective action but penalties in the form of back-pay awards for past
discrimination—were viewed as sanctions that would deter potential
discriminators and punish those discriminators who were caught. These
concerns help to explain the rush to enact in 1991 new civil rights
legislation aimed at restoring the status of antidiscrimination remedies
in employment. Untouched, at least as of this writing, are a large range
of antidiscrimination efforts in other markets.

Often overlooked in the current debate about the weakening of
affirmative action and other remedies to discrimination is the impreci-
sion of the actual measuring and detecting of discriminatory behaviors
that are in violation of existing statutes and constitutional provisions.
The older statistical standards for measuring and detecting discrimina-

tion were arguably vague and inconsistent. Plaintiffs in discrimination suits, however, often paid little attention to these now troubling flaws in the methods used to establish discrimination. Much of this inattention can be attributed to the fact that, until the Supreme Court cases of 1989, the burden of proof in establishing impermissible discrimination has not rested on the shoulders of the victims of discrimination. Despite the existence of a wide variety of sophisticated techniques for satisfying the most demanding standards for establishing illegal discrimination, most plaintiffs continued to use rudimentary and unpersuasive statistical arguments in bringing discrimination complaints before the courts. Yet, now, with an apparent victory in the passage of the 1991 Civil Rights Act, things remain as murky as ever.

This chapter summarizes the main approaches to "proving" discrimination under different legal "theories" and sets forth the equation structure needed for each approach. I do not address the broader issue of whether remedies under attack are adequate for redressing discrimination or whether they go too far. These and other issues are central to the public debate about affirmative action and such race-based policies as minority business set-asides and preferential hiring. Instead, the focus is on the methodological and statistical issues that must be resolved in order to advance the larger public policy debates beyond the present impasse.

One statistical approach discussed is the familiar Blinder-Oaxaca-Duncan residual difference method. Unfortunately, few court cases have attempted to go so far as to specify and estimate the relations suggested here. Nevertheless, a three-step procedure that goes beyond the residual difference method is offered to accommodate more recent challenges to discrimination suits based on "business necessity" or related cost justifications for otherwise illegal discriminating behavior.

In the post-civil rights era, when the burden of proof upon the plaintiffs seems to be heightened, this three-step method serves as a potentially useful tool in seeking a balance between the social goal of equal opportunity and the economic objective of protecting legitimate business interests. It is probably the only tool available to plaintiffs in a certain class of discrimination suits. In particular, this method seems potentially useful in the analysis of discrimination in punishment, an area not specifically covered by the civil rights laws of the 1960s and explicitly excluded from recent antidiscrimination legislation.

What Is Discrimination?

Discrimination refers to differential treatment of otherwise equally qualified persons. The classical notion of discrimination used by psychologists in relation to learning theory is not what is meant here. For the psychologist the appropriate term and the associated theory relates to prejudice. This prejudice is often regarded as "irrational" and not motivated by objective consideration of facts. Of course, this notion of discrimination may be inconsistent with purposeful differential treatment designed to deny particular rights and privileges to members of particular groups.

In his now famous treatise on the economics of discrimination, Gary Becker (1971) skirts the difficult issues posed in the sociopsychological literature that concern the definition of discrimination. He chooses the simple route of providing essentially his own definition:

> If an individual has a "taste for discrimination," he must act *as if* he were willing to pay something either directly or in the form of a reduced income to be associated with some persons instead of others. When actual discrimination occurs, he must, in fact, either pay or forfeit income for this privilege. This simple way of looking at the matter gets to the essence of prejudice and discrimination. (p. 14)

Becker's intent is to place discrimination into an explicit market context. The context he chooses, however, is that of individualistic self-interested maximization. As such, the definition, simple and appealing as it is, misses some of the salient issues of relevance to legal studies and social analyses of discrimination in the contemporary United States.

David Kaye (1982), a legal scholar as well as a statistician, provides a profile of four essential types of discrimination. Each corresponds loosely to the definition used frequently by affirmative action officers. Discrimination is unequal treatment of equal individuals.[1] Kaye notes, however, that even equal treatment of individuals may have a discriminatory impact.

According to Kaye, the first type of discrimination involves ad hoc decisions that are not based on clearly defined standards or rules of general applicability. Kaye (1982) asserts that the disparate treatment that follows may establish a discriminatory motive, for "it cannot plausibly be explained without reference to presumable irrelevant classification [criteria]" (p. 774). Discrimination in the application of a rule is a second type. Here, a rule that in and of itself is not discriminatory may be applied in such a way that there is disparate treatment of otherwise identical individuals. Then there is discriminatory intent, when the *formation* of a rule has the direct effect of classification according to prohibited criteria. This is *de jure* discrimination, or discrimination on its face. Finally, there is discrimination in the *operation* of a rule. When the uniform application of a rule has a disparate impact on a protected class the result is called *de facto* discrimination.

In an attempt to clarify the distinction between differential treatment and differential impact implicit in Kaye's topology, Lea Brilmayer (1982) comments, "The essence of disparate treatment is that the employer is differentiating on the basis of some illegal factor such as race or sex; of disparate impact, that the employer is differentiating on the basis of some factor that is *correlated* with an illegal factor such as race or sex" (p. 789). Brilmayer's central legal point is that disparate impact is not illegal per se. In fact, it is known that in most antidiscrimination statutes certain exemptions for disparate impact are available as defenses against charges of discrimination, such as business necessity. Brilmayer concludes, "Differences in legal treatment of disparate impact and disparate treatment reflect, in large part, the legal importance of discriminatory motive, which is the characteristic that singled out disparate treatment as 'the most obvious evil Congress had in mind when it enacted Title VII' " (p. 789).

From the statistical point of view, it is not obvious how or why disparate treatment establishes discriminatory motive. Particularly in light of the inability of good empirical analysis to control for every "relevant classification criterion," the search for a statistical proof of "motive" seems elusive. But that does not diminish the importance of quantitatively distinguishing between disparate impact and disparate treatment. Disparate impact implies that there are differential outcomes. Those outcomes need not be the consequence of differential treatment; they may result from differences in characteristics of individuals.

The Law and Discrimination

The Fourteenth Amendment to the U.S. Constitution was enacted specifically to provide due process and equal protection before the law for the newly enfranchised former Black slaves. For nearly 100 years, this amendment was one of the sole sources of legal protection that Blacks and other disadvantaged groups could turn to for relief from discriminatory actions by public bodies. The central limitations of the Fourteenth Amendment are that it provides no systematic remedy for discriminatory behavior and it fails to regulate the discriminatory behavior of private firms and individuals. In the minds of many, these limitations render the amendment ineffective in reversing the second-class status of African Americans.

The Civil Rights Act of 1964 sought to give the goal of equal opportunity the substance that earlier Reconstruction civil rights statutes and the Fourteenth Amendment lacked. In particular, Title VII, which bars discrimination on the basis of race, sex, ethnic origin, and color in employment, arose as one of the major tools for two decades of equal rights litigation efforts. Many of the precedents reached in housing discrimination, credit discrimination, death penalty punishment, and other criminal justice discrimination cases flow from important litigation filed under this statute. But this legislation also has caused much confusion about just what constitutes illegal discrimination. Legal scholar Robert Belton (1981) writes:

> Title VII of the Civil Rights Act of 1964 is the principal statute under which the major substantive theories of discrimination law have developed. Congress enacted Title VII to prohibit discrimination on the basis of race, religion, sex, or national origin. The goal of Title VII could have been accomplished in a variety of ways. Congress could have expressed the prohibition in terms of motive or intent, or it could have defined discrimination solely in terms of effect. Unfortunately, the statutory language that Congress chose did not identify clearly which of these concepts is necessary for a finding of unlawful discrimination. The Supreme Court, however, has interpreted Title VII to embrace both substantive concepts. (p. 1226)

There is confusion about whether discriminatory intent must exist in order for there to be illegal discrimination or if there simply must be evidence of a discriminatory effect. Belton recognizes that the Civil Rights Act of 1964 was passed at a time when much discrimination in American life embodied both intent and effect. In subsequent years, the nature of discrimination changed:

> It is increasingly rare to encounter the kinds of direct and overt practices that originally prompted Congress to enact the discrimination laws. Many claims of discrimination today deal with systemic, subtle, and stereotypical practices—which developed when overt discrimination was lawful—and are imbedded in basic institutional and organizational structures. (p. 1224)

Overt discrimination as it was practiced throughout much of the history of the United States—unequal employment opportunities, segregated workplaces and public accommodations, explicit differences in treatment of Blacks and whites in every conceivable aspect of economic life—has diminished considerably in recent generations. Covert discrimination, however, by its very nature, is difficult to uncover through observation alone. And without proof of discriminatory motive or evidence of specific harm to identifiable victims, institutionalized covert discrimination is arguably more difficult to establish using simple numerical comparisons.

The initial introduction of numerical comparisons into litigation on discrimination, however, helped establish a particular type of statistical reasoning in civil rights cases. Until recently, often the only "proof" of discrimination offered by plaintiffs in Title VII and related cases has been to show a statistical disparity. Campbell (1984) relates:

> To determine whether discrimination exists, the percentage of a particular group in a given work force is compared with that group's percentage in the appropriate selection pool or the general population. If there are large differences between the two percentages, and they do not result merely from the chance of selection of an atypical sample, a court may properly infer discriminatory practices. (p. 1299)

The sort of discrimination that this comparison is suited to uncover is what David Kaye considers "ad hoc," or employer decisions that are not based on clearly defined standards or rules. In many respects, this type of discrimination is precisely the sort that economists such as Gary Becker would believe cannot exist in the long run in competitive markets. If the disparate outcomes "cannot plausibly be explained without reference to presumably irrelevant classification [criteria]" (Kaye, 1982, p. 774), then they must be economically inefficient. And if that were the case, then the market would correct these inefficiencies.

In the first decade after the passage of the 1964 Civil Rights Act, courts in a wide variety of cases have found these simple comparisons insufficient to establish a plaintiff's claim of discrimination. Defendants in these cases have often prevailed in part because these simple comparisons failed to account for legitimate differentiating factors that could appear to reflect discrimination. As Campbell (1984) correctly notes:

> Where a number of qualifications are necessary in an occupation, however, a simple comparison of percentages will not satisfy the plaintiff's burden of

proof. . . . In these cases . . . multiple regressions have found frequent use. (pp. 1299-1300; complete citations in the original)

Yet regression analyses designed to account for qualifications, for example, have not been accepted without objection. The arguments against them combine legal issues with standard arguments found in the labor econometrics literature about regression-based models of wage or earnings disparities. Campbell reviews the key objections expressed by courts in rejecting regression analyses that purport to show discrimination or to counter discrimination claims. These include the following: (a) The explanatory variables are themselves tainted by discrimination, (b) the size of the sample is insufficient to support the statistical conclusions, (c) important variables are excluded from the model, (d) different groups are incorrectly aggregated into the same regression, and (e) the regression includes observations from a time when discrimination was not illegal. Courts have not systematically addressed other important qualifications to regression analyses, including model specification, estimation issues, attendant problems of selection bias, unobservables, and errors in variables. No standards have been established for how much of the underlying variance must be explained by the statistical model in order for the model to be acceptable. Nor have standards for tests of robustness of alternative specifications been resolved. The effect is that more sophisticated issues of what constitutes discrimination have remained obscured in all but the most obvious and blatantly overt instances.

The burden of proof, from the earliest litigation of employment discrimination cases, in proving discrimination in violation of Title VII has rested with the plaintiff. The plaintiff has had the initial burden of persuading the court that there was a valid claim and the ultimate burden of proving that claim.[2] Although simple numerical comparisons have met the initial burden of persuasion in such discrimination suits, ultimately more was needed to prove discrimination. Depending on the type of discrimination the plaintiff wished to prove—intentional discrimination or merely discrimination that followed from otherwise legal acts—the next steps in proving illegal discrimination varied. For nearly two decades the courts were guided by two legal theories: disparate impact and disparate treatment.

In *Griggs v. Duke Power Co.* (1971), the U.S. Supreme Court embraced an "effects test." A practice that on its face was racially neutral could be found in violation of the Civil Rights Act if it had the *effect* of discriminating against a protected group. The Court specifically rejected the argument that discriminatory motive or intent was an essential element in violation of Title VII. It was from this landmark case that the disparate impact theory arose. Racially neutral practices that have an adverse impact on the opportunities of members of protected classes—practices that on their face do not separate or classify according to inadmissible criteria—are unlawful unless the practice is shown to be mandated by business necessity or to have a manifest relationship to some legitimate interest of the defendant (Belton, 1981).

In *McDonnell Douglas Corp. v. Green* (1973), the Supreme Court enunciated the disparate treatment theory. According to this theory, in order to prove discrimination, evidence of discriminatory motive or intent can be inferred from differential treatment that more likely than not was "based on a discriminatory criterion illegal under the Act." This theory requires a finding of specific intent to discriminate, although proof of discriminatory intent can be inferred from circumstantial evidence.

Belton (1981) attributes the rise of these opposing theories of discrimination law held by the court to varying interpretations of section 703(h) of the Civil Rights Act, which says that a particular employment practice is not unlawful if it is pursuant to a bona fide seniority or merit system or if it relies on a professionally developed ability test, provided that the differences that result are not the consequence of intentional discrimination.

Both theories suggest three-step procedures for proving illegal discrimination. The difference is in who has the burden of proving what. Under the disparate impact theory, the plaintiff has the initial burden of proving that the policy or practice has a substantive impact on members of a protected class. The defendant must prove that the practice is mandated by business necessity or that the practice has a manifest relationship to the defendant's business. The plaintiff then must show that other practices or policies with a lesser differential impact on the protected class would serve the defendant's legitimate interest (Belton, 1981).

Under the disparate treatment theory, the plaintiff must establish a *prima facie* case of discrimination. The defendant must articulate a legitimate, nondiscriminatory explanation for his or her conduct. The plaintiff must then prove that the defendant's presumptively valid justification was in fact merely a pretext for discriminatory conduct (Belton, 1981).

The economically meaningful difference between these two theories rests in the second steps. Implicit under the disparate impact theory is the notion that a discriminatory practice can be "justified" on grounds of economic efficiency or cost-effectiveness. Under the disparate treatment

theory, any objective function could satisfy the defendant's less demanding need to justify his or her actions. If the firm has other objectives beyond profit maximization, then the steps need not be the same.
Yet in both cases the third step can be reached by taking the objective
that the firm itself expresses as its goal and estimating the impact of a
discrimination-free environment on the outcome measure of legitimate
concern to the defendant.[3]

A legally meaningful distinction between the two theories concerns
"proof" versus "articulation." Under the disparate treatment theory, the
defendant need only articulate a legitimate reason for his or her conduct. Under the disparate impact theory, the defendant must prove that
his or her actions were based on business necessity.

Wards Cove Packing introduces a major new interpretation of disparate impact theory. What might be called "Wards Cove disparate impact
theory" shifts the burden of proof in the second step from the defendant
to the plaintiff. The defendant, in the second step, need only produce
evidence of a business necessity.[4] In its essential elements of what is to
be proven, the Wards Cove version of the disparate impact theory is the
same as the earlier version enunciated in *Griggs v. Duke Power Co.* In
its allocation of burden of proof, of course, the Wards Cove version is
a major departure from the earlier interpretations.

These three theories, disparate impact, disparate treatment, and Wards
Cove disparate impact, still provide for a less burdensome proof of discrimination than a constitutional theory based on the Fourteenth Amendment. The equal protection aspect theoretically protects against racial
discrimination, but an "invidious discriminatory purpose" must be
proven to establish racial discrimination in violation of the Fourteenth
Amendment (*Washington v. Davis,* 1976). Without evidence of discriminatory intent, the state need only show a "rational relationship" to
legitimate legislative goals. Moreover, with evidence of discriminatory
intent, which can be inferred from differential treatment, the state must
then demonstrate a "compelling state interest." These steps suggest that
the third step in a constitutional theory must clearly refute the claim of
compelling state interest, even if discriminatory intent can be inferred.

Statistical Tests of Discrimination

Precisely what do the foregoing differences mean for a convincing
statistical test? Under the disparate impact theory, a regression model

must first establish that the practice has a discriminatory impact. The Wards Cove disparate impact theory clearly suggests a more demanding showing of discrimination because the plaintiff must show that the disparity is unjustified on business necessity grounds. The disparate treatment theory, which assumes a showing of intent that can be inferred from evidence on differential treatment, is best approached by estimating separate equations for protected and nonprotected group members to test for what has come to be known as "residual discrimination." An even more demanding third step seems warranted in a constitutional challenge. It will require the production of an efficiency test.

Disparate Impact Theory

In this interpretation of discrimination, a desirable factor, such as X_i, used by the firm to screen among applicants, has the *effect* of disadvantaging members of the protected group if values of X_i are smaller among the protected group members than among the unprotected group members.

Assume that the factor X_i^B for Blacks is smaller than X_i^W for whites. Further, assume that the effects of X_i on outcomes, Y, are identical for Blacks and whites, then

$$Y^B \leq Y^W, \text{ for } X_i^B \leq X_i^W,$$

where

$$Y^B = \alpha^B + \sum \beta_j^B Z_j^B + \gamma_i^B X_i^B,$$

$$Y^W = \alpha^W + \sum \beta_j^W Z_j^W + \gamma_i^W X_i^W,$$

and where

$$\alpha^B = \alpha^W, \quad \beta^B = \beta^W, \quad \gamma^B = \gamma^W, \quad \text{and } Z^D = Z^W.$$

The outcome measure for Blacks will be lower than for whites simply because the factor X_i is smaller for Blacks than for whites. The use of this factor in distinguishing among applicants has the impact of lowering the outcome measure, Y, for Blacks. If the defendant is unable to demonstrate a business justification for including X in his or her decision apparatus, or if a business justification is claimed but the plaintiff is able to demonstrate an alternative, and not necessarily less costly, way to reach the same objective, then the resulting decision apparatus will be deemed impermissibly discriminatory.

The logic of the foregoing analysis does not depend upon the assumption that all other legally relevant factors are identical between protected and unprotected group members. Nor does the analysis require that the impacts of these factors be the same between the two groups. To isolate the discriminatory impact directly attributable to X one need only compute

$$Y^{B\prime} - Y^B = \gamma^B(X_i^W - X_i^B),$$

where

$$Y^{B\prime} = \alpha^B + \sum \beta_j^B Z_j^B + \gamma_i^B X_i^W,$$

and

$$Y^B = \alpha^B + \sum \beta_j^B Z_j^B + \gamma_i^B X_i^B.$$

In other words, the disparate impact on group B of using factor X_i in the decision process is measured by the difference in what the value of Y would be for B-group members if they had W-group members' values of X_i, and the value of Y using B-group's own values of X_i. This is equal to the weighted difference in X between W- and B-group members. The defendant, then, has the burden of showing that there was a business justification for using X_i in the decision process.[5]

Wards Cove Disparate Impact Theory

Here, there are two additional burdens on the plaintiff beyond those established in disparate impact theory. First, the plaintiff must "isolate and identify the specific employment practices that are allegedly responsible for any alleged statistical disparity" (109 S. Ct. 211 S, Z124, 1989). In addition, the plaintiff must disprove "the employer's assertion that the adverse employment action or practice was based solely on a legitimate neutral consideration" (490 US 642, 660, 1989).

The first of these two requirements suggests the need to decompose the effects of X_i from those of γ_i. After all, both of these contribute to the disparate impact; a determination of "the specific employment practices that are allegedly responsible for any observed statistical disparities" must address this fact.

The required decomposition is as follows:

$$Y^{B\prime} - Y^B = \gamma^B(X_i^W - X_i^B),$$

and

$$Y^{B\prime\prime} - Y^B = (\gamma^W - \gamma^B)X_i^B,$$

where

$$Y^{B\prime\prime} = \alpha^B + \sum \beta_j^B Z_j^B + \gamma_i^B X_i^B.$$

(Note that it is not possible to obtain a direct measure of $Y^{B\prime\prime}$, however. The coefficients in each equation are specific to the identified subgroup. It is valid when the only area of difference between Blacks and whites is the valuation of X.)

The first measure, $\gamma^B(X_i^W - X_i^B)$, is the disparate impact due to differences in X. The second, $(\gamma^W - \gamma^B)X_i^B$, is the disparate impact due to differences in how the employer values X. It appears that it will be more difficult to sustain a discrimination charge based on differences in what are usually termed "endowments" or "characteristics" of victims than one based on differential treatment of those characteristics. And, because differential treatment of characteristics introduces the additional consideration of discriminatory motive, it appears in the best interest of the plaintiff to uncover these possible disparities.

The Wards Cove case, however, makes it clear that even if there are disparate impacts, the plaintiff must disprove any claim advanced by the defendant that those impacts are necessitated by legitimate business factors.

Let the business factor introduced by the defendant be Ω, composed of two parts: a value specific to the employee, Q, and the employer's evaluation of that value in the determination of Y, ω. Then, the new equations to be estimated are as follows:

$$Y^{B*} = \alpha^B + \sum \beta_j^B Z_j^B + \gamma_i^B X_i^B + \Omega^B,$$

$$Y^{W*} = \alpha^W + \sum \beta_j^W Z_j^W + \gamma_i^W X_i^W + \Omega^W,$$

where $\Omega = \omega Q$. A finding either that there is no effect of Q on Y—that is, $\omega = 0$—or that there are no differences in Q between the two groups will defeat the business necessity defense.

Disparate Treatment Theory

Disparate treatment differs from disparate impact in the crucial aspect of motive or intent. In this class of discrimination case, the burden falls upon the plaintiff to "prove" intentional discrimination. But the courts have interpreted statistical proof of intent or motive to mean that an inference of discriminatory behavior can be made from evidence of differential treatment. Other evidence, such as historical documentation of past discriminatory acts and anecdotal evidence of continuing discriminatory behavior, must buttress this statistical proof.

The objective of a statistical test for the disparate treatment theory is to compute a "discrimination-free" measure of the outcome variable for the plaintiff. This measure is compared with the actual outcome variable. Significant differences between the two would permit the inference that substantially equal persons were treated unequally because of the discriminatory intent or motive of the firm.

This is nothing more than the standard Blinder-Oaxaca-Duncan residual discrimination methodology.[6] Using the same notation as before, we have

$$Y^B = \alpha^B + \sum \beta_j^B Z_j^B + \gamma_i^B X_i^B,$$

$$Y^W = \alpha^W + \sum \beta_j^W Z_j^W + \gamma_i^W X_i^W,$$

except that now we make no assumptions about the relationships among the αs, βs, and γs for Blacks and whites. We compute the following residual difference:

$$D = \hat{Y}^B - Y^B,$$

where

$$\hat{Y}^B = \alpha^W + \sum \beta_j^W Z_j^B + \gamma_i^W X_i^B.$$

In other words, we compute the difference in Y between a world where Blacks are treated like whites and the world they actually face. In the absence of differential treatment of equally qualified persons, this difference will be zero. Even with differential treatment, however, there may still be no residual difference, if the factors favoring Black workers outweigh those that disfavor them.

To disprove a business necessity defense, moreover, the plaintiff must demonstrate that upon reestimation of the outcome equations including Ω, the residual difference remains. Thus we must estimate

$$Y^{B*} = \alpha^B + \sum \beta_j^B Z_j^B + \gamma_i^B X_i^B + \omega^B Q^B,$$

and

$$Y^{W*} = \alpha^W + \sum \beta_j^W Z_j^W + \gamma_i^W X_i^W + \omega^W Q^W.$$

The revised residual difference is

$$D' = \hat{Y}^B - Y^B,$$

where

$$\tilde{Y}^B = \alpha^W + \sum \beta_j^W Z_j^B + \gamma_i^W X_i^B + \omega^W Q^B.$$

If $D' \geq 0$, the plaintiff will survive a business justification contention by the defendant.

Fourteenth Amendment Theory

The demand that a plaintiff show irrational, capricious, or arbitrary behavior in order to counter a claim that an alleged discriminatory act fulfills a compelling state objective requires more than the sort of test envisioned in the business necessity test. I propose an efficiency test. First, the standard residual is estimated. Then an objective function, dependent upon the outcome variable, is estimated. The objective function might be a cost function, a profit function, or a general social welfare function. In the case of state parole boards, for example, the objective function might be the rate, C, at which released offenders return to crime. This, ostensibly, depends on the form of release, Y, and the time of release, T. The objective of the parole board is to pick persons for parole release so as to minimize postincarceration criminal involvement. Denote this objective by C. Then, a discriminatory outcome on Y is inefficient if

$$C^B \geq \hat{C}^B,$$

where

$$C^B = f(\tau^B T^B; v^B Y^B),$$

and

$$\hat{C}^B = f(\tau^B T^B; v^B \tilde{Y}^B),$$

where the second expression is the value of C under a discrimination-free environment. One advantage to performing this efficiency test is that even if the plaintiff fails to find the discrimination-free environment less costly than the discriminatory environment, it is possible to argue, buttressed by evidence of historical patterns of discrimination, that the price for rectifying the observed disparity is minuscule when compared with the continued harm to the plaintiff. The state, in turn, would prevail if the computation reveals significant economies in the presence of the disparate treatment.

Implicit in such challenges as those posed by *Croson*, which question whether race-based remedies to alleged discrimination are themselves impermissible due to the equal protection provisions of the Fourteenth Amendment, is the need to demonstrate *through historical evidence* patterns and practices establishing invidious discriminatory motive. Thus statistical evidence, even such evidence as suggested by the "efficiency test" proposed above, is unlikely to be sufficient to meet the standards established in *Croson*.

The Special Case
of Discrimination in Punishment[7]

A Black man named Green, who went to prison because he failed to report for military induction, applied for a job as a clerk with the Missouri Pacific Railroad. He was denied the job because of the railroad's long-standing policy of refusing to hire applicants with conviction records. Green contended that the railroad's employment policy resulted in greater proportions of Blacks than whites being excluded from jobs. A class action suit was filed alleging violation of Title VII of the Civil Rights Act of 1964. The case was tried in the U.S. District Court for the Eastern District of Missouri and was dismissed on the grounds that while Blacks were disproportionately among those with arrest and conviction records, the actual number of Blacks so rejected from employment on these grounds was quite small. The *"de minimis* discriminatory effect," uncovered in the district court, was one where 16% of the population was Black, while only 2.05% of all applicants rejected were Blacks with conviction records.

Green appealed to the U.S. Court of Appeals, Eighth Circuit. That court held that the railroad's rule against hiring ex-offenders was racially discriminatory and could not be justified by business necessity (*Green v. Missouri Pacific Railroad,* 1975; see also "Conviction Records," 1976). In addition, it stated:

> The issue to be examined statistically is whether the questioned employment practice operates in a disparate manner upon a minority race or group, *not whether the individuals actually suffering from a discriminatory practice are statistically large in number.* (*Green v. Missouri Pacific Railroad,* 1975, p. 1295; emphasis added)

The court went on to say that "an employment practice must be examined for its operation on a racially exclusionary basis—thus its effect must be measured upon blacks separately and whites separately."

What this case reaffirmed was that however small the resulting harm may be from a discriminatory practice, the statistical examination must direct itself to the *existence* of that practice. Also, it confirmed that the statistical issue must address differential effects for Blacks and whites. At least in employment discrimination cases, then, the ruling makes unambiguous how much discrimination or differential treatment of Blacks and whites should be considered desirable or, in economists' jargon, "socially optimal." As long as there is a statistically significant disparity, a *prima facie* case of discrimination can be established.[8]

In addition to establishing firmly that businesses' unjustified hiring criteria have discriminatory impacts on minority group members, *Green v. Missouri Pacific* uncovered substantial evidence of discriminatory impacts of criminal justice policies. In the expert testimony, evidence was submitted contending that Blacks are three to six times more likely to be arrested or convicted of criminal offenses than are whites. For example, while it was estimated that from 11.6% to 16.8% of all white persons in urban areas would have conviction records in their lifetimes, from 36.9% to 78.1% of all Black persons would acquire conviction records. Whether such disparate outcomes are violative of any civil rights statutes was not an issue in this case and therefore was not addressed. Still, the Eighth and Fourteenth Amendments to the U.S. Constitution have been interpreted as prohibiting racially discriminatory punishment practices.[9] Thus whether or not racial discrimination in punishment exists is more than a narrow statistical concern; it involves important legal considerations.

But what have social science researchers had to say on the existence of racial discrimination in punishment? A recent National Academy of Sciences report that purports to undertake a systematic and thorough review of previous research on sentencing provides a bleak summary. It concludes that observed racial disparities in punishment are due primarily to the overrepresentation of Blacks among those committing more serious crimes. The conclusion of that distinguished panel, which included eminent statisticians and econometricians, is that the evidence does not support the contention that Blacks are discriminated against in sentencing decisions. This conclusion is buttressed by a review of several, but not all, statistical analyses of previous studies of racial discrimination in punishment. While an extensive and detailed account is given of the bias that is likely to occur when single-equation models are estimated in the face of omitted or unobservable variables, the NAS report does not mention the appropriateness of dummy variable techniques for measuring discrimination.[10] The National Academy of Sciences study, therefore, leaves unexplored the question of how to detect and measure differential treatment in punishment. Moreover, the report utterly ignores the issue resolved by *Green v. Missouri* of how much discrimination is enough to make such discrimination illegal.

The implication left by recent reviews of racial disparities in punishment, such as those by Hagan and Bumiller (1983), Petersilia (1983), Pope (1979), and others, is that the overrepresentation of Blacks among the criminal population is a possible, if not plausible, explanation for at least some of the racial disparities in punishment. That Blacks are more likely than whites to be arrested and convicted (evidence of which is provided in Peterson & Braiker, 1980; Wolfgang & Cohen, 1970, p. 31) or that Blacks serve longer prison sentences than whites (evidence of which is provided in Myers, 1985b; Petersilia, 1983, p. 67) is often justified by the presumption that Blacks are more criminally violent than whites, and that violent crimes are more harshly punished than other crimes. It is not difficult to find evidence that Blacks are more criminally violent. Wolfgang (1983), for example, using the now famous Philadelphia Birth Cohort data, reports that the officially recorded offense rate for serious assaultive crimes is 4 to 11 times higher among Blacks than it is among whites. He also calculates that 80% of all offenses involving physical injury to the victims are accounted for by minority offenders (p. 9). But such findings hardly provide a basis for concluding that Blacks are not discriminated against. Offering evidence that differences between groups exist, as shown by unequal outcomes from a process, does not provide an acceptable explanation in support of the hypothesis of equality of treatment. What the courts have contended in numerous employment discrimination cases is that the pertinent evidence must address the problem of disparate impacts. Because of the extensive litigation of civil rights cases in the employment area, substantive empirical meaning has been lent to the concepts "differences between groups" and "disparate impacts."

There are nonetheless important differences between employment and punishment disparities. Much of the law concerning racial discrimination in employment has evolved from the Civil Rights Act of 1964, which made differential treatment in hiring, wages, and other aspects of employment illegal if such differentials could not be justified on the grounds of business necessity. The Fourteenth Amendment is more demanding. In a recent death penalty case the Eleventh Circuit Court of Appeals wrote:

> Disparate impact alone is insufficient to establish a violation of the Fourteenth Amendment. There must be a showing of an intent to discriminate. . . . Only if the evidence of disparate impact is so strong that the only permissible inference is one of intentional discrimination will it alone suffice. (*Adams v. Wainwright*, 1988, p. 1449)

The burden of proving intent and racially disparate impact has become even more difficult, especially in light of sentencing guidelines, determinate sentencing laws, and appellate review of capital cases, all of which purport to eliminate disparities in punishment. Thus if historical patterns of punishment—which may themselves be racially discriminatory—become rationalized through race-neutral legislation, then future findings of racial disparities in punishment may fail to meet the test in *Adams v. Wainwright*. Moreover, the courts increasingly have gravitated toward the position that statistical evidence of "large" and "significant" levels of discrimination must be tendered before constitutional claims of excessive or nonproportional punishment will be entertained. Although there is as yet no definition of what is "large" or "significant," there does appear to be a standard, however imprecise, that requires the statistical analysis to leave no other conclusion *except* a finding of intentional and irrational discrimination.[11]

How useful can econometric analysis be in formalizing a method for detecting and measuring racial discrimination in punishment? It seems ambitious to hope that statistical tools will ever be very persuasive as a means of establishing intent. And there are several questions that deserve answers before social scientists leap to that challenge. How does one measure differential treatment in sentencing? What sort of bias is introduced by using the labor econometric method of measuring discrimination when there are omitted or unobservable variables, such as violent behavior, that legitimately enter into the sentencing decision? And how serious is the bias likely to be?

Legal Issues and Discrimination in Punishment

What sort of evidence must be marshaled to establish discrimination in punishment? In Eubanks v. Louisiana (1957) the Supreme Court established that indictments and verdicts that resulted from a jury selection procedure that systematically excluded Blacks could be overturned because by such blatant discrimination Blacks were deprived of equal protection under the law. Until that case, no Blacks had ever served on juries. The evidence hardly required a fine-tuned statistical analysis. The court found:

> Although Negroes comprise about one-third of the population of the parish, the uncontradicted testimony of the various witnesses established that only one Negro had been picked for grand jury duty within recent memory. And this lone exception apparently resulted from the mistaken impression that the juror was white. . . . out of 432 jurors selected only a single Negro was chosen. . . . We are reluctantly forced to conclude that the uniform and long-continued exclusion of Negroes from grand juries shown by this record cannot be attributed to chance, [or] to accident. (p. 586)

Allegations of racial discrimination in punishment and supporting statistical evidence, however, are now being met with strongly worded and often antagonistic responses from the federal courts. For example, in *Smith v. Balkcom* (1982) a challenge to Georgia's death penalty was mounted on the grounds that racial factors were evident in sentencing patterns. The statistical analysis in that case was discredited because "the raw data selected for the statistical study bear no more than a highly attenuated relationship to capital cases actually presented for trial in the state [and] the leap from that data to the conclusion of discriminatory intent or purpose leaves untouched countless racially neutral variables" (5th Cir. 671 F.2d 858, 859, 1982).

In a footnote, the Fifth Circuit Court of Appeals explained that the number of unsupported assumptions underlying the data analysis rendered the statistical results useless. The analysis failed to include information on whether the charges or indictments stemmed from the reported incident or whether there were aggravating or mitigating circumstances surrounding the individual crimes. The analysis also failed to account for not-guilty verdicts. The court concluded, "The statistics are not inconsistent with the proper application of the structured capital punishment law of the state" (p. 859). It said:

> The tender of statistical evidence must account for nonracial variables so as to render the statistics so strong that the results would permit no other inference but that they are the results of racially discriminatory intent or purpose. (p. 859)

In another case, where a 17-year-old Black male was convicted and sentenced to death for murdering a white state trooper following a drunken spree, the Fifth Circuit Court of Appeals again asserted that the burden of the statistical analysis should be to establish beyond any reasonable doubt the existence of *intentional* discrimination against the particular petitioner (*Prejean v. Blackburn,* 1984). An important example of an attempt to carry that burden is the statistical analysis of David Baldus in *McCleskey v. Kemp* (1985). In that case, a Black male was arrested and charged with the murder of a police officer during an armed robbery of a furniture store. He was sentenced to death for the murder of the police officer and to consecutive life sentences for two counts of armed robbery. After exhausting several appeals to state and federal courts, the defendant filed a petition in federal court raising several constitutional issues, including the constitutionality of the application of Georgia's death penalty. McCleskey contended that his death sentence was unconstitutional because Georgia's death penalty was discriminatorily applied on the basis of the races of the offender and the victim. Blacks who kill whites, he contended, were more likely to receive a sentence of death than whites who kill whites or whites who kill Blacks.

To support this contention, Professor David Baldus estimated a logistic model for the probability of a death sentence, using a Georgia-based stratified random sample of 1,966 cases of individuals indicted for murder between 1973 and 1978. More than 100 independent variables were included to measure every conceivable aspect of the murder case. The Baldus study found that murderers who killed whites were six percentage points more likely to receive a death sentence than if the victim were Black. Although the dummy variable for Black offenders was found to be insignificant, the study concluded that significant disparities in sentencing did arise, particularly in the middle range of crime aggravation.

The majority of the members of the Eleventh Circuit Court of Appeals rejected these findings.[12] That court continued the established pattern concerning the need to demonstrate intent. It found that a constitutional claim of racial discrimination could be met by a showing of disproportional impact alone. There had to be a showing that no other reasonable inference could be drawn from the statistical analysis other than that there was discriminatory intent. Moreover, the majority of that court held that the discriminatory impact had to be great enough to compel the conclusion that the system was unprincipled, irrational, arbitrary, and capricious in order for the disparate impact to be sufficient to invalidate a capital sentencing system.

It did not help that at the district court hearings the quality of the research was called into question. Flaws in the data base, the low predictive validity of the models, and the high levels of multicollinearity were cited. Because the statistical analysis failed to show that prosecutors were systematically discriminating against Blacks, no finding of intentional discrimination could be supported merely by the evidence.

Interestingly, Baldus appears not to have included a full set of interaction terms or to have estimated his equation separately for Blacks and whites. The finding that the race dummy for the offender is insignificant may be a consequence of the fact that Blacks are more likely to kill other Blacks than to kill whites. Because offenders with Black victims are sentenced less severely, the single dummy variable for race captures mixed and opposite effects. What Baldus should have demonstrated was that Blacks who kill whites are treated more harshly than whites who kill whites. To establish this, either separate equations for Blacks and whites or a single equation with a fully loaded set of interaction terms should have been estimated.

But the majority in the *McCleskey v. Kemp* case still have a point that remains unresolved. Even if Baldus had used the residual approach with an appropriate functional specification, would the disparate effects so found be enough?

The constitutional protections of prisoners are frequently called into question. In *Hudson v. Palmer* (1984) the Supreme Court held that prisoners, while enjoying many of the protections of the Constitution, lose certain protections because imprisonment makes necessary particular practices consistent with the needs and objectives of the prisons. The primary objectives of prison officials, the court argued, are internal security and safety. Thus random searches and destruction of personal property that would be in violation of the Fourth Amendment rights of other citizens are necessary practices in prisons. Citing the violent nature of America's prisons, the Court contended that otherwise unconstitutional search and seizure practices are appropriate in prisons in order to foster legitimate institutional interests.

Prisoners seem to have lost other constitutional rights as well. In a 1960s challenge to racial segregation in the prisons, the Supreme Court held that "prison authorities have the right, acting in good faith and in particularized circumstances, to take into account racial tensions in maintaining security, discipline, and good order in prisons and jails" (*Lee v. Washington*, 1968, p. 334).

These instances of curbs on the constitutional protections of prisoners seem akin to the business necessity rule in employment discrimination cases. It was established in *Griggs v. Duke Power Co.* (1971) that business necessity might be a sustainable justification for discriminatory treatment. The burden of proving business necessity, however, requires showing that the discriminatory practice fosters employee productivity and that no acceptable alternative exists that has a lesser discriminatory impact. The business necessity of random search and seizure in inmates' cells is to assure the safety and security of correctional facilities. The business necessity of racial disparities in punishment has never been questioned directly by the courts, but the reluctance to rule outright that any racial disparity in punishment is indicative of racial discrimination hints that the business necessity rule may be at work.[13] The business necessity of racially disparate punishments may be to perform the legitimate functions of the prisons and the criminal justice system: to deter, rehabilitate, and so on. This is a perspective that forms the basis for a novel statistical test of discrimination in punishment.

Conclusion

The limited victories attendant to the passage of the 1991 Civil Rights Act must be placed within a broader context of retreat from the ideal of equal outcomes at all costs. The equality of outcome ideal, as distinct from the ideal of equal opportunity, has fostered the growth of plans, timetables, affirmative action efforts, set-asides, and a wide array of other race-based or gender-based strategies. These strategies, implemented during a period of often overt discriminatory behavior in both the private sector and the public sector, were once seen as virtually the only means of reversing centuries of discrimination. Ironically, the one constitutional provision specifically enacted for the purpose of addressing unequal treatment faced by newly freed slaves is now invoked to challenge programs that have evolved to hasten the drive toward racial equality.

Yet, proponents of equality of outcomes cannot rest comfortably as long as the standards for proving what constitutes discrimination remain unresolved. There is little guidance and even less reassurance provided by the language of the 1991 Civil Rights Act, which ironically is being hailed by many as the solution to the problems created by the 1989 spate of Supreme Court decisions calling for strict scrutiny of all policies that infringe on the constitutional provisions of equal protection under the law. Indeed, in areas such as criminal justice, which are not specifically covered by the new legislation, the status of statistical tests of discrimination remains undisturbed. There remains a substantial burden that plaintiffs must bear, and that burden is unmet by the simple statistical comparisons that evolved under the older civil rights litigation.

The more demanding tests suggested in this chapter, combined with careful historical documentation of discriminatory practices and policies, offer the hope of uncovering illegal discrimination and at the same time addressing legitimate defenses for unequal outcomes in a variety of settings. The logic of examining whether a discriminatory pattern is "business justified" or based on a "compelling state objective" is not in question. What we address here is how to perform this and related tests.

Not all inequality is the result of discrimination, and not all discrimination results in inequality. Knowing the difference can mean much for advancing the state of the art in research on race and economic well-being.

Notes

1. Kaye (1982) states: "Although there are many such laws governing racial and other forms of discrimination, it is possible to think of all these laws as expressions of one deceptively simple principle: 'like' cases are to be treated alike, and 'unlike' cases are to be treated differently. . . . discrimination . . . consists in departing from this principle of equal treatment" (p. 773).

2. "In a Title VII case the plaintiff has the ultimate burden of proof and the initial burden of persuasion" (Campbell, 1984, p. 1308; citing *Texas Department of Community Affairs v. Burdine*, 1981, pp. 252-253).

3. This third step actually exceeds the legal requirements under the disparate impact theory. In such instances, the plaintiff must show that an alternative practice exists. The alternative found does not have to be less costly than the alleged discriminatory practice, the plaintiff need only demonstrate that an alternative practice prevails. Economists generally object to this last requirement because it fails to compare adequately the costs of enforcing the antidiscrimination legislation against other social costs, including those that would result in increased burdens on the alleged victims of discrimination. For example, credit market discrimination against female heads of families might result from the higher credit risks these persons carry into the market. Family status might be a legitimate indicator of creditworthiness, and the exclusion of this variable in credit scoring schemes may result in an increase in defaults and thus a rise in the cost of borrowing. The increased borrowing costs, according to this reasoning, would have to be shared by all borrowers, including creditworthy female heads of families.

4. Justice White wrote in the *Wards Cove* majority opinion: "The employer carries the burden of producing evidence of a business justification for his employment practice. The burden of persuasion, however, remains with the disparate-impact plaintiff." Yet the cornerstones of the third step remain unchanged: "If respondents cannot persuade the trier of fact on the question of petitioners' business necessity defense, respondents may still be able to prevail [by] com[ing] forward with an alternative to petitioner's hiring practice." The major alteration in the third step is the contention that the cost of the alternative must be considered and the alternative must be equally effective as the existing practice in achieving legitimate employment goals.

5. An interesting alternative, however, is to demonstrate that X has no impact on Y for Blacks or whites. In that case, there is no disparate impact.

6. I do not consider here several of the many alternatives to this methodology, including the "reverse regression" method (Conway & Roberts, 1983) and the Cotton (1988) correction.

7. This section is based in part on Myers (1985a).

8. For a complete discussion of how the courts have come to regard the arbitrary 5% level as "statistically significant," see Kaye (1982).

9. As will be discussed below, the majority of punishment disparity cases that have made their way to the federal courts on the basis of constitutional claims have been death penalty cases. In those cases, and elsewhere, it has been established that "systemwide racial discrimination" violates the equal protection clause of the Fourteenth Amendment while a capriciously and irrationally operating system of capital punishment violates the Eighth Amendment. See *McCleskey v. Kemp* (1985).

10. This is a procedure that I will argue amounts to assuming that the coefficients on the "race-neutral" variables are identical for Blacks and whites. Or, stated differently, it is a procedure that assumes that there is no differential treatment of Blacks and whites—a highly questionable assumption given the requirements put forth in *Green v. Missouri Pacific*.

11. The contradiction of requiring that the statistical analysis show irrationality and intent apparently never has been addressed.

12. After several failed attempts to obtain further Supreme Court review, McCleskey was executed in the fall of 1991.

13. The motives and intent perspective is possibly a red herring. The point may be less whether a criminal justice system has been operating in a systematically and consciously racially discriminatory fashion than whether there is a plausible explanation for the differential effects.

10

Psychoeducational Assessment
of Gifted and Talented
African Americans

JAMES M. PATTON

A man with wisdom is better off than a stupid man with any amount of charm and superstition.

African proverb

It is essential that any treatise on the topic of theory and methodology related to identifying gifts and talents among young African American learners place this subject within the larger historical, philosophical, sociocultural, political, and educational contexts associated with the development and use of intelligence tests during the past 250 years. The present treatise begins along this path. It continues by critiquing certain traditional Western-inspired and -oriented psychoeducational assessment theories and methodologies that define intelligence in unidimensional terms. The conclusion presents a schema designed to serve as a guide to theory building and the development of assessment methodology and assessment systems based on African American worldviews and aspects of deep-structure culture. Such theory building should enhance our capacities to identify gifts and talents among young African American learners ages 4 through 13.

Evolution and Critique of
Traditional Assessment Theory and Methodology

My hypothesis in this chapter is that psychoeducational assessment theories and methodologies grounded in worldviews and cultural characteristics of African Americans are needed to guide the development of psychoeducational assessment of African American learners with gifts and talents. In advance of exploring a schema that offers a model in this regard, I offer a brief review of the historical and contemporary cultural and sociopolitical contexts of theory development, methodology, and practices in psychoeducational assessment. A comprehensive review of the historical origins and sociopolitical contexts of the intelligence testing movement is beyond the scope of this chapter. However, I will outline a synthesis of this body of literature, which provides the fundamental underpinnings of contemporary theory, methodology, and practice in psychoeducational assessment.

An examination of the work of many of the early European pioneers of psychometrics, their aims, assumptions, and general theoretical and methodological orientations, leads one to conclude that many of these individuals shared a particular worldview and developed a set of theories and methodologies related to the intelligence construct and intelligence testing consistent with these worldviews.

Dixon (1976) has argued that theoretical assumptions emanate partially from a philosophical worldview whose form shapes specific modes of knowing and ways of organizing and verifying knowledge, all of which are culture bound and influenced. He continues by observing that there exist distinct differences *in kind* between major Euro-American and African American philosophical characteristics that subsequently lead to "worldview-specific" theories, methodologies, tests, and practices. The Euro-American tradition of positivism and penchant for valuing knowledge that can be reduced to discrete measurement, and that implies hierarchical levels of abilities within a unidimensional construct of intelligence, became, early on, *the* standard against which all knowledge and intelligence were compared. In contrast, assessment theories and methodologies derived from African and African American cultural worldviews have rarely been valued or affirmed by past or present leaders in the development of assessment theory and practice.

The fact that European, positivist-oriented psychoeducational assessment theory, methodology, and testing of African Americans have played critical roles in the continued justification of the sociopolitical, cultural, and educational oppression of Americans of African descent is indisputable. The early nineteenth-century leaders in the development of measurement theories, paradigms, instruments, and methodologies may have differed in their conceptualizations of the proportional weight attributed to causes of, or factors related to, intelligence (e.g., polygenists versus monogenists, evolutionists versus creationists, hereditarians versus environmentalists), but they never questioned the central idea of European and Euro-American superiority and African and African American inferiority.[1] The assault on African Americans through the political use of purported scientific methodology and psychometric instruments has a long and rich history.

The seminal works of Gould (1977, 1981), Chase (1980), Hilliard (1984), Nobles (1983), and Kamin (1974, 1975) have provided a detailed and thorough history of the shared cultural, philosophical, and political worldviews of the early European and Euro-American intelligence test developers. An exploration of the metaphysical, epistemological, and conceptual universes held by these major developers of the early conceptual, theoretical, and methodological approaches to psychoeducational assessment provides insight into the fundamental tenets of the testing movement and intelligence tests, and their sociopolitical purpose and use. It is important to understand the connection between an individual's philosophical worldview and subsequent theory and methodology developed by that person. Gordon (1985), like Dixon, reminds us that theory, methodology, and practice in the social sciences emanate from individuals' fundamental belief systems, which are shaped partially by their racial, cultural, and class identities. More recently, Gordon, Miller, and Rollock (1990) have informed us that the communicentric bias and a priori prejudices traditionally held by many Euro-American social science knowledge producers have generated fallacious and distorted social science theories, paradigms, and methodologies that deny the cultural integrity of African Americans and exalt Eurocentric culture and worldviews.

The early theoretical and methodological work of measurement and testing pioneers such as Broca (1861) and other masters of craniometry and the hereditarians such as Galton (1884), Terman (1916), Goddard (1919), Yerkes (1917), Spearman (1923), Thorndike (1940), and Jensen (1969, 1979), as well as Binet (1909) and Binet and Simon (1912, 1916), provide numerous rich examples of Eurocentric worldviews and perspectives. The aforementioned represent a veritable "who's who" of the historical lineage of leaders in the assessment movement in Europe and America. It is evident that the origins of the testing movement rested in the leadership and guidance of these individuals and others who harbored, in too many instances, a priori prejudices and often manufactured and reported on distorted data that led inevitably to invalid conclusions. The works of Goddard (1912) and Sir Cyril Burt (1966) exemplify the manner in which a priori bias can contribute to biased results and represent classic examples of the falsification and alteration of data to support racial and cultural predilections for the superiority of the Euro-American culture.

Goddard, the earliest American to call for the use of the Binet Scale of Intelligence, epitomized an early hereditarian worldview in 1920 when he wrote:

> Stated in its boldest form, our thesis is that the chief determiner of human conduct is a unitary mental process which we call intelligence; that this process is conditioned by a nervous mechanism which is inborn; that the degree of efficiency to be attained by that nervous mechanism and the consequent grade of intellectual or mental level for each individual is determined by the kind of chromosomes that come together with the union of germ cells; that is but little affected by any later influences except serious accidents that may destroy part of the mechanism. (quoted in Tuddenham, 1962, p. 491)

Terman, another early and major advocate of the Binet scale, certainly shared Goddard's view. His inclination to ascribe innate inheritance to intelligence can be seen in three questions he posed in 1916:

> Is the place of the so called lower classes in the social and industrial scale the result of their inferior native endowment, or is their apparent inferiority merely a result of their inferior home and school training? Is genius more common among children of the educated classes than among the children of the ignorant and poor? Are the inferior races really inferior, or are they merely unfortunate in their lack of opportunity to learn? (pp. 19-20)

The works of Terman, Galton, Goddard, and others who shared their sociocultural and conceptual universe have influenced current assessment theory, methodology, and practice. They have been seen also as a strong source of influence in the lives of several generations of politicians, social scientists, educators, and researchers. Today, the assault on African Americans, as observed by Nobles (1987), is not as openly and crudely advanced as it was by the earlier craniometrists or hereditarian pioneers. The contemporary world and modern approaches have called for different types of assaults—subtler in their conceptual and psychometric manifestations. As Gould (1981) has pointed out "the crudities of the cranial index have given way to the complexity of intelligence testing" (p. 143). The pseudoobjective "scientific" approaches of contemporary practice in psychometry have disguised many biases still inherent in many of today's intelligence and standardized testing paradigms. Kamin's (1975) question, "What shall we say of the voices of today's mental testers?" (p. 322) still begs to be answered.

It should be noted at this point that some of the earliest criticisms of intelligence constructs, theories, methodologies, and improper use of intelligence tests were advanced during the late 1800s and early 1900s by African American social scientists. Individuals such as W. E. B. Du Bois, Howard Hale Long, Horace Mann Bond, Martin D. Jenkins, Joseph St. Clair Price, and Doxey Wilkerson, to name a few, refuted the African American intelligence deficit conjectures offered by the leading Eurocentric scientists of their era (Franklin, 1976). These individuals attacked the generally accepted construct of intelligence and beliefs about the methodological soundness of measuring intelligence through the use of IQ tests. As early as 1924, Bond challenged the traditionally held view that the Army Alpha tests measured innate or native intellectual abilities and found in a 1924 study that African American children scored significantly higher on the Stanford-Binet IQ test than had been reported previously by Terman (p. 63). Earlier, Martin Jenkins (1936) found that African American children scored significantly higher on IQ tests when the tests were administered by individuals who established positive rapport with the children.

Nobles (1987) has identified "cultural antimony" as a major source of problems in psychoeducational assessment theory, and methodology, today as it has been in the past. According to Nobles, the "Eurocentric cultural paradigm which guides the assessment and evaluation of reality stands in contradistinction to the cultural laws which are consistent with the cultural deep structure of African people" (p. 3). The resulting contradiction between these two laws (i.e., cultural antimony), says Nobles, is in the direction of assumed white superiority (p. 54). Intertwined with this view is the proposition advanced by Nobles that the historical Euro-American perceived necessity to "verify the falsification of the historical presence and position of African people in relation to Europeans" is another problem in the assessment of African Americans today (p. 54).

As noted above, contemporary intelligence tests were developed partially out of shared Eurocentric, culture-bound theories concerning the nature of intelligence and the presumed inferiority of African Americans. Chief among the shared paradigms advanced by these assessment theorists and test developers were notions that intelligence tests accurately measure intelligence and tap mental aptitudes and abilities that are universal. It has been shown that intelligence tests, in fact, more closely sample discrete, Eurocentric, middle-class, culturally and linguistically valued cognitive skills, not universal cognitive capacities or processes (Cole & Scribner, 1973; Guthrie, 1976; Hilliard, 1984; Nobles, 1987; Ogbu, 1988; Sattler, Hilliard, Lambert, Albee, & Jensen, 1981; Vernon, 1969). These tests could, therefore, be viewed as isomorphic to middle class American values.

Continuing this analysis of traditional Western assessment theory and methodology, Ogbu (1988) has distinguished between intelligence as cognitive capacities, which are universal, and cognitive skills, which are relative and vary from culture to culture. Intelligence tests, according to Ogbu's schema, measure specific Eurocentric cognitive skills that are specific to Western culture. Therefore, since these tests are grounded on samplings of cognitive universes and behaviors valued by "the middle class in Western societies, they inevitably discriminate against members of other cultures" and cannot adequately measure "intelligence" of African Americans (Ogbu, 1988, p. 29).

Jones (1979), Reschly (1980), Cronbach (1984), and Sharma (1986) inform us that the problem of test bias is multifaceted and that biases emanating from deep-structure cultural dissonance between African American and Euro-American assessment procedures often create biases at several levels. Biases have been found to exist at the level of test content (e.g., the noninclusion of test items reflective of the unique cultural perspectives, language,[2] and experiences of African Americans) and at the levels of testee readiness, motivation, and response set (e.g., nonresponsiveness to cultural influences and manifestations of motivation). These researchers have also found biases to exist at the test standardization level (e.g., noninclusion of significant numbers of African Americans in the normative samples), examiner and test administration levels (e.g., noninclusion of individuals knowledgeable of and sensitive to African American culture in test administration and interpretation), reliability and validity levels (e.g., nonresponsiveness to cultural influences), and decision-making level (e.g., noninclusion of individuals knowledgeable of and sensitive to African American culture in test interpretation). Reschly and Ross-Reynolds (1982) have found biases at these levels particularly manifested when applied to gifted African American learners.

Many of the questions and concerns regarding test and testing bias manifested at the aforementioned levels have been addressed primarily by technical efforts aimed at developing new tests and/or methodologies that would not discriminate unfairly against diverse racial and ethnic groups. As Cronbach (1984) and Drew (1973) argue, however, there has been little response challenging the theoretical precision, purposes, and decision making on the basis of these tests and test scores. Issues surrounding the achievement of conceptual clarity related to the purposes and uses of test results are clearly primary concerns and, when related to testing the African American child, must be resolved by maintaining and advancing the integrity and deep-structure cultural elements of African Americans.

Toward the Development of Models for Assessing African American Learners

Theory has been defined as a symbolic representation of experience (Kaplan, 1964). As such, theory serves as a medium through which experiences can be reconstructed and subsequently analyzed, synthesized, measured, interpreted, and criticized. The methodological process in psychoeducational assessment is guided, shaped, and influenced by theory. The use, then, of a particular methodological approach or test presupposes some type of implicit or explicit *prior* theorizations about the construct or attribute of the thing or person to be measured and the inquiry method to be employed (Kaplan, 1964). These theory-building and methodological selection processes, as previously advanced, flow from the individual's culture-based philosophical worldview and can, as a result, influence results.

The concern about the discriminatory use of intelligence tests emanates from the fact that African American learners have historically been underrepresented in classes for the gifted and talented and overrepresented in special education classes for the mentally retarded. Although there appears to be abundant evidence implicating contemporary psychometry and standardized tests in the continued sociopolitical, economic, and educational exploitation of African Americans, the exclusive use of intelligence tests and other norm-referenced tests continues unabated. Judge Peckham's ban on the use of IQ tests in assessing African American learners in California is clearly an exception to today's heavy reliance on the use of these tests (Jensen, 1979). In fact, my colleagues and I found in a recent national study that 88.5% of the states responding to a national survey indicated some use of traditional, norm-referenced tests in the identification of at-risk gifted learners (Patton, Prillaman, & VanTassel-Baska, 1990).

In spite of the fact that African Americans constitute approximately 16.2% of individuals enrolled in America's public schools, they make up only about 8.4% of those enrolled in programs for the gifted (Alamprese & Erlanger, 1988). The exploration and creation of psychoeducational assessment theories, methodologies, and tests that are consistent with the philosophical worldviews and cultural systems and styles of African Americans, should enhance our ability to differentiate and identify increased numbers of gifted African Americans.[3] Stated differently, what I am calling for here is the creation and use of culture-specific and culture-sensitive assessment and identification paradigms to be used in attempts to locate gifts and talents in African American learners. Accordingly, I present the following schema needed for conceptualizing and understanding the interrelatedness and connections among African American worldviews, theoretical paradigms, and assessment methodologies, which might serve to guide the psychoeducational assessment of African American learners with gifts and talents. This schema is followed by examples of existing screening, assessment, and identification approaches that are at least somewhat consistent with this model.

Table 10.1 identifies a "pure" and traditional African American philosophical and theoretical system that could serve to guide the development of constructs of intelligence and giftedness and certain consistent and distinct assessment methodologies and approaches suggested in Table 10.2. The theoretical/conceptual system displayed in Table 10.1 is identified as "pure" and traditional because it represents historical, deep-structure cultural characteristics of African Americans that provide the foundation for a "cultural signature" unique to African Americans.[4] All African Americans do not embrace this "pure" cosmological system. It is important to acknowledge that intragroup differences do exist; these are being further explored elsewhere (e.g., Frasier, 1989). Differences in degrees of internalizing this system exist but do not negate the reality that many African Americans relate strongly to the conceptual system outlined in Table 10.1 and, accordingly, reconstruct

Table 10.1 Some Fundamental Dimensions of Classical African American-Oriented Philosophical Worldviews and Theoretical Orientations

Metaphysics	Axiology	Epistemology	Logic
Dualist/holist view of reality	Importance of person-to-person relations	Affective orientation	Diunital
Viewing the whole and the interconnectedness of the parts	Viewing interpersonal relationships as holding the highest value	Using the affect to know through symbolic imagery and rhythm	Union of opposites; viewing things as apart and united at the same time

SOURCE: Information in the metaphysics, axiology, and logic sections is drawn from the philosophical and conceptual works of Dixon (1976), E. J. Nichols (1976), Maurier (1979), J. A. Baldwin (1991), and Nobles (1983, 1987). That in the epistemology section is drawn from these authors as well as the theoretical work of Boykin (1983).

experiences in life through lenses affected by fundamental realities incorporated in this table.

Concerns and questions related to ultimate reality and values are metaphysical and axiological in nature. Table 10.1 sets forth a schema for understanding the basic metaphysical and axiological orientations of African Americans. These metaphysical and axiological systems also include notions of time and the relationship of individuals to nature. Implicit is the belief that individuals should be in *harmony* with nature (or the nonself) and that time is relative and "continuously felt."

As stated earlier, theoretical orientations inform the method of inquiry employed to investigate a certain phenomenon. There should be some consonance between theory and methodology. The latter should flow from the former. Concepts of multiple manifestations and forms of intelligence, gifts, and talents are consistent with the worldview set forth in Table 10.1. Table 10.2 suggests some useful constructs of African American intelligence and giftedness and certain psychoeducational assessment methodologies that are consistent with African Americans' worldviews and theoretical orientations, as set forth in Table 10.1. Table 10.3 then provides an outline of selected assessment approaches and procedures suggested for use in the development of systems to assess and identify giftedness among African American learners that, in turn, provides a close fit to the basic philosophical orientations postulated in Table 10.1.

The tests and approaches shown in Table 10.3 incorporate knowledge and understanding of African American culture in their theoretical and methodological orientations, including test designs and practices that allow, to some extent, for the use of culturally relevant data and approaches, and that allow for identification through student responsiveness to program stimuli.

It should be noted that this schema postulates a context- and culture-specific theoretical and methodological system for assessing and identifying African American learners with gifts and talents. It is intended that such a system feature characteristics that are consistent internally and across the various areas advanced in Tables 10.1-10.3. With this schema serving as a frame of reference, the remaining discussion provides a description of selective assessment procedures, approaches, and tests that are potentially useful in assessing and identifying African American learners with gifts and talents. A previous effort, the National Identification Conference in 1981, attempted to identify a comprehensive listing of promising practices in the identification of so-called at-risk students (Richert, Alvino, & McDonnel, 1982). The listing and descriptions

Table 10.2 Some Methodological Considerations for Assessing and Identifying Gifted and Talented African American Learners

Construct of Intelligence	*Assessment Approaches and Procedures*
Multiple forms of intelligence and giftedness, with multiple domains for manifesting intelligence that allow for cultural and learning differences (Gardner, 1983; Sternberg, 1991).	Assessment systems and tests grounded on assessing and interpreting cognition, behavior, and creativity emanating from a normative structure of African American culture, history, and experiences (J. A. Baldwin, 1991; Hilliard, 1976; Nobles, 1987; Ogbu, 1988).
	Utilization of an open assessment system that employs multiple criteria and assessment in multiple contexts and recognizes both quantitative and qualitative data. In addition to traditional and nontraditional measures of aptitude, achievement, and creativity, such a system requires the inclusion of areas such as motivation, leadership, and affective development in the assessment process. Peer, community, and parent nominations, as well as evaluation of student products, are used in these assessment systems (Frasier, 1989; Renzulli, 1983; Torrance, 1987).
	Use of action-oriented and dynamic assessment methodology (Feuerstein, 1977; Hilliard, 1976).
	Use of test, teach, retest, teach curriculum-based assessment approaches.

Table 10.3 Selective Assessment Approaches, Tests, and Checklists Potentially Useful in Screening, Assessing, and Identifying Gifted and Talented African American Learners

Screening Measures That Attempt to Incorporate Knowledge and Understanding of African American Worldviews	*Assessment Measures With Psychometric Designs and Practices That Recognize Culturally Relevant Data and Approaches*	*Assessment Models Useful in Intervention Planning*
"Who" and "O" Checklists (Hilliard, 1976)	Coloured, Standard, and Advanced Progressive Matrices (Raven, 1938, 1947a, 1947b)	Baldwin Identification Matrix (A. Y. Baldwin, 1984)
Checklist of Creative Positives (CCP) (Torrance, 1977)	Matrix Analogies Test, Expanded and Short Forms (MAT-EF and MAT-SF) (Naglieri, 1985a, 1985b; Naglieri &Prewett, 1990)	Frasier Talent Assessment Profile (F-TAP) (Frasier, 1990)
	Kaufman Assessment Battery for Children (K-ABC) (Kaufman & Kaufman, 1983)	Preselection activity-based assessment models (Feuerstein, 1968, 1977; Haywood, 1988)
	Torrance Test for Creative Thinking (TTCT) (Torrance, 1987)	Program of Assessment Diagnosis and Instruction (PADI) (Johnson et al., 1985)
		Potentially Gifted Minority Student Project (U.S. Department of Education, 1989)

209

offered herein, however, are selective, based upon a review of consistencies in the extant research and literature base and my own research and experience. Time and space do not permit a detailed description of each identified test or procedure or a comprehensive listing of all tests or assessment procedures appropriate for gifted African American learners.

Screening

While local school districts may vary in the processes they use to identify and select students for gifted and talented programs, most engage in an identification model that involves an initial prescreening and/or screening phase in order to establish a pool of potentially eligible students, followed by an assessment phase during which standardized and nonstandardized instruments are used to collect additional and more discrete data, and concluding with the selection of individuals for gifted programs.

Hilliard (1976) and Torrance (1977) have developed and advocated the use of screening checklists and rating scales that are based upon identifying distinct social, psychological, and behavior indicators reflective of distinct African American culture. The rating scales and checklists developed by these individuals have been included in attempts to screen and identify gifted and talented African American learners.

Hilliard (1976), at the request of the San Francisco Unified School District, attempted to devise prescreening measures that would recognize the "basic African American cultural contributions to patterns of human behavior" (p. 14). Accordingly, his resulting checklists, the "Who" and "O," are purported to be based upon unique and common deep-structure culture of African Americans. These checklists emphasize synthetic-personal stylistic characteristics of African American learners and, if used in concert with certain traditional prescreening procedures, have been found to identify previously overlooked gifted African American learners (Hilliard, 1976).

The "Who" and the "O" have been designed as prescreening devices to be used in concert with postscreening tests and procedures. Hilliard suggests that it would be important to collect the cultural and behavioral style information resulting from the use of the "Who" and "O" to utilize as a base for developing *new* culturally sensitive second-level screening instruments.

Torrance (1969) has identified a set of behaviors of African Americans that provides the basis for the development of the Checklist of Creative Positives (CCP; Torrance, 1977). He identifies a "set of characteristics that helped to guide the search for strengths of culturally different students for giftedness among such students" (p. 25). The resulting 18 characteristics are called "creative positives." Torrance argues that indicators of these creative positives, such as articulateness in role playing, sociodrama, storytelling, and use of expressive speech, responsiveness to the kinesthetic, originality of ideas in problem solving, and humor can best be assessed through observation, with results recorded on a checklist.

One additional checklist should be mentioned that has been found to provide culturally relevant information useful in the screening and identification process. The Renzulli-Hartman Scales for Rating the Behavioral Characteristics of Superior Students (Renzulli, 1983; Renzulli & Hartman, 1971) enjoy wide use among teachers of the gifted, and the use of some of Renzulli and Hartman's subscales (motivation and leadership) has been reported to result in increasing the numbers of young African Americans identified as gifted. The five subscales of these rating instruments measure characteristics of creativity as well as sociopsychological characteristics such as leadership and motivation.

Identification

As discussed previously, the exclusive use of traditional intelligence tests to identify African American learners with gifts and talents has not resulted in a proportionate identification of these learners as being gifted. Some intelligence tests, as a result of their conceptual, technical, and cultural sensitivity approximations, however, have been used successfully as one component in the assessment and identification of young gifted and talented African American learners.

A recent national study by VanTassel Baska, Patton, and Prillaman (1989), as well as the work of Baska (1986) and Frasier (1989), informs us that the Coloured, Advanced, and Standard Progressive Matrices (Raven, 1938, 1947a, 1947b) are intelligence tests frequently used by local school systems nationwide in attempts to increase the number and types of African American learners in gifted programs. While the heavy use of these tests for identification purposes, in and of itself, is not sufficient to recommend their use, their high to moderate positive correlations with other intelligence and achievement tests, their high concurrent validity of use with African Americans (Court & Raven, 1982; Sattler, 1982; Valencia, 1979), and their predominant nonverbal administration and content make these tests appealing when applied to African American learners. Other attractive features of these tests include their quick and simple administration, which is untimed, and the option of individual or group administration.

Two other aptitude measures, the Matrix Analogies Test—Expanded Form and the Matrix Analogies Test—Short Form (MAT-EF and MAT-SF; Naglieri, 1985a, 1985b; Naglieri & Prewett, 1990), are purported to be normed on a very large and recent representative sample of individuals in the United States, with controls for race, class, gender, and geographic region. These tests measure nonverbal ability through the use of figural matrices and are said to be useful with individuals whose scores may be influenced by speed (Naglieri & Prewett, 1990). They have been reported to have a high degree of internal reliability and evidence of validity (Naglieri & Prewett, 1990).

Frasier (1989) reports that considerable evidence indicates the Kaufman Assessment Battery for Children (K-ABC; Kaufman & Kaufman, 1983) "is fair to minorities" (p. 218). African Americans, as a group, have generally scored higher on the K-ABC than on other more traditional intelligence tests. The test developers attribute these higher scores to the test's emphasis on a multidimensional concept of intelligence and "deemphasis of applied skills and verbal expression" (Kaufman & Harrison, 1986, p. 151). While these tests have resulted in yields of higher scores for African Americans, they have been faulted for their low ceiling for gifted populations (Sattler, 1982) and lack of demonstrating evidence of validity (Salvia & Ysseldyke, 1988).

An assessment system consistent with the schema advanced here would, by definition, include some measures of creativity. One would be safe to include the use of the Torrance Test of Creative Thinking (TTCT; Torrance, 1987) in assessment efforts designed to identify gifted African American learners. Not only does this test measure an important dimension of giftedness, creativity, but it has been found to be culturally fair, particularly its figural form. The TTCT enjoys moderate levels of reliability based on recent data obtained from longitudinal studies attesting to its ability to "predict quantity and quality of public personal creative achievements" (Torrance, in press). While the time-consuming nature and complexity of the scoring may restrain the use of the TTCT, its quick and easy administration (30 minutes) and wide application (individual or group; grades K through graduate school) make the use of this test very appealing, particularly in light of the paucity of tests that measure the domain of creativity.

Achievement is another component that should be included in a gifted and talented assessment system. The SRA Achievement Series, which assesses skill development in basic curriculum areas, has been used to assess achievement in a number of programs designed to locate gifted African American learners (Alamprese & Erlanger, 1988; Dabney, 1988). The appeal of these tests lies primarily in the inclusion of several factors in their psychometric construction. The tests purport to have used a large and diverse norming sample and explored race and gender bias in the various phases of test development.

Matrix and Profile Systems

Several assessment models have been developed that view giftedness as a multidimensional construct and employ a more comprehensive and holistic approach to *identifying* and *nurturing* the development of gifted African American learners. When a multimodal assessment approach is used, the domains of intelligence often considered are aptitude measures, achievement, creativity, and psychosocial characteristics (e.g., motivation, leadership, task commitment). The Baldwin Identification Matrix (BIM; A. Y. Baldwin, 1984) and subsequent modifications (Dabney, 1983, 1988) have been reported to be able to increase the number and kinds of gifted African American learners. These matrix approaches have been designed to allow the user to arrange the results of multiple objective and subjective data sources into a matrix format, so that data from multiple sources can be collected, reviewed, and interpreted before decisions are made about the selection of individuals for inclusion in programs for the gifted. These earlier matrix approaches, however, usually resulted in the reduction of the disparate data to a single score.

More recently, Frasier's development of an assessment "profile" approach holds promise for enhancing our capacity to discover gifted African American learners often overlooked by more traditional approaches. The Frasier Talent Assessment Profile (F-TAP; Frasier, 1990) has been designed to allow the user to gather both quantitative and qualitative data on individual students that provide a potpourri of important information from multiple sources (e.g., teachers, parents, community sponsors, tests, case study data, student products). This process results in an individual "biography," or profile, that includes collected information from which identification and selection decisions can subsequently be made. Judgment about program inclusion is based, then, upon multiple and broad areas of indicators of giftedness or potential giftedness and is withheld until all information is collected, profiled, and reviewed.

Several assessment models that employ curriculum-based assessments have been found useful in increasing the inclusion of African American learners in programs for the gifted and talented. Based primarily upon dynamic assessment models advocated by Haywood (1988) and popularized previously by Feuerstein (1968, 1977), an identification through responsiveness to programs approach is utilized in these models as the basis for assessment, identification, and instruction. This approach allows students to be taught certain concepts and strategies that are a part of a gifted program, to be tested after receiving such instruction, and then to be retaught. This process, as discussed by Johnson, Starnes, Gregory, and Blaylock (1985), allows students to develop and display cognitive and affective skills and abilities over extended periods of time, thus enabling them to further refine these skills while the project staff crystallize, over time, their judgments about the abilities and talents of students to meet the demands of the gifted program. These researchers' experience with the Program of Assessment, Diagnosis, and Instruction (PADI) has led them to believe responsiveness to differentiated classroom curriculum, then, becomes a part of the gifted program assessment and identification paradigm, thus allowing for an appropriate linking of identification and curriculum.

The Program of Assessment, Diagnosis, and Instruction, as reported by Johnson et al. (1985) and the Potentially Gifted Minority Student Project, recently described by Alamprese, Erlanger, and Brigham (1989), report that a preselection activity approach has been successful in identifying high numbers of gifted and talented or potentially gifted African American learners. In addition to the "identification through teaching" approach, both of these programs employ several features that reflect practices found to result in increased numbers of African Americans identified as gifted and talented. First, the philosophical orientation used by these programs to undergird the selection of diagnostic and identification instruments and procedures consists of an attempt to select those diagnostic instruments *known to be able* to tap reasoning and creativity potential of African American learners (Johnson et al., 1985). Thus the ability of a given instrument or procedure to identify and diagnose the strengths, skills, and needs of potentially gifted African American learners became a major criterion that guided the selection of measures and procedures for inclusion in the diagnostic batteries used by these two programs. Second, both programs employ multidimensional diagnostic batteries composed of assessment instruments and procedures that obtain objective and subjective information from multiple data sources and are reflective, therefore, of an expanded vision of the giftedness construct. Third, both programs' emphasis on early identification and intervention exemplify an inclusive and developmental philosophical perspective toward intervention, a view often shared by African Americans. Last, these programs emphasize curriculum-based measurement (CBM), in which the school's curriculum and instruction and the students' responses to it allow teachers to use assessment data to teach students rather than to rank them.

Summary

This chapter has sought to offer both historical and sociopolitical contexts for exploring theoretical and methodological issues and concerns related to the psychoeducational assessment and testing of African American learners, especially those with gifts and talents. It is important to acknowledge that while much progress has been made in contemporary psychometric theory and instrumentation, more work remains. As Nobles (1987) reminds us, the traditional Western fixation with pseudoscientific testing approaches continues to hinder the development of new conceptions for the assessment and identification of African Americans with gifts and talents.

It is essential to understand that tests are not neutral. They reflect, generally, in their content, style, administration, and interpretation, the predominant culture of their developers and interpreters. This fact has led to the political use of psychoeducational assessment and testing to the disservice of African Americans as a collective body. There are ways to overcome this problem. New and more expanded visions of the constructs "intelligence" and "gifted" have emerged (Asante, 1988; Feldman, 1983; Gardner, 1983; Harris & Ford, 1991; Ogbu, 1988; Sternberg, 1985, 1991). Pluralistic procedures for identifying gifted African Americans are emerging. Curriculum-based measurement approaches hold promise and should be explored further. Alternatives to paper-and-pencil assessment such as assessing student portfolios and products are increasing in use and should be refined and developed further. Increased usage of pluralistic procedures, CBM approaches, and student products as assessment tools should move psychoeducational assessment in the direction of assessing for the purpose of teaching rather than ranking students.

While the deep-structure culture of African Americans is unique and shared by people of African descent, there exists much diversity in its sociopsychological manifestations. A recognition and understanding of this reality should lead to the development of psychoeducational assessment theory, methodology, instruments, and practices based upon intragroup research and study. More work needs to be undertaken to uncover intragroup differences in cognition, behavior, and motivation before comparisons can continue to be made between two different cultural groups (Gordon, 1985).

The identification of gifted and talented African American learners continues to loom as a challenge. New theories, paradigms, methodologies, tests, and practices are begging for attention. A reconceptualization of theory and methodology related to assessment, testing, and giftedness constructs represents an essential first step in this theory-building process. Equally essential in this process is the recognition and use of Afrocentric worldviews to guide and serve as a foundation for this reconceptualized theory building. Until these actions are taken, neither psychometry nor the field of gifted education will enjoy the liberating qualities needed for progress in the social sciences.

Notes

1. I am referring here specifically to those individuals who shared the philosophical and cultural traditions of the European Enlightenment and the American Revolution. This examination of the issues does recognize the prerevolutionary roots and styles of scientific racism as expressed through monogenetic and polygenetic theories, but I will not explore these specific roots at this time. I refer the reader to Gould's (1981) analysis of David Hume, Charles White and Louis Agassiz, and others for an accounting of the prerevolutionary justifications for assumptions of racial inferiority.

2. Shuy's (1977) study of the language of test items, which built upon the previous cultural linguistic work of Chomsky (1957) and Lévi-Strauss (1966), shows clearly the variability of semantic meanings among individuals and groups that can and has been shown to create measurement error when language is used in tests. Shuy's work and that of other cultural linguists previously cited clearly demonstrates the culturally specific nature of manifestations of intelligence.

3. For a more detailed explication of Afrocentric metaphysical, epistemological, and axiological cultural systems, the reader is referred to the works of Molefi Kete Asante, Wade Nobles, Na'im Akbar, John S. Mbiti, Asa G. Hilliard III, George S. James, Edwin J. Nichols, Vernon J. Dixon, and John H. Stanfield II, to name a few social scientists and theoreticians who write in this tradition.

4. The African American community is a quite diverse one in which regional, class, gender, and other types of differences can and do occur. The attempt here, however, is to offer a set of constructs that represents generalizable historical, philosophical, and conceptual groundings and orientations of African Americans.

11

Survey Research on African Americans

Methodological Innovations

A. WADE SMITH

The attitudes white Americans hold toward their Black counterparts probably constitute the longest-running topic in public opinion research. Yet despite this prominence of race relations in scientific sample surveys, until recently Black Americans—long the minority group most identified with "racial matters" in the United States—were virtually invisible to serious students of American values. But even having this statistical visibility does not necessarily mean that when survey research data are gathered from Blacks a great deal is learned about the Black community per se.

What has driven survey researchers to include Blacks at all is the imperative to compare Blacks and (most often) whites systematically. In the process, survey analysts oversimplify many of the differences *among* Blacks. Currently, when even the most amateurish poll user

AUTHOR'S NOTE: An earlier version of this chapter was read at the 1986 meetings of the Association of Black Sociologists, and also appeared in the March/April 1987 issue of the *American Behavioral Scientist*. Shirley Hatchett, June Meitz, Aldon Morris, and John Stanfield deserve recognition for their critical readings of earlier drafts. However, I am solely responsible for all findings, errors, and omissions. Direct all correspondence to A. Wade Smith, Department of Sociology, Arizona State University, Tempe, AZ 95287.

(e.g., a TV news commentator) knows to look at differences among population subgroups (by age, sex, region, and so on) when making reports based on survey data, standard survey samples seldom include enough Blacks so that such differences within the Black population can be observed. This results in a false homogeneity wherein Black Americans are all but inscrutable: They are all presumed to think alike.

Historical Overview

Before the late 1940s, primitive sampling procedures governed most survey data collection efforts (Yeric & Todd, 1983). The ease with which a telephone could be used for interviewing initially led many early analysts to view telephone surveys with some degree of reverence, despite the less than uniform distribution of telephones in American homes. Later, when more complex issues and more diverse populations came to be of interest, personal interviewing began to supplant telephone surveys. However, samples were drawn from lists that were less than complete. For instance, because political issues were more complex than marketing concerns, most often samples were drawn from voter registration rolls. Thus, even toward the end of the 1940s, the legal and illegal exclusion of Blacks (especially southern Blacks) from voter registration records also eliminated their participation in many political polls, and led to a serious—if not total—underrepresentation of Blacks in most national surveys. Here, the period of "modern" national surveys begins with the 1948 SRC National Election Study. (The unreliability of previous surveys was responsible for such findings as "Dewey Beats Truman.")

Of course, in soundly constructed national, cross-sectional surveys, Blacks should turn up proportionately. Still, a statistically valid national sample of 1,500 cases produces only roughly 150 Black respondents. Of mathematical necessity, the following will be true:

1. Results from the subset of Blacks will be less reliable. Roughly speaking, percentages from whites will have a 3% margin of error, whereas those from the Black subsample will have a 20% margin of error.[1]
2. The subset of Blacks will not be large enough to allow for subgroup breakdowns and statistical controls, which are the heart of modern data analysis.

Over time, especially as Black-white relations came to prominence both politically and socially, survey researchers responded to the demand for more data on race relations. First, questions on racial issues found consistent placement in many of the studies fielded by the national survey organizations that dominated survey research from the late 1950s until the 1970s. These organizations are the American Institute of Public Opinion (Gallup); Harris, Inc.; the National Opinion Research Center (NORC); and the Survey Research Center (SRC) of the University of Michigan. This trend culminated with a survey sponsored by the National Advisory Commission on Civil Disorders (Campbell & Schuman, 1968). The study (which required the combined efforts of NORC and SRC) extensively sampled both Blacks and whites in 15 major urban areas, querying them on a variety of racial issues.

All of this concern over numbers of respondents should not overshadow the fact that surveys seldom include extra questions applicable only to small fractions of the respondents. It is true that as the public debate over racial equality increased because of civil rights activity, the survey research community investigated each issue in detail, frequently replacing passé questions with more relevant items. But it is also true that most of the time Blacks were not allowed to respond to race relations questions. (Sporadically, the National Urban League has attempted national surveys of the Black population, sometimes with the specific intention to fill the void of Black public opinion on racial issues. By its own admission, these surveys have been decidedly less rigorous than traditional surveys; see National Urban League, 1980.) The survey scientists responsible for the instruments not only felt that Myrdal (1944) was correct in locating "the race problem— in the minds of whites (mostly southern or lower-class whites), but also that Blacks' opinions on racial matters were obvious. As early as 1942, in its attempt to assess support for U.S. involvement in World War II "in the light of American racial norms," the National Opinion Research Center designed separate surveys for whites and for Blacks, so that a separate questionnaire—one devoid of all items on racial attitudes—could be administered to the latter.

Until relatively recently, most modern surveys continued to skip over racial attitude questions for interviews with Black respondents. In part, this was done to compensate for effects of the race of the interviewer on respondents' answers (for excellent treatments of the literature in this area, see Schaeffer, 1982; Schuman & Hatchett, 1974). Because most of the interviewers in survey organizations were white, unless special efforts were taken to ensure race matching with the interviewee, there was a good likelihood of interviewer's race affecting the response. Thus, given the perspective toward Blacks historically dominating the industry and its own race problem, the solution taken in the survey research community simply was not to investigate Blacks' attitudes on racial matters. Moreover, there were suspicions among survey investigators that Blacks and whites might interpret questions quite differently (*especially* racial issues). Specifically, the white research community thought that Blacks' responses to race relations items were "obvious," and therefore it was not really necessary to ask. There was also an assumption among survey researchers that—in general—the Black community would be less receptive to interviewers, who were most often white. As a result of both the relatively narrow focus on certain topics in the survey research community and the predominantly white field staffs produced by discriminatory personnel policies of most survey organizations, the *issues* important to Blacks—including, but not limited to, race relations— were historically as invisible in surveys as were Blacks themselves.

Although exceedingly slow, by the 1960s a realization was developing among scholars that studying the responses to questions about race relations in traditional national surveys was not producing much knowledge about public opinion among Blacks. In part this realization was forced on survey researchers (especially the academicians) by their collective failure to warn the nation of the impending racial crisis, leading to widespread collective civil rights activity and to the race riots that followed. Commissioning the 15-city study noted above was akin to closing the barn door after the horse had fled.

Although it was obvious that there were significant limitations of both Black respondents and the number of questionnaire items devoted to Black people's concerns in general cross-sectional surveys, still there were few *national* surveys specifically of Blacks. Until recently, the best surveys of Blacks were localized efforts, epitomized by Du Bois's (1899) classic study of the Philadelphia Black community. Du Bois canvassed (i.e., did not sample, but interviewed at every household) an entire Black city ward. Moreover, he used Black interviewers and a well-grounded interview schedule, and supplemented his data with tabulations from the U.S. Census and other sources. The product was the earliest known empirical study in the United States.

Before the 1980s, there were only nine cross-sectional surveys with 900 or more Black cases. Only three of the nine attempted to sample the general U.S. Black population; the rest were limited to particular communities or regions. None of the three national surveys was of the (by then) scientifically desirable full-probability design, partially because the cost of such a sample of Blacks was prohibitive. Almost 9 of every 10 contacts found using traditional probability techniques would not be Black, and the costs incurred while making these contacts were irretrievable.

Consequences of the Status Quo

Thus by the early 1980s, despite advances in research methodology as well as the application of increasingly sophisticated technological tools (e.g., computers for random-digit dialing, direct data entry, probability sampling, coding), the treatment of Blacks in survey research had not changed much since the inception of modern sample surveys. Survey researchers have attempted to field few studies of Blacks in the past 30 years, meaning that the most intensely studied questions in survey research—racial issues—have not been applied to those few Black respondents typically found in modern surveys (for a notable exception, see Davis & Smith, 1983, p. 383). By deduction, this situation has at least five undesirable consequences:

The statistically "invisible man." Although public opinion data on whites are common and important contributors to public policy discussions, no such input is available regarding Black Americans. For example, both social scientists and journalists almost always report southern data without separating Blacks from whites. As whites are the larger group, we tend to think of *southern white opinion* as *southern opinion,* although one can easily think of matters in which southern whites do not have full consensus with southern Blacks.

The statistically "inscrutable man." Because there exist few reliable data on age, sex, social class, religious, or regional differences among Blacks on various attitudes and policy issues, there is a tendency to assume that such differences do not exist. This is little more than a form of stereotyping, an *underestimation* of the variability of opinions among Blacks. This leads to an *overestimation* of the contribution of race, per se, to Black/white differences.

Unreliable information on race problems. If the media are to be believed, Blacks were strongly in favor of integration during the late 1950s and early 1960s, had come to reject participation in predominantly white institutions by the late 1960s and early 1970s, and since then have shifted toward a less separatist stance. Is this true? What is known about white opinion leads us to doubt this hypothesis. Bellisfield

(1973) used survey data to compare whites' racial attitudes before and after the urban riots of the mid-1960s, controlling for cities with and without riots. The conclusion offers "no support" that the much-heralded "white backlash" resulted from Blacks' rioting (p. 584). In both riot-torn as well as nonriot locales, there was "increasing acceptance of integration" over this period. Thus, in the absence of data to the contrary, there is no reason to assume that popular hypotheses about Black opinion are any more accurate than those about white opinion.

Poor research. It has not been generally recognized that an entire generation of Black scholars was developed on the basis of survey research on Black subject populations. According to Boyd and Hyman (1975), some of the works providing the earliest survey evidence about Black people's attitudes include those by Davis and Dollard (1940), C. S. Johnson (1941), Frazier (1949b), and Warner, Junker, and Adams (1941). These works, and the surveys on which they are based, afforded opportunities to an entire generation of Black scholars. Although Johnson, Frazier, Adams, and Davis had numerous and significant productions before as well as after the works listed above, they were also engaged in the research training of other Blacks—often from their own staffs.

At present, scholars concerned with Blacks have no better attitude data than do policymakers. Of necessity, such research is dependent on scraps from the table of general national surveys (see above), on small, unrepresentative samples, or, all too often, on sheer uninformed speculation. Obviously, this approach is not likely to build sound, cumulative scholarship about Blacks, or to advance the scientific standing of the Black scholars concerned with such matters. Moreover, the advocacy of social policy has tended to originate from the Black political, as opposed to scholarly, community.

Handicaps for national leadership. Political and social leaders of whites have continual access to public and private poll data on their followers. For example, national pollsters frequently publish findings on what "citizens" (a priori, mostly white) consider the major problems facing the nation. (Whether public institutions and officials can or should follow the polls when making decisions is not the issue here; the point is that the data are available.) For leaders and organizations embracing Black constituencies, such crucial information does not exist. Beyond the level of the precinct, church, or school, both Black and white leaderships must guess what their Black constituencies want, or must rely on self-appointed spokespersons of unverified credibility.

In the end, the latter practice may have much higher costs and lower utility than all but the most undesirable approaches to surveying Blacks.

Beyond the fact that even one first-class national political campaign such as Jesse Jackson's bid for the 1984 Democratic party nomination could finance dozens of high-quality national surveys of Blacks, the political advocacy of social change may have other negative consequences for Blacks as well. There is some survey evidence that when Blacks develop even the intent to compete for significant political positions (e.g., Jackson's bid), this only brings to the surface reactionary attitudes (even among white liberal elites) that may be exploited by the opposition (W. A. Smith, 1985). Obviously, scientific survey data to be used in developing social policies could be obtained without incurring such rancor.

Methodological Developments in Surveying Blacks

The 1980s have finally seen the development of three national surveys of Blacks. Even so, these studies all use methods that differ in their abilities to produce scientifically desirable Black samples cost-effectively. Below, each of these methods is described in detail, and its potential applications to future survey research efforts are noted.

Intergenerational Research

With the intent to concentrate on family structure and mental health issues among Black Americans, in 1979-1980 the University of Michigan's Institute for Social Research (ISR) developed a National Survey of Black Americans (NSBA) from which it extrapolated samples for two additional generations. The assembled triad of interviews constituted the Three Generation Family Study (TGFS). The intentions were (a) to interview a representative national sample of Black Americans on a variety of typical survey items (including many questions specifically designed for Blacks); (b) to obtain data from additional generations that, *when weighted,* would form new probability samples (e.g., of the elderly); but then (c) to concentrate on mental health indicators in the TGFS. Obviously, the quality of the sample for the three-generation study is "highly dependent upon the quality of the parent survey" (Jackson & Hatchett, 1985).

According to Jackson and Hatchett (1985), from 76 primary sampling units in which the measure of size (MOS) is the number of Black households, ISR obtained a sample of more than 2,000 completed interviews. Typical of multistage area probability procedures, smaller geographic units (places, clusters of places, blocks, and groups of blocks) were defined with the same MOS, and were *randomly* chosen from larger strata.

Moreover, the NSBA uses a race-stratified screening system for household selection. In very Black areas, the interviewer began by determining a set of "reference housing units" by randomly selecting households from a complete listing of the assigned area, then resorting to the relatively standard procedure of screening for race of respondent at the door. But in areas suspected of having small Black populations, a few "pre-designated households (distributed around the cluster)" were selected and asked of the presence of Black households in the immediate area (Hess, 1985). Then—*based on information provided by those screening interviews—the interviewer proceeded directly (and only) to other households with Blacks known to those respondents.* Only Black households identified using this procedure were listed, and later selected for full-schedule interviews.

Using the interview obtained for the NSBA as the informant, ISR created the TGFS by screening *this* sample for respondents with living linear relatives in any two other generations (i.e., parent-grandparent, child-grandchild, or parent-child) that would complete a contiguous triad. To be eligible, these relatives had to be at least 14 years old. Whenever possible, the relatives of the informant were interviewed by the same interviewer. However, because an unexpected number of the linear relatives of the informants resided outside of the areas selected for the NSBA, approximately one-third of them were interviewed by telephone.

Although admirable in many respects, both the NSBA and TGFS are open to serious methodological criticisms. What the national cross section obtained was not the most representative sample of Black Americans possible. Because every area had an equal probability of selection at each sampling stage, the size of an area (irrespective of its Black population) disproportionately contributed to its potential for selection.

Moreover, stratifying sampling units (of any level) by race because of their concentrations of Blacks is known to have limited utility (Kish, 1965, pp. 409-410). Thus the overabundance of Blacks from urban areas reported by Jackson and Hatchett (1985) is not unexpected. The intent for every Black household in the United States to have an equal probability of selection was realized, but because Blacks are more concentrated in the South and in urban areas, southern and urban Blacks too often appeared in the sample. Similarly, because Black households disproportionately have female heads, and perhaps older heads as well, the NSBA also overrepresents them.

As for the TGFS, by Jackson and Hatchett's (1985) own admission, weights must be assigned if any one of the generations is to be considered alone as a national sample. But the most problematic aspect of TGFS is that it is a mixture of personal and telephone interviewing. Although telephone interviewing is purported to generate data of quality comparable to personal interviewing (Sudman, 1967), there is overwhelming evidence throughout the period of modern survey research that *the two should not be mixed* (Cahalan, 1960; Colombotos, 1969; Hochstim, 1962, 1967; Larsen, 1952; Rosenthal, 1966). Although the TGFS undoubtedly fills a void, if and when these data actually enter the public domain, researchers are advised to approach with extreme caution.

Finding Blacks for Surveys

Survey research investigations of Black Americans have labored under two reciprocal constraints. On the one hand, Blacks are generally unevenly distributed over the landscape, and therefore are usually expensive to locate and interview. For instance, if 10 households must be contacted in order to find one that contains Blacks, roughly 90% of preinterview field costs are probably lost. On the other hand, most of the methods employed to cut field costs including the technique used in the NSBA described above—can easily be demonstrated to produce poorer-quality data because, theoretically, they are predicted on a relatively even distribution of the target populations (Hansen, Hurwitz, Marks, & Mauldin, 1951; Kish, 1965, pp. 404-415).

Modern national probability samples are constructed on the basis of a size criterion—the estimate of the *total* population in any given geographic area. A given place (i.e., county, SMSA, primary sampling unit, segment, or block) has a probability of being included in a sample that is roughly proportionate to its size. Many places end up in a sample on such a basis, but they may have few Blacks, therefore a majority of the households might be disqualified from any survey interested solely in Blacks. Moreover, when looking particularly for Blacks, one tactic is to overrepresent systematically places having higher *concentrations* of them. This is the procedure followed in the NSBA, as described above.

But what if a particular place were to be chosen for a sample on the basis of a *combination* of the properties of Blacks in its boundaries, as well as its total population? Obviously, this procedure would be much more efficient than oversampling because many of the areas chosen would have *large numbers,* if not a majority, of Blacks. In those areas where the numbers of Blacks are insubstantial, interviewers could stop searching for them once the expected number of Black interviews is reached. If the object is to construct a sample of Blacks by making the probability of an area's selection proportionate to the size of its Black (as opposed to total) population, this can be called *ppsb* sampling.

As part of an experiment, the 1982 General Social Survey (GSS) collected additional interviews from Blacks, beyond the 156 Blacks found as part of the regular GSS sampling procedures. Some of these additional Black cases were collected by oversampling a regular national probability sampling frame. In this oversample, the only deviations from regular GSS interviewing procedures were that no non-Blacks were interviewed and all Blacks were interviewed by Black interviewers. With the addition of 10 questions specifically addressed to Blacks, all respondents were administered the same questionnaire as non-Blacks.

The remainder of the additional interviews resulted from the development of a survey-specific sampling frame with selection probabilities proportional to the size of the Black population at every stage. In the *ppsb* subsample were 17 primary sampling units, 51 secondary units, and 51 segments selected from these secondary units, which resulted in 1,400 selections listed at the household level. *Every* household was contacted for a list of its occupants, and whenever a Black over 18 years of age was present, that household was denoted eligible. This *ppsb* sample had an extremely low eligibility rate (.17) because, a priori, all whites were out of the sample. Further, approximately half of the Blacks in this subsample were interviewed by whites, and, as with the oversample, all Blacks were asked 10 additional questions. Nevertheless, its response, refusal, and availability rates all equal or surpass those of the (predominantly white) regular 1982 GSS (Davis & Smith, 1983).

The *ppsb* frame employed in the 1982 GSS yielded 247 completed interviews of Blacks; the oversample contains 107 cases. Not only does this experiment demonstrate that it is possible to survey Blacks with the same degree of efficiency and economy, and to the same standards as in the highest-quality (and mostly white) national surveys, but, as a residual benefit, when the oversample and the subsample are combined with the 156 Black cases found in the "regular" 1982 GSS, 510 Black cases are available for analysis.

Thus not only is *ppsb* sampling intuitively and theoretically more cost-efficient than oversampling Blacks (Draper & Guttman, 1969; Kish, 1961), as a result of the GSS experiment the former has been demonstrated actually to expend fewer dollars per completed interview (Tourangeau & Smith, 1985) while yielding substantially similar results (A. W. Smith, 1984). (There were benefits to NORC as well: A substantial Black component to its field staff now exists and, alone, it has demonstrated the ability to conduct a survey in which systematic race-of-interview effects are absent.) Moreover, the application of *ppsb* sampling need not be confined to national surveys. This technique can be used to develop regional, state, metropolitan, and even neighborhood Black samples. There is no longer any reason for not fielding surveys of Blacks. The costs incurred are no greater than they would be in any other high-quality survey.

Although the "Black GSS" experiment demonstrates the efficacy of surveying Blacks, it does have at least one drawback. First, the questionnaire schedule contained very few items that would actually be included unless (as in this case) the purpose is to replicate long-running general social indicators. In other words, the Black GSS offers little to investigators interested specifically in Blacks, *unless their subjects are ones covered in the regular GSS*. In fact, the remnant skepticism about the ability to sample and interview Blacks effectively forced NORC to abandon its original proposal for two series of all-Black surveys: one that would emulate the GSS and another that would specifically allow researchers to place new and different topics before Black respondents. In order to obtain any funding at all, NORC had to settle for demonstrating that *ppsb* sampling could actually yield high-quality data without resorting to dubious field procedures (as with the NSBA above).

But perhaps more important, data from the Black GSS are already in the public domain (all GSSs are released within six months after data collection is completed). Some methodological and technical sophistication is required to be able to determine when it is best to use all 510 Black GSS cases, just those generated via sampling *ppsb*, or just the 156 appearing in the regular GSS (Davis & Smith, 1983, p. 383; A. W. Smith, 1984). Therefore, although the Black GSS is of a more rigorous design than the NSBA or TGFS, its utility to Black scholars in general is actually increasing to the extent that papers, both those to guide users and those with substantive findings from the 1982 Black GSS, obtain publication in major social science research journals. Finally, the 1987 GSS (to be released this summer) will include enough additional interviews of Blacks—alas, generated via "traditional" oversampling techniques—to ensure the presence of approximately 500 Black cases.

Telephone Sampling of Blacks

Before and after the 1984 presidential election, ISR conducted telephone interviews with a national sample of Black Americans. Although those data have yet to become available to non-ISR researchers, the National Black Election Study (NBES) represents perhaps the best example of survey research on Blacks. The NBES is state of the art.

In the NBES, the sample for the preelection wave was obtained by using a disproportionate random-digit dialing design. ISR learned from a pilot study that, given an equal probability design (in which every phone in the United States has the same chance of being selected), the eligibility of working numbers for Black households would be too low and thus too costly (Inglis, Groves, & Heeringa, 1985). Instead, the NBES assigned all telephone exchanges in the United States to one of three "Black household density" strata. These strata were defined as follows:

1. *High Black density:* exchanges in all large SMSAs with a Black population of 15% or more
2. *Medium Black density:* exchanges in small SMSAs and in all of Alabama, Florida, Georgia, Louisiana, Mississippi, North Carolina, South Carolina, and Virginia
3. *Low Black density:* all remaining exchanges

The selection rate for the high-density stratum was three times that for the low-density stratum, and the rate for the medium-density stratum was twice that of the low-density stratum.

There were 200 secondary numbers (four-digit followers) generated from each exchange. The racial composition of the household was determined by including a direct question about race in the screening instrument. All working numbers of households with at least one Black occupant were eligible. The overall Waksberg (1978) cluster size was 7.5, including the exchange (Inglis et al., 1985). A total of 1,151 respondents were interviewed before the 1984 election, and 873 in the reinterview.

Perhaps the most serious fault to be found with NBES is that, as of two years after the election, there were no concrete plans to place it in the public domain. Eventually, as usual with ISR-generated studies, it will be distributed by the Inter-University Consortium for Political and Social Research (ICPSR). In the meantime, only a few investigators have access to these valuable data. NBES personnel are attempting to devise a strategy whereby Black scholars will have the first opportunity to use the data and a little lead time before the data are to be distributed by ICPSR.

Prospects for the Future

Given the advances in studying Black Americans noted above, the potential for applying sample surveys to the study of the Black community appears to be limited only by the collective vision of researchers and funders of research. For the first time, tools and techniques are available that can bring the scientific rigor and costs of studying Blacks to the same (or better) levels traditionally associated with racial comparative research. Although this chapter has used examples of research that sought data representative of Blacks nationwide, there is no reason the procedures detailed above cannot be applied in regional, state, or even more local studies. There is also no reason two or more aspects of the research designs discussed here could not be incorporated within a single study.

In the final analysis, the scholarly and funding communities have never had a better opportunity to survey Blacks. This discussion has sought to demonstrate that this can be done to the highest standards of modern survey research, that several methods exist to facilitate it, and that the Black community cooperates with *sensitive* survey inquiries at the same level obtained among non-Blacks. If, under these circumstances, there fails to be an increase in survey investigations centering on Blacks, it would only raise new questions about the purposes and values of researchers and funders alike.

Note

1. For the technician: I start with the standard table for 95% confidence limits on a proportion of .50, "discounting" the white subset of the same to 1,000 and the Black subset to 100—the usual rule of thumb to compensate for clustering. Given the extent to which Blacks are subjected to housing segregation, the discount of Blacks is probably too *small* to offset their heavier clustering. The true situation is probably worse than these figures.

PART IV

Historical/Comparative Methods

12

Toward a Multidimensional Historical Comparative Methodology

Context, Process, and Causality

DUANE CHAMPAGNE

In 1856, the Chickasaw formed a constitutional government modeled on principles similar to those of the U.S. government. This nineteenth-century Indian society, however, was an unlikely case for such a transformation if one considers structural arguments only. The Chickasaw occupied the present northern Louisiana-Alabama and western Kentucky region. Between 1700 and 1820, they engaged in fur trade with European traders. From the early 1800s, a small percentage of Chickasaw families organized Black slave labor and produced cotton and other agricultural products for market and export. The Choctaw, Cherokee, and Creek also occupied territory in the South, and therefore make natural comparisons with the Chickasaw. All four Indian nations encountered the same sequences of world-system incorporation, formed capitalistic planter classes, and experienced increased U.S. political pressure for removal west during the 1820s and 1830s.

Social order among the four nations, however, differed significantly. Although socially and symbolically unified by seven national clans and associated ceremonial relations, villages and regions formed the primary political units in the Cherokee national polity. Under U.S. pressure for land, the Cherokee formed a unified political nationality between 1809 and 1810 and adopted a democratic constitution in 1827. Under similar conditions, the Chickasaw, Creek, and Choctaw did not follow the Cherokee plan of forming a nation-state in order to preserve territory and national independence. Chickasaw clans organized and celebrated national ceremonies, which indicated a greater degree of centralized national ceremonial order than among the Cherokee. Unlike among the Cherokee, however, the Chickasaw polity was embedded within kinship and ceremonial institutions, because specific clans held rights to national religious and political offices. Thus the Chickasaw had greater institutional obstacles to adopting a secular, non-kin-based nation-state than the politically better-integrated and institutionally differentiated Cherokee. These institutional differences between the Cherokee and Chickasaw help explain why the Cherokee were more likely to adopt political change and the Chickasaw were more reluctant. A polity with overlapping kinship, solidary, religious, and cultural institutions is difficult to change by consensual social action. In such situations innovators contend with multiple overlapping group prerogatives and often must introduce fundamental changes in traditional orientations between polity and cultural order. All else being equal, a polity is more amenable to consensual change when it is autonomous from kinship, social solidary, and religious institutional relations. In such cases, innovators contend with fewer overlapping group prerogatives and need not introduce fundamental changes in cultural and normative order (Champagne, 1989, 1992).

Thus there are institutional antecedents for explaining Chickasaw traditionalism compared with Cherokee change within their common geopolitical and world-system contexts of the 1820s and 1830s. Given similar world-system and geopolitical contexts as the Cherokee, overlapping political, cultural, and kinship institutions help explain Chickasaw reluctance to adopt political change. An anomaly, however, arises at this juncture. If we rely on the structural arguments given above, we cannot explain the formation of the Chickasaw democratic government in 1856. We therefore must appeal to other factors and/or different levels of analysis in order to give an explanation for Chickasaw traditionalism in one context and political change in another. We can move beyond the structural explanation by including the analysis of historically contingent group struggles within the context of institutional and transsocietal relations. This approach implies that an appropriate vision of causality includes the effects of interdependent transsocietal and institutional contexts and historically contingent group interactions that lead to enduring change in a social order. Before continuing with my analysis of Chickasaw political change, I will discuss institutional and trans-societal context, microgroup processes, and multidimensional (or cybernetic) causality as central to theoretical and empirical progress in comparative-historical analysis.

Issues in Historical Comparative Methods

Much contemporary comparative work focuses on cross-sectional survey comparisons among nation-states. Underlying this approach are positivist assumptions about methods and social action. Positivist methodologies and epistemologies encourage collection of survey and statistical data, which yield static slices of social phenomena. When attention turns to the study of process, change, and institution building, the positivist assumptions are less suitable. Positivism tends to look past normative and cultural contexts and group interpretations and actions in historically contingent events (Andreski, 1965, pp. 66-67, 82-83; Przeworski & Teune, 1970, pp. 144, 182-183; Roth, 1971, pp. 80-82). The researcher who seeks to explain change in institutional order must ultimately refer to the historical sequences and human actions that account for such events. In my view, positivism and statistical methods cannot satisfactorily explain processes of institutional change. I am not willing to constrain my analysis with the assumption that historical sequences conform to one or more probability functions that underlie statistical theory. Explanation of institutional change in historical social orders demands a more multidimensional epistemology and method than contemporary positivism now bears (Alexander, 1983; Dogan & Pelassy, 1984, p. 18; Parsons, 1937; Roth, 1971, p. 80; Sica, 1988).

My explanatory goals dictate use of a multidimensional method. I seek to explain processes of institutionalized change, and in my view this may require interdependent change in culture, values, social solidarity, political solidarity, political order, and/or economic order. From the outset I assume that consensual social change requires interdependent adjustments among normative, organizational, and material conditions of life. Parsons (1977a) argues that economy and polity condition relations of normative order, values, and culture, while values and culture control social action within the polity and economy. In Parsons's model, control means that norms, values, and culture inform and motivate social action within (and sometimes beyond) the context of political and economic situations or conditions. The relative primacy of normative or material relations is a major issue in macrosociological theory. Parsons argues that, in long-term evolutionary change, culture and normative systems control social action within the systems of polity and economy. Many, however, contest this argument. Nevertheless, Parsons argues that normative and cultural primacy is less applicable to short-term historical change, where explanatory emphasis may take a variety of interdependent configurations among material and normative factors (p. 240). For the student of historical comparative methods, the shorter-term historical period is of most interest. In the shorter run, Parsons's theory leaves open the question of interdependent relations among normative and material factors.

In my view, researchers should set aside the materialist-normative debate. More fruitful may prove study of historically interdependent normative and material conditions that help explain processes of institutional change. Such a method requires specification of empirical interdependencies between material and normative factors (or environments) and transsocietal conditions. Furthermore, explanation should not be reduced to a single factor or variable, but retained as part of the explanation of the interdependent relations among institutional, transsocietal, and material conditions. A multidimensional view of causality will indicate necessary but not sufficient causes (parameters or preconditions), and sufficient conditions (effective causes or cybernetic controlling factors or environments) (Andreski, 1965, p. 83; Dogan & Pelassy, 1984, pp. 16, 164-165; Roth, 1971; Smelser, 1976, pp. 131-134).

As the Chickasaw example shows, structural factors do not necessarily give a complete explanation for change. Analyses of social change should take into account the micro-level group processes that negotiate, reconstruct, and maintain the institutional order (R. Collins, 1988, pp. 264-300; Stryker, 1980). Group actions and historically contingent events, which occur within the context of interdependent material and institutional relations, however, provide an additional dimension of analysis. Contemporary theory suggests a social movements approach to institutional change, and focuses attention on concrete actors and groups (elites, classes, class segments, local communities). Outcomes are determined through conflicts and/or consensus formation among prochange, conservative, and accommodationist leaders and groups (Alexander & Colomy, 1985; Colomy, 1985, 1990a, 1990b; Eisenstadt, 1964a, 1964b, 1990). Institutional, transsocietal, and material conditions provide a context for group struggles and negotiation. Nevertheless, processes of change depend on group interactions as they break down, maintain, and/or create and legitimate new forms of institutional organization. In the explanation of social change, micro-level group processes and historically contingent events complement and extend explanations based on interdependent macro-level transsocietal and institutional contexts (Abrams, 1982). In the following sections I expand upon the arguments given above.

The Transsocietal Context

Transsocietal context refers to geopolitical relations, world-system relations, and global cultural and normative interchanges. Skocpol (1979) argues that geopolitical relations are analytically independent from world-system economic relations (see also Hintze, 1975a, 1975b). In other words, interstate competition has autonomous effects on processes of social change. World-system and neo-Marxist theorists (Wallerstein, 1974; Wolf, 1982), however, often assume that geopolitical context is reducible to economic class interests. Similarly, group acceptance of colonial or transsocietal institutional models, religions, new cultural, and normative views are potential elements for an explanation of change. Again, arguments can be made to reduce transsocietal cultural and institutional influences to economic incorporation or geopolitical-colonial hegemony. For example, do missionaries follow their national flags (colonial hegemony) or do the flags follow the missionaries? These situations can vary by case, region, and historical period. Therefore, I prefer to handle transsocietal cultural and normative interchanges as analytically independent from world-system incorporation and geopolitical context. The interdependent relations among transsocietal impacts are left to empirical study within historically specific contexts. Each transsocietal factor is potentially dominant. The relative causal effects of transsocietal relations on any particular society are a matter for empirical investigation (Champagne, 1990). Such questions should not be decided before the historical and/or comparative analysis begins.

Let us return to the example of the Chickasaw and outline their transsocietal context. The Chickasaw traded regularly with the English and French by the early 1700s and were subject to trade and diplomatic entreaties from both colonial powers. Like most other eastern Native American societies, the Chickasaw quickly became dependent on trade. They bartered furs and skins—usually deerskins, but beaver primarily among the northern Indian nations—in exchange for European manufactured goods. Being dependent on European trade for guns, ammunition, metal goods, and other industrially manufactured materials, the Chickasaw sought alliance with one or another of the European colonial powers. During the early 1700s, the French planned to forge a line of forts and Indian alliances along the Mississippi Valley and to restrict the English colonies to the eastern seaboard. The English countered the French plan by attempting to win over the strategically located Chickasaw with more abundant, cheaper, and better trade goods. Throughout most of the 1730-1760 period the Chickasaw were in almost constant warfare with the French colonies and Indian allies. The Chickasaw usually allied with the British, although some clans formed a minority pro-French faction. After 1763, in a treaty that confirmed French defeat in the Seven Years War, the British assumed hegemony over present eastern North America. During the American Revolutionary War, however, the Spanish recaptured West Florida from the British.

During the late 1780s and early 1790s, the Spanish and the Americans vied for Chickasaw trade and military alliance. By the late 1790s the pro-American party (old pro-English clans) gained the upper hand in favor of trade and alliance with the U.S. government. During the 1800 to 1820 period, the fur trade steadily declined owing to falling prices and declining demand. As a result, most Chickasaw adopted subsistence agriculture and husbandry during the 1820s. A small percentage of families, who exploited Black slave labor, moved from trade and/or merchandising into plantation production and export of cotton, corn, and cattle. The Chickasaw, like the Cherokee, Choctaw, and Creek in the Southeast, increasingly stratified into two culturally and economically distinct classes—a small market-oriented planter class and a large majority of culturally conservative subsistence farmers.

After 1795 and even more so after the War of 1812, the United States gained increasingly dominant hegemonic power over the territory east of the Mississippi River. By the late 1820s the American government and newly created southern states were pressing the southern Indians to remove west of the Mississippi River. Before 1817 there were few missionaries among the Chickasaw and before removal west in the late 1830s the missionaries had little success among most Chickasaw. The Chickasaw planter class welcomed teachers who taught literacy and business skills to their children but did not necessarily encourage their children toward Christian conversion. The availability of Western cultural orientations had little significant effect on Chickasaw institutional order before 1837. The Chickasaw and other major southern Indian nations participated in the southern export economy and were subject to strong pressures from the United States to sell their homelands and migrate west. Furthermore, they were exposed to U.S. models of education, Christianity, and economic and political organization. These latter relations constitute the transsocietal context for the southern Indian nations during the 1817 to 1840 period (Baird, 1974; Barden, 1953, p. 249; Champagne, 1989, pp. 59-61; Eaton, 1830; M234, n.d., roll 135, pp. 154-158).

The Institutional Context

Theoretical assumptions influence the selection of variables, their relative weights, and relations of interdependence. Assuming the analyst strives for an argument of interdependent conditions and factors, it is advisable to adopt fewer reductionist arguments, as they entail simplification of institutional relations that may not hold in many empirical situations. For example, an orthodox Marxist analysis might reduce culture and moral order to an ancillary role with respect to capitalist class interests. Such an argument, however, may overlook the empirical influence of culture and normative order in historical processes of institutional change. Most theories and epistemologies make reductionist assumptions at some level. For example, positivism underemphasizes faculties of the human mind for interpreting cultural, normative, and situational contexts. Advocates of the so-called rational model also understate the causal effects of cultural, normative, and institutional contexts (Andreski, 1965, pp. 66-67, 82-83; Marsh, 1967, pp. 18-20; Przeworski & Teune, 1970, pp. 182-183; Smelser, 1976, pp. 65-67). The tendency toward reductionist assumptions about social action and institutional order has been a great stumbling block to the development of a sophisticated cross-cultural comparative analysis.

My particular theoretical biases suggest analytic separation of cultural and normative relations from economy, polity, and personality. In an analogous way, the disciplines of psychology, economics, political science, sociology, and anthropology have staked out their principal analytic terrains. Without doubt, the social sciences have progressed with this academic division of labor. In the study of institutional change, however, even more significant are the interdependent relations among cultural, political, solidary, economic, and personality institutions. Theoretically, it is possible to specify interchanges between various subsystems, as

Parsons (1956, 1977b) has done. Rather than pursue abstract systems analysis like Parsons (K. D. Bailey, 1990, pp. 43-44), I prefer to analyze concrete historical configurations of interdependence among culture, polity, normative order, economy, and personality (or configurations of institutional differentiation). Furthermore, I seek to know how these empirical configurations vary throughout the world and across history. After determining the configuration of institutional differentiation of a society, the next step is to study its processes of change through time. Observation of patterns of change shown by empirical institutional orders within the various historical contexts will provide data for understanding a broad range of social change processes.

I disagree fundamentally with the comparative method of Stinchcombe (1978), who disregards transsocietal and institutional context and compares organizations and social action across contexts. As Stinchcombe and others say, totalistic units of analysis such as nation-state, society, and empire are too diffuse and need analytic decomposition (Przeworski & Teune, 1970, pp. 169-171, 208). Nevertheless, the units of analysis (i.e., units of institutional differentiation) should decompose totalistic units into comparable subunits, yet retain the *sui generis* character of the totalistic order or unit of analysis (Durkheim, 1984). Others, such as Geertz (1971; see also Bendix, 1977; Skocpol, 1984a, pp. 368-374; E. P. Thompson, 1966), use contextual analyses for elaborating differences among societal orders that share some common institutions or traditions such as Islamic religion. Unlike Weber, Geertz does not present causal arguments for explaining institutional change. In Weber's (1958, 1963, 1981) comparative studies, he investigated social, economic, political, and cultural differences in order to explain how they comparatively or directly helped explain the rise of Western capitalism. Understanding the institutional and transsocietal context of a causal argument is a prerequisite of providing a meaningful and adequate explanation; otherwise, researchers risk abstract applications that disregard important features that may contribute to or refine an explanation.

Comparative conceptualization of institutional orders, however, requires a common analytic language capable of expressing and defining relations within all social orders (Crimshaw, 1973, pp. 3-6; Dogan & Pelassy, 1984, p. 10; Marsh, 1967, p. 6; Przeworski & Teune, 1970, p. 10). A corollary to this premise suggests that the analytic principles of institutional order are similar for all human societies. In other words, a comparative understanding of institutional order and processes of change posits that human societies are analyzable by a common set of organizational principles. Variations in institutional order derive from permutations generated by a set of fundamental principles. The assumptions made about the principles of institutional order thus have bearing on the analysis of institutional order and processes for change. I argue that the theory of differentiation and associated arguments of social and political solidarity provide fundamental principles and a universal language for comparative analysis of institutional change.

The arguments for social and/or political solidarity are required for explaining consensual institution building and institutional stability and continuity. As emphasized above, processes of stable, consensual institutional change require adjustment not only in economic and political order, but also in normative and cultural order. Groups that impose major institutional change (i.e., the formation of a state) without accompanying changes in cultural, normative order and values will have to maintain order through vigilant coercion. Coercively controlled institutional orders can persist for extended periods. Such societies or institutions, however, will experience instabilities caused by groups who are resistant to the imposed order (Durkheim, 1984, pp. 310-322; Parsons, 1977a, p. 25). Analysis of stability and consensual change in institutional orders requires investigation of processes of solidarity formation and cultural legitimacy.

As I have argued the necessity of observing interdependent relations among cultural, normative, political, and economic institutions, Parsons's functionalist paradigm comes to mind. Parsons, however, presents a paradigm consisting of four functions: pattern maintenance, integration, goal attainment, and adaptation. The four functions, however, do not have a one to one correspondence to empirical institutions (Parsons, 1977b). Parsons does not make a concentrated effort to apply his analysis to empirical processes of social change. He therefore leaves the historical comparativist at something of a loss. Nevertheless, Parsons emphasizes systemic interdependencies within the institutional order. For those who seek to understand processes of institutional change, this key insight sets the stage for transcending more reductionist views of institutional order and change. Instead of employing Parsons's emphasis on systems theory, I, however, prefer returning to Weber's emphasis on studying concrete empirical institutional orders, but aided by an empirical version of Parsons's differentiation theory.

The theory of differentiation is implicit within Parsons's interdependent functional paradigm, and it argues that more differentiated societies have greater generalized capacity to manage relations with their environments than do less differentiated societies. For Parsons, environments are multiple, consisting of cultural, social, and organic as well as "the environment"—the physical environment. This level of analysis, however, is not usually one that interests the comparativist, especially given that Parsons's (1977a) evolutionary theory does not focus on concrete historical processes of change. Nevertheless, the theory of differentiation provides a set of principles for understanding institutional relations within societies. The theory hypothesizes that, everything else being equal, more institutionally differentiated societies will exhibit greater capacity for change and adaptation than less differentiated societies. As a historical comparative sociologist, I find the latter statement somewhat general and lacking due respect for historical contingency. Nevertheless, I accept the argument as a guiding hypothesis, but withhold my final judgment awaiting further empirical evidence.

In terms of institutional context, the theory of differentiation directs attention to relations of autonomy and interdependence among major societal institutions. In order to start an analysis of institutional context, we need to describe a society's primary features: cultural worldview, political organization, normative order, and economic order. We also need to know the degree of mutual autonomy or interdependence among political, cultural, solidary, and economic institutions. The first steps in analysis of institutional context are to conceptualize the cultural, normative, political, and economic order and, just as important, to describe the relations of differentiation among the same major institutions. Having done these, the researcher has a benchmark institutional configuration from which to gauge change.

Now we can again return to the Chickasaw case study. Above, I briefly outlined early Chickasaw institutional order. While there is no space to give an elaborate description, I extracted this information from documents, oral histories, ceremonies and myths, and observations by travelers and traders (Champagne, 1992). The Chickasaw study, as I have conceived it, seeks to explain the formation of a differentiated constitutional government. Therefore, the analysis of early Chickasaw society concentrated on the organization of the Chickasaw polity and its relations of differentiation with culture, normative order, and economy. As mentioned above, the Chickasaw held traditionalistic cultural orientations that predisposed well-socialized Chickasaw to prefer preservation of the old institutional order (Adair, 1968, pp. 34-46, 99-101; Gibson, 1971; Nairne, 1988, pp. 40-42). The early Chickasaw polity was embedded within local clans and religious-ceremonial organization

(Adair, 1968, pp. 31-33; Baird, 1974; Gibson, 1971, pp. 12-30; Malone, 1922, pp. 211-213). By the early 1800s, one report states that the Chickasaw national council no longer met in a sacred ceremonial square, indicating a trend toward secularization of Chickasaw political order (Jennings, 1947).

Hence the Chickasaw had traditionalistic cultural orientations and a relatively nondifferentiated polity and we expect them to resist major institutional change. Interestingly enough, the Chickasaw acted in accordance to the above theoretical prediction during the preremoval period. During the 1820s and 1830s, the Chickasaw polity did not change significantly, despite the presence of strong U.S. geopolitical pressures, incorporation into the southern export economy, the presence of a market-oriented planter class, and American agents and missionaries who worked to convince the Chickasaw to adopt U.S. forms of agriculture and democratic political order and to adopt Christianity (Barden, 1953, pp. 222-229; M234, n.d., roll 135, pp. 135, 155, 194, 259, 693-695). Thus the Chickasaw case upholds an argument that institutional order—a traditionalistic worldview, and a polity embedded in kinship, solidary, and religious relations—helps explain Chickasaw resistance to change despite intense pressures for adaptive change.

So far so good, but now we meet the dilemma presented above. The Chickasaw formed a differentiated constitutional government in 1856, when the intensity of U.S. pressure for land temporarily receded and while many Chickasaw preferred the old institutional order. How can we use the same transsocietal and institutional arguments to explain Chickasaw traditionalism before 1837 and political change in 1856? The answer to this question is that we cannot. Such arguments work better for explaining Chickasaw traditionalism than for explaining change. Sole reliance on geopolitical context, class formation, nondifferentiated political order, and world-system incorporation cannot explain Chickasaw state formation. Nevertheless, empirically this is what happened and therefore we must look to other modes of analysis, because sole reliance on structural arguments fails.

Group Interaction, Historical Contingency, and Causality

Turning again to theory, macrosociological arguments have often relied heavily on structural arguments. In particular, Parsons's evolutionary theory understates the issues of process and change between levels of societal differentiation. Even to understand processes of evolution there must be historical causes for major changes in institutional order. A serviceable theory of social change must explain change and transition between types of institutional order. Such explanations will necessarily involve actions by groups and contain narratives of group actions played out within transsocietal and institutional contexts. Several theorists have contributed arguments toward a theory of institutional change based on social movements theory (Alexander & Colomy, 1985; Colomy, 1985, 1990a, 1990b; Eisenstadt, 1964a, 1964b, 1990; Smelser, 1959, 1985, 1990). In this view, changing structural or contextual conditions can create dissatisfactions or opportunities for the introduction of institutional innovations. These innovations may lead to a path of increased institutional differentiation or they may also lead to less differentiated institutional orders. Several groups may offer competing innovations, but the mere introduction of a particular innovation will not necessarily lead to its adoption. The mere desire for change does not mean that institutional entrepreneurs will succeed in gaining adoption of their innovations. The likelihood that an innovation will become institutionalized depends on a variety of conditions, some of which are the strengths and interests of opposition groups and organizations, cultural acceptability of the innovation, the level and configuration of preexisting institutional differentiation, the social solidarity of the innovators, the form of social and political solidarity of the society, and the ability of the innovators to gather widespread support, commitment, and resources from the major groups in the society. It is quite likely that more traditional social movements' literature can extend and broaden the institutional change perspective, but I will not explore that possibility here (Morris, 1984; Oberschall, 1973; Smelser, 1963; Turner & Killian, 1972). This view of institutional change indicates that we must look to group interactions and sequences of historically contingent events to explain processes of institutional change.

Now we have tools for analyzing Chickasaw state formation. Until the late 1830s the Chickasaw were reluctant to make major changes in their political system, where kinship groups and hereditary chiefs held traditional rights to political office. Under similar transsocietal conditions, the Cherokee, with a more politically solidary and differentiated society, formed a differentiated constitutional government in 1827. The other two major southeastern nations, the Creek and Choctaw, however, did not follow the Cherokee path of political centralization and increased differentiation. In the late 1820s, a small group of Christianized Choctaw planters attempted to form a centralized constitutional government. This attempt failed, however, owing to the political resurgence of traditional regional leaders, who mobilized considerable support against centralization and differentiation of the Choctaw polity. The decentralized and nondifferentiated Choctaw political order helps explain their resistance to political change. The Choctaw polity relied on social and political loyalties to kin groups and consisted of a federation of local clans and regions. Similarly, the symbolically ordered and politically and culturally decentralized Creek responded much like the Chickasaw and willfully and collectively refused to adopt the plan of change taken by the Cherokee.

The Choctaw and Creek formed centralized constitutional governments in 1860 and 1867, respectively. In both cases, an alliance between the U.S. government and a small group of prochange-oriented planters imposed differentiated constitutional governments over reluctant conservative majorities. U.S.-supported planters applied force to create the Choctaw and Creek constitutional governments, while Cherokee constitution building was more consensual and came 30 to 40 years earlier. Earlier and more consensual political change was more possible within the politically solidary and differentiated Cherokee society than among the locally solidary and less differentiated Creek and Choctaw societies. With U.S. support, Creek and Choctaw institutional entrepreneurs created constitutional governments without strong support from conservatives who preferred adherence to less differentiated and decentralized political and institutional orders (Champagne, 1989, 1992). Similarly, Chickasaw planters, with backing from U.S. officials, dismantled the kin based political order. Nevertheless, after these events greater national political solidarity supported the formation of a Chickasaw constitutional government, but not among the Creek and Choctaw. A historical narrative of group interests, struggles, and contingent events that transpired within the institutional and transsocietal conditions of the 1840s and 1850s will illustrate this turn of events. The Cherokee, Creek, and Choctaw movements toward political change also deserve treatment, but the concentration here is on the critical Chickasaw case.

By the early 1830s, Chickasaw society stratified into a majority of subsistence farmers and a minority of market-oriented planters, merchants, and cattlemen. The market-oriented groups did not challenge the old political authorities, in part because some leading planters had access to political decision making by means of inherited political office and through honorary chiefships. The conservative majority allowed the planters and merchants to benefit privately from managing Chickasaw relations with the United States. In exchange, the conservatives hoped to gain protection against American land and removal pressures. In the late 1820s the planters engineered the adoption of some laws regulating market relations, but the political order remained organized by a hereditary principal chief and hereditary subordinate chiefs. The Chickasaw, under considerable federal and local state pressures, reluctantly agreed to sign removal treaties in 1830, 1832, and 1836, but could not find a suitable homeland in the West. The Treaty of 1834 established a Chickasaw Commission and delegated to it management of Chickasaw legal issues arising from removal. The Chickasaw Commission acted as a de facto government and administered Chickasaw grievances that emerged during the removal period. In fact, the Chickasaw Commission contained the most important hereditary chiefs, including the principal chief, or "king," as the English and Americans called him. Nevertheless, the king led a majority of Chickasaw, who before 1837 had little interest in changing the kin-based political order (Litton, 1939; M234, n.d., roll 135, pp. 281-182; roll 136, pp. 21-22).

Between 1837 and 1845 a series of events led to the official dismantling of the Chickasaw kin-based government. Desperate for a place to settle after suffering the intrusion of American settlers and legal harassment from nearby states, a group of planters negotiated a treaty with the Choctaw in 1837. By this time most Choctaw were living in the West. In the early 1830s, the United States pressured the Choctaw to resettle in what is now eastern Oklahoma. Previous negotiations ended in failure because the Choctaw would not cede land, but were willing to grant citizenship to the Chickasaw. Most Chickasaw, however, did not wish to surrender their independent nationality, and they therefore refused the Choctaw offer. By 1837 conditions in the East deteriorated so far that the Chickasaw agreed to surrender their nationality and become citizens of the Choctaw nation.

Under pressure from the United States, the Choctaw formed a decentralized constitutional government in 1834. The new Choctaw national council consisted of 30 delegates elected from three districts. The three traditional regional chiefs formed the national executive branch, but none had jurisdiction outside his own district (Baird, 1979; Foreman, n.d., vol. 25, p. 330; M234, n.d., roll 170, pp. 414-420, 880; roll 171, pp. 452-453). According to the 1837 treaty, the Chickasaw created a fourth district within the Choctaw nation. In 1838 the Choctaw revised their constitution, which now included the Chickasaw. Thereafter, the Choctaw and U.S. governments expected the Chickasaw to conform to Choctaw law and political order. This, however, required the Chickasaw to abandon their old political system and adopt the electoral system of the Choctaw. By 1843, a group of Christians and planters took up residence in the Chickasaw district and elected a district chief in conformity with Choctaw law and the treaty of 1837. Most Chickasaw, however, hesitated to settle in the Chickasaw district during the early 1840s. The area was subject to intermittent raids by Plains Indians who still claimed the land (Debo, 1934, pp. 64-77; Gibson, 1971, pp. 216-219, 223, 242; M234, n.d., roll 172, pp. 278-280; roll 137, pp. 144, 296-298; Wright, 1929).

A large group of conservative Chickasaw, probably a small national majority at the time, refused to accept abolition of the kin-based government and were disheartened over the loss of national autonomy. Between 1843 and 1845, three interconnected groups vied for official U.S. recognition and control over Chickasaw affairs—the king and his conservative following, the Chickasaw Commission, and the Chickasaw district chief. The American government refused recognition to any Chickasaw government other than the Chickasaw district government. Planters led in the district, and they actively campaigned against the old government and for adoption of the Choctaw constitutional government. Despite this setback, the conservatives openly started to advocate nationalist separation from the Choctaw government (Baird, 1974, pp. 52-55; Gibson, 1971, pp. 246-248; M234, n.d., roll 139, pp. 142, 148-149, 153-154, 219, 227, 236-239; Wright, 1929, pp. 401-402).

In the late 1840s, the planters of the Chickasaw district agreed to pursue nationalist separation and the conservatives agreed to accept a constitutional government if established independent of the Choctaw government. In 1846, Chickasaw district government adopted an early constitutional declaration. In 1848, the constitution was revised to include separation of powers between executive and legislative branches and election of a unicameral national council composed of 30 "captains"—the old name given to clan headmen by the Spanish. The captains were elected from throughout the districts of the Choctaw nation, because many Chickasaw did not reside in the Chickasaw district. Of the 30 delegates, 17 were elected from the Chickasaw district. The Chickasaw district chief was named "the chief of the Chickasaw People," and he had the right to convene the national council whenever necessary. The constitution went on to create laws for the organization of government bodies and stated that the Chickasaw government strongly supported education and economic development for its citizens. With this constitution the Chickasaw declared that they had the right to make their own laws and to manage their own financial affairs. At this time, the U.S. government recognized the Chickasaw district within the Choctaw government, and delivered funds from treaty agreements to the Chickasaw district chief (CKN, 1977, roll 4, 1848-1856). The constitution of 1848 showed a clear break with past political organization. While the name "captain" was retained, men no longer occupied offices according to clan and heredity. All offices were now elective, and the polity was formally differentiated from kinship ties and from Chickasaw religious ceremonial order.

In 1850 the Chickasaw again revised the constitution of their "unofficial" government, this time taking a more nationalist turn by electing a chief—the "financial chief"—who was independent of the U.S.- and Choctaw-supported Chickasaw district chief. In late 1850 the Chickasaw council elected a chief who for them had superior authority over the Chickasaw district chief, who served the Choctaw government. The number of delegates to the unicameral national council was reduced from 30 to 12. After election of the new chief, the national council convened in secret session and considered the question of nationalist separation from the Choctaw government (CKN, 1977, roll 4, 1848; Gibson, 1971, p. 248; M234, n.d., roll 139, pp. 253-254, 456, 522; roll 140, pp. 171-177, 502-505; Wright 1929, pp. 401-402).

Between 1850 and 1855, a united movement to secede from the Choctaw nation and create an independent national government galvanized a new Chickasaw political nationality. As among the Cherokee, the formation of a mobilized and unified national political identity preceded the consensual formation of the differentiated constitutional government. In October of 1851, the Chickasaw held a convention to revise their constitution further. The new constitution declared that the general council under the provisions of the Chickasaw constitution had plenary power to manage Chickasaw funds. This was the Chickasaw solution to the struggle dating from the early 1840s over who controlled Chickasaw funds and government authority. The United States, the Choctaw, and many Chickasaw planters then agreed that the Chickasaw district chief would control the funds. By 1851, the Chickasaw conservatives and planters were united within a constitutional government and were pursuing control over their own national affairs from the Choctaw and the United States. The Chickasaw Constitution of 1851 created a bicameral legislature composed of 13 captains and 13 representatives.

Of the captains, 11 were elected to four-year terms and 2 were prominent conservative leaders who were granted office "for life and always
entitled to be members of the council" (CKN roll 4, 1851). The chief
was elected by the general council for two-year terms and was granted
a salary. From 1852 to 1855, the financial chief was granted powers to
appoint a committee and seek separation from the Choctaw nation. In
early 1852 the Chickasaw council declared:

> Be it enacted by the Chickasaw in General Council that the Chickasaws will
> no longer submit to the oppression of the Choctaws or the enforcement of the
> Choctaw laws in the Chickasaw District until our rights are acknowledged
> that the expenses of the Chickasaw District, as a district of the Choctaw
> Nation, shall not hereafter be paid out of the funds of the Chickasaws. (CKN,
> 1977, roll 4 1852; roll 4, 1850, pp. 33, 45; roll 4, 1851; M234, n.d., roll 140,
> pp. 296-297, 340-342; roll 141, pp. 193; roll 142, pp. 139, 300-302, 304, 308)

The formation of a Chickasaw constitutional government, however,
depended on U.S. officials who forced the Choctaw to grant national
independence to the Chickasaw in the Treaty of 1855. Negotiations with
the Choctaw for separation repeatedly failed, because the Choctaw saw
such a move as resulting in permanent loss of Choctaw national territory. U.S. officials ultimately intervened on behalf of the Chickasaw
and arranged the Treaty of 1855 (CKN, 1977, roll 4, 1855; Gibson,
1971, pp. 225-228, 231, 249-257; Wright, 1929, pp. 400-403), which
allowed the Chickasaw to form an independent government after paying
the Choctaw substantial amounts for land and withdrawal from Choctaw
citizenship.

In August of 1856 the Chickasaw convened a constitutional convention. The financial chief, the elected captains under the Chickasaw
Constitution, and elected delegates from the Chickasaw precincts composed the body of the convention. They adopted a differentiated constitutional government formally modeled after U.S. federal and state
constitutional governments. The new Chickasaw government included
a bill of rights, separation of church and state, freedom of speech, right to
trial, equality before the law, and separation of powers among executive,
legislative, and judicial branches. The Constitution also included a slave
code that prohibited the government from emancipating slaves without
agreement from and compensation to the owners. The slave code was
struck down after the American Civil War, in which most Chickasaw allied
with the South (CKN, 1977, roll 4, 1856; roll 8, 1856-1889; M234, n.d.,
roll 142, pp. 139-169; Wright, 1929, pp. 409-410).

The Chickasaw Constitution of 1856 defined a polity that was differentiated from religious and kinship organization. The election of delegates to office indicated a differentiation of polity from society. The new government also included separation of executive, judicial, and legislative powers, all of which increased institutional differentiation within the organization of the polity itself. By the middle 1870s, the Chickasaw created formal political parties, another indication of further organizational differentiation within the polity and further differentiation of polity from society. If we were to continue the analysis it could be shown that although the Chickasaw adopted a highly differentiated polity, there was considerable continuity of Chickasaw culture, values, norms, political culture, and social organization that gave social and political relations a very different dynamic than was found within the U.S. polity.

In the Chickasaw case there was no evolutionary or systemic progression from the kin-based political order to a differentiated constitutional government. An alliance of U.S. officials and Chickasaw planters willfully dismantled the old Chickasaw political order. U.S. and planter repression of the kin-based political order removed overt religious and kin-based resistance to the consensual acceptance of a constitutional government in the 1850s. A new and more centralized national political solidarity emerged from the Chickasaw movement to regain nationalist independence. The new national solidarity contributed to a political consensus that was relatively independent of the old nondifferentiated religious-kinship-political consensus that supported the kin-based political order. The mobilization for nationalist separation by the Chickasaw conservatives included planter leaders who carried and supported a U.S. model of political organization. Chickasaw planters eventually supported separation, but not a return to the old political system. The conservatives, however, were forced to abandon the traditional political order in the face of U.S. and planter opposition. Conservatives enlisted the aid of Chickasaw planters and U.S. officials in their quest for national independence by submitting to U.S. and planter interests in forming a constitutional government. Ultimately, groups and organizations are the creators and modifiers of institutional orders. The outcomes of struggles between the major social groupings are the effective causes of institutional change, although always conditioned by their transsocietal and institutional contexts.

Discussion

I have advocated an inductive and empirical method for studying processes of social-institutional change. To be sure, method must be informed by theoretical arguments if researchers are to identify significant controls and salient features of cultural and social order and to define the process of change itself. But theory must not dictate results to research and method, as I believe has been the case in macrohistorical studies of social change, which in sociology have tended to incorporate evolutionary or modernist teleologies implicitly. The method I propose here curbs some of the more strident and predictive claims of current theory and forces sociologists to show how their theories fare within concrete historical situations. By considering institutional, cultural, world-system, and geopolitical contexts, a healthy respect for analyzing processes of stability and change within varying situations should be obtained. Our theories should not abstract past historical contexts, but enlighten us as to how societies change and/or remain stable from context to context. This can be done with specific analyses of case studies and comparative studies of societies within regions within the modern world-system and throughout history. This is work for a discipline over long periods of scholarly activity. Certainly there are many obstacles, because many historical data are missing and the magnitude of the project is large, but I believe such a project promises a better and more thorough understanding of human societies, their variations, and likely future. Therefore, I believe that such a difficult undertaking is well worth the effort, and will pay great rewards in our understanding of the past and future of human societies.

Embedded in the method is a strong antievolutionary and antistructural ist bent. A multidimensional method demands much care in the understanding of political, cultural, social, geopolitical, and world-system contexts, and consideration of their relative conditioning and effective cause for explaining social change. This method seeks to understand the variations in institutional orders among societies, and to explain their differential paths of social change. Hence there can be no inherent teleology of modernism or evolution or convergence. An inductive empirical approach can isolate historical trends of centralization, bureaucratization, market expansion, and increased institutional differentiation, but such trends should not be extrapolated into evolutionary principles for all time or for the next several centuries. Knowledge of history should give the researcher and theorist a healthy respect for the decline and fall of numerous great civilizations. Similarly, it should not be posited, as Parsons does, that the modernization of U.S. society will continue into the next several centuries. Such a position ignores the possibility that world and domestic economic conditions may change drastically, and that democracy in the United States is upheld by a continually negotiated process, and is not structurally ordained, and that just as the Republic of Rome passed ultimately to centralized authoritarian leadership, specific historical conditions may yet arise that foster similar authoritarian developments within the U.S. polity. It should be our task to understand how specific historical societies and their constituent groups behave under varying contextual conditions. A primary objective of historical-comparative sociology should be to develop grounded generalizations about group action and institutional change within varying historical contexts. Our methods and theories should seek ways of understanding the complexity and diversity of all human societies and should study the variations in their trends in stability and change. Hence small societies such as the Chickasaw of North America or the Pygmies of Africa become worthy of study as well as the larger-scale societies that are currently featured in sociological studies. Only after completing many empirical studies about the social change processes of historical and contemporary societies can we formulate a general theory of social change that more accurately reflects the diversity of the human institutional order and more accurately accounts for the diverse possibilities of future societal change.

Transsocietal conditions and institutional contexts identify the parameters of institutional change, but they do not by themselves necessarily account for processes or causality in institutional change. Processes of change take place within transsocietal and institutional contexts. Change in transsocietal contexts conditions group action and is analyzable as sequences of group actions and historical events effecting change in institutional order. Application of this method will help us to identify a variety of historical and contemporary institutional configurations and sequences of change. By studying group processes of institutional change within their transsocietal and institutional contexts, we can accumulate empirical knowledge about historically specific processes of social change. Based on this evidence, theory can be generated by inductive means, through comparisons of results from accumulated historical and comparative studies. Researchers who combine empirical investigation of transsocietal and institutional contexts with group processes of change will necessarily address fundamental theoretical issues of social order and social change. For example, the arguments for institutional order, social movements, world-system, and geopolitics draw on theories current within macrosociology. Consequently, both empirical analysis and theoretical analysis will go forward, hand in hand. A multidimensional method will not only include interdependent material and normative arguments, macro and micro arguments, but will also help reconcile theory and historical comparative data.

13

The Comparative Study of Ethnicity

Methodological and Conceptual Issues

CHARLES C. RAGIN
JEREMY HEIN

"Studies that now represent the core of knowledge in the field of race and ethnic relations are increasingly those based on macro-comparative research, studies that often contrast race or ethnic relations in one society with those in other societies" (See & Wilson, 1988, p. 223). We agree with See and Wilson that comparative study is essential in the field of race and ethnic relations. Although essential, comparative study is also highly problematic. In this chapter we discuss some of the methodological and conceptual difficulties that beset the comparative study of ethnicity, especially small-N case-oriented studies in which one ethnic situation is contrasted with one or a small number of other situations.

Essentially, our argument is that because ethnicity is much more socially constructed and situated than most other forms of social inequality (e.g., social class), the diversity of ethnic situations is extreme, so much so that each ethnic situation may appear to be unique and unparalleled. Clearly, the more unusual each case seems, the less plausible the comparison of cases becomes. Although the task of comparison appears daunting when cases are very different, we argue that the comparative study of ethnicity offers many opportunities for the development or elaboration of concepts, and we outline analytic strategies appropriate for this goal. Although we focus much of our discussion on the category of *ethnicity,* most, if not all, of our arguments apply with equal force to the larger category of *race and ethnicity.*

Our discussion opens with an analysis of the diversity of ethnic situations and different ways this diversity can be conceptualized. We then address aspects of case-oriented comparative analysis, especially its holistic orientation, relevant to the study of complex social phenomena. Unfortunately, most applications of comparative methodology resort to truncated, rhetorical comparisons that give the appearance but have little of the substance of a natural experiment. We show that the two-case comparison is limited in its ability to test theories regarding causal regularities and thus refine and extend some of the complaints presented in rudimentary form by Lieberson (1992). However, the two-case comparison is useful for better defining cases, creating typologies, developing ideal types, and, if carried far enough, differentiating competing conceptual frameworks. To illustrate our argument, we present preliminary material from a study comparing two "civil rights eras"—the United States from 1954 to 1968 and France from 1981 to 1990 (Hein, 1991).

The Contextual and Interactive Nature of Ethnicity

Ethnicity is usually conceptualized as a common origin or culture resulting from shared activities and identity based on some mixture of language, religion, race, and/or ancestry (Yinger, 1985). Obviously, social scientists would like to know more about the precise differences between "origin" and "culture," as the debate between the neoprimordial (van den Berghe, 1981) and emergent (Barth, 1969) schools of ethnicity suggests. Similarly, the nature of the relation between "activities" and "identity" has fueled controversy over which comes first (for example, entrepreneurship or group cohesiveness among Japanese Americans; see Bonacich & Modell, 1980; Jiobu, 1988). Finally, although the constituent elements of ethnicity are well established (Isaacs, 1977), the "and/or" relationships among these elements remain unclear, a controversy that includes the issue of whether race should be considered a variant of ethnicity. Although perplexing, these conceptual enigmas are key findings from several decades of research showing that ethnicity is profoundly *contextual* (it takes many forms, depending on associated conditions) and deeply *interactive* (it is closely intertwined with political and economic institutions, events, and processes).

The contextual nature of ethnic identity is well illustrated by changing identities among white Americans, for whom "the character of ethnicity has shifted over the last fifty years. It was once a primary axis of socioeconomic stratification and institutional segregation; it is now a symbol of cultural and political differentiation" (Hirschman, 1983, p. 416). Where the category WASP once defined the core of American society, a new category of European American is emerging as assimilation erodes the structural supports of English, German, and related identities (Alba, 1990). Remaining ethnic identities among Polish, Irish, Italian, and other white Americans stem from the need to belong to a "costless community" that allows individuals to differentiate themselves but requires little group loyalty (Waters, 1990).

Indeed, when asked about their ancestry, a growing number of U.S. residents report that they are "Americans" and do not give any affiliation with a European country (Lieberson, 1985; Lieberson & Waters, 1988). Among whites, these "unhyphenated Americans" constitute the sixth-largest ethnic group after English, Germans, Irish, French, and Italian, and they exceed the last two when residents who report no ancestry are included with them. The simple passage of time since immigration to this country and intermarriage across white ethnic lines account for part of this shift, but larger processes of ethnic definition are at work as well. Studies using the General Social Survey have shown that the majority of self-labeled "Americans" are nonwhite. And in the 1980 U.S. Census, 21 million residents reported their race as Black, but only 12 million reported their ethnicity as Black.

The complex relationships among the identities white, Black, and American in the United States reveal that race and ethnicity are historically shaped in the sense that a claim to a racial or ethnic identity also can be considered a claim to a collective history. Sometimes the people in a nation-state share only a small portion of their respective histories, and the sense of national collective history and identity is weak. In other nation-states there is one dominant collective history, and the sense of national collective identity is strong. In still other settings there are two opposed histories that are nonetheless closely intertwined.

The "American dilemma" between racial equality and racial subordination is a good example of the last of these possibilities. American conceptions of liberty developed not in spite of slavery, but because property rights and the wealth produced from slavery were given priority over other rights (Davis, 1975; Morgan, 1975). Black servitude was incorporated into the Constitution in order to avoid sectional disputes and remained legal for eight decades after independence (Robinson, 1971). Thus American citizenship and national identity developed as much from racial inequality as from civic rights (Jordon, 1974). Even after 1865, the economic mobility of European immigrants often came at the expense of Blacks (Lieberson, 1980). As a result, whites and Blacks in the United States share a common history, but derive very different identities from it. From this perspective, racial and ethnic designations can be seen as residue of large-scale historical forces: wars, migrations, conquests, colonizations, acts of political and economic imperialism, and international economic changes.

Since the French Revolution and especially since World War I, the relevant political context for racial and ethnic categories is most often national (Young, 1976), especially in the advanced countries. As nations and their politics change, so do these categories. Northern Ireland provides a vivid example. As part of Britain, Protestants in Northern Ireland have the option of asserting their Britishness. In an independent Northern Ireland Protestants would lose this official Britishness, but still dominate as Orangemen in Ulster because of the coincidence of class and religion. If Northern Ireland were joined to the Republic of Ireland, the Orangemen would be a vulnerable minority of Irish Protestants in a Catholic nation, especially given their history in Northern Ireland.

The importance of national contexts for ethnic categories is further reinforced by the simple fact that conceptions of nationhood are fundamentally ethnic in form (A. D. Smith, 1986). Ideally, the nation is a community of descent, sharing not only territory, history, government, language, and culture, but also symbols of group membership and common allegiances to authority. However, it is rare for the population contained within the territorial boundaries of a state to possess a single collective history. Indeed, ethnicity is not only nationally situated but internationally situated, because national boundaries force qualitative political change on human geography (Rothschild, 1981). For example, many ethnic minorities in Western Europe reside near the territorial boundaries of adjacent countries (e.g., French Alsatians and Finnish Swedes). These ethnic minorities exist because almost all national boundaries are determined by a complex intersection of political forces, not by the goal of drawing boundaries around culturally similar collectivities (impossible to achieve in most instances). The current ethnic-national crises in Eastern European countries (e.g., Serbs and Croatians in Yugoslavia) and the former Soviet Union provide vivid illustrations of the persistent problem of political boundaries. The interactive effect of state making and unmaking on ethnicity is further influenced by the fact that an ethnic minority in one country (e.g., Irish Catholics in the United Kingdom and Quebecois in Canada) may be a majority in another (Ireland and France, respectively). In these instances, the coethnic nation-state provides an important international resource for ethnic minorities.

Economic institutions also interact with ethnic distinctions because markets and modes of production mediate and shape intergroup contact and subsequent relations. For example, proximity to trade routes was a key variable in the development of nation-states in Europe from the Middle Ages onward (Rokkan, 1975). Shifting demands for unskilled labor in core societies during the colonial, industrial, and post-World War II periods led to extensive international migration and thus ethnic pluralism in these core nations and in their political dependencies (Portes & Walton, 1981). Levels of ethnic antagonism are heavily influenced by labor market conditions as well (Bonacich, 1972). For example, historical shifts in the employment of African Americans from agriculture to industry and then to the service sector (especially government jobs) have profoundly altered the dynamics of racial inequality in the United States (W. J. Wilson, 1978).

However, ethnicity is not dependent on economic subordination for its maintenance. Ethnic minorities may be more economically advanced than the culturally dominant core, as in the Catalan and Basque areas of Spain (Linz, 1973). Such peripheral areas are exploited to the extent that they lack political power commensurate with their relative economic wealth. Other ethnic groups exist because of the specific economic tasks they performed at a much earlier point in time, such as the Chinese in Southeast Asia who arrived during the colonial period (Esman, 1975). In short, the international system presents an impressive array of ethnic situations shaped by local contexts and by interaction with political and economic institutions and processes.

Analytic Consequences

Race and ethnicity take multiple forms and have close relationships to other social structures, complicating the analytic tasks of the researcher. The socially situated nature of ethnicity is made even more complex by the many different ways it is situated (e.g., nationally, politically, historically, internationally) and the many different ways it is mediated (e.g., by economic inequality, by territory, by language, by physical markers).

Rothschild's (1981) attempt to provide a basic conceptual map for understanding what he calls "ethnopolitical" situations illustrates the immensity of the diversity (see also Schermerhorn, 1970/1978). Our distillation of the major factors he considers (labeled A through N) includes the following:

characteristics of the politically dominant ethnic group(s)

A = numerical majority, plurality, or minority?

B = culturally homogeneous or heterogeneous?

C = also economically dominant or only politically dominant?

D = regionally concentrated or geographically dispersed?

characteristics of the politically subordinate group(s)?

E = numerical majority, plurality, or minority?

F = culturally homogeneous or heterogeneous?

G = economically dominant or politically *and* economically subordinate?

H = regionally concentrated or geographically dispersed?

formal/legal status of ethnicity

I = ethnicity recognized in the law? (e.g., United States, affirmative action)

J = citizenship mediated by corporate ethnic membership? (e.g., former Soviet Union)

K = if J, openly inegalitarian? (e.g., South Africa)

nature of the international situation

L = subordinate group has international resources (e.g., Arabs in Israel)

M = dominant group has international resources (e.g., colonial situation)

locus of ethnopolitical struggle

N = control of central versus local governments (e.g., Belgium, United States)

Altogether, 14 characteristics are listed. Treated as simple dichotomies, these 14 characteristics yield 16,384 logically possible combinations— thousands and thousands of different ethnic situations.

Clearly, not all these different ethnic situations exist, and many combinations of characteristics are logically impossible or empirically implausible. Diversity is also limited because some sets of characteristics cohere in meaningful clusters—they tend to be present or absent in unison. Still, many of these different combinations of characteristics may be relevant in a given comparative investigation because small-N case-oriented research is *holistic* in its approach to social phenomena. This holism is manifested in a variety of ways. For example, comparativists often ask questions about the possible consequences of a single altered circumstance. (For example: What would have been the political fate of this minority if it had been more culturally homogeneous?) A holistic orientation to cases takes as a basic premise the idea that two cases that differ on only one characteristic may be qualitatively different from each other, so much so that they may represent wholly different types. This way of thinking about cases contrasts sharply with most statistically based approaches, which would see two cases that are similar in all respects save one as virtually identical. In case-oriented analysis, sharp qualitative differences often emerge when key circumstances change from one case to the next, even in the face of a broad range of similarities.

This concern for whole cases and for configurations of characteristics carries over into causal reasoning. To assess, for example, the political consequences of cultural heterogeneity for politically subordinate ethnic groups, it would be necessary to compare cases that differ on only this one feature because the investigator would expect the political consequences of cultural heterogeneity to vary by context. Similarly, any conclusions that might be drawn regarding the impact of cultural heterogeneity would be specific to the context compared—to the characteristics that the cases in the study share. In simpler terms: The impact of cultural heterogeneity might be very different for different types of cases. For some types of cases this factor may be decisive; for others it may be irrelevant.

Because ethnicity is deeply contextual and interactive, the number of conditions relevant to any analysis is great and the possibility of matching cases in the manner just described (i.e., so that they differ on only one factor) is correspondingly reduced. The methodological consequences of these aspects of comparative methodology are explored in the contrast offered below between "truncated" and "fully elaborated" comparisons. Many comparative studies offer only truncated comparisons. Such comparisons have much of the appearance but little of the substance of experimental design.

The Logic and Rhetoric
of Small-N Comparative Research

Small-N case-based comparisons have become increasingly popular among social scientists concerned with grounding their studies in time and place (Ragin, 1987, 1991; Skocpol, 1984b; Tilly, 1984). Many of these studies attempt to implement a comparative design that follows the pattern of an experiment (see Ragin, 1987). The general approach can be illustrated with the factors used by Rothschild (1981) to map ethnopolitical situations and listed in distilled form above. With an uppercase letter denoting the presence of a factor and a lowercase letter denoting its absence, a fully elaborated two-case comparison would take the following form (O is the outcome of interest, perhaps some form of ethnic political mobilization such as the coalescence of an ethnic political party):

        Case 1: ABCDEFGHIJKLMN   O
        Case 2: ABCDEFGHIJKLMn   o

(Causal conditions A through N are listed first, followed by the outcome variable O; please note that none of the examples presented in this section attempts explicit substantive linking of combinations of letters to the listing of characteristics presented above.) Careful selection of cases allows the investigator to hold all possibly relevant conditions (A though M) constant, and to argue that it is the presence of condition N that accounts for the difference in ethnic mobilization (O). This matching of cases with different outcomes and only one discordant causal condition is an example of Mill's method of difference. Of course, it is extremely rare for two cases to match perfectly. Usually there are many differences across two cases even when, at first glance, they appear to be very similar. A more likely pattern of similarities and differences might be as follows:

        Case 1: AbCDEFgHIjKLMN   O
        Case 2: ABCdEFGHIJKlmn   o

The two cases again differ on condition N and outcome O, supporting the idea that N causes O, but they differ on many other characteristics as well. For example, it may be the absence of J in the first case that accounts for the presence of O.

Typically, when investigators are confronted with such imperfect fully elaborated comparisons, they resort to rhetorical strategies using truncated comparisons. For example, if the investigator wants to argue that N causes O, then he or she is likely to present the following truncated comparison:

Case 1: ACEFHIKN   O
Case 2: ACEFHIKn   o

The researcher thereby presents the favored contrast (N combined with O versus n combined with o) against a backdrop of similarities (ACEFHIK). In this rhetorical strategy, the greater the number and variety of similarities that can be delineated, the greater the confidence the investigator may display in arguing that condition N causes outcome O. Similar rhetorical strategies are often used to rescue applications of Mill's method of agreement from this same state of indeterminacy. With the method of agreement, two cases should differ on all causal conditions except one, and share the same outcome. The ideal application of the method of agreement thus takes the form:

Case 1: ABCDEFGHIJKLMN   O
Case 2: abcdefghijklmN   O

Comparing these two cases, condition N appears to be the cause of O because the two cases share outcome O and only one condition (N). Empirical cases are rarely this neat, of course. A more likely pattern might be as follows:

Case 1: AbcDEFGhiJkLmN   O
Case 2: abCdefGhijKlmN   O

This indicates that there are many possible causes of outcome O in addition to condition N. Both cases agree in displaying an absence of M, for example. Faced with this discordant two-case comparison, an investigator would take the tack of emphasizing the favored similarity (N) against a backdrop of differences and present the following truncated comparison as an application of Mill's method of agreement:

Case 1: AcDEFJkLN   O
Case 2: aCdefjKlN   O

This rhetorical strategy presents agreement on condition N against a backdrop of disagreement on other conditions. Thus the method of agreement in this rhetorical strategy supports the conclusion that condition N causes outcome O.

It is important to emphasize that both rhetorical strategies presented above are common in comparative social science but clearly inadequate from the perspective of formal logic applied to fully elaborated comparisons. Truncated comparisons are often persuasive, especially when presented to audiences lacking sufficient substantive knowledge of the relevant cases (the usual situation in sociology). Truncated comparisons give the appearance of careful evaluation of evidence but fail usual tests of analytic rigor. The problem of truncated comparisons is particularly acute in the comparative study of ethnicity because there are many relevant conditions that must be considered in any comparative analysis. As noted, ethnicity is deeply contextual and highly interactive; it is socially situated in a variety of ways and mediated through many different mechanisms. The preliminary task of detailing the relevant conditions that should appear in a fully elaborated comparison is in itself a difficult assignment.

The problem of truncated comparisons is compounded by the general state of ignorance among social scientists regarding the strict causal logic of the comparative method. As before, this ignorance derives from the substitution of rhetorical strategy for logically sound analytic strategy. Consider the application of the method of difference to the very first pair of cases discussed above. Recall that in this fully elaborated comparison the two cases differ on the outcome O and on *only* condition N, among all possibly relevant conditions. The conclusion that most investigators would draw from this evidence is that condition N is the cause of outcome O (i.e., N → O). But the logically correct conclusion is *not* that N causes O, but that *in the presence of ABCDEFGHIJKLM* condition N causes outcome O (i.e., if ABCDEFGHIJKLM, then N → O). It is possible that under altered conditions (say, the absence of A: aBCDEFGHIJKLM), N may not cause O. In fact, to be able to argue that N is *the* cause of O, it would be necessary to observe condition N paired with outcome O and n paired with outcome o in all logically possible combinations of conditions A through M ($2^{13} + 2^{13} = 16,384$ combinations of relevant characteristics, assuming all characteristics are relevant to outcome O). This requirement follows from the holism of comparative analysis—from the premise that if two cases differ on only one characteristic, they may differ qualitatively from each other. These same logical requirements apply to conclusions drawn from applications of the method of agreement. Obviously, the strict requirements of the logic of the comparative method, as just formulated, negate the possibility of the comparative analysis of small Ns. Social phenomena such as ethnicity are simultaneously too complex and too limited in their diversity, at least from a strictly logical point of view, to permit systematic analysis.

To summarize: Truncated comparisons, the most common types of comparisons in the social sciences, are suspect—they are rhetorical devices. Fully elaborated comparisons, by contrast, are both difficult to construct (all relevant conditions must be specified) and limited as a basis for generalization, especially when applied to complex phenomena. Thus the comparative analysis of small Ns is highly problematic in the study of complexly situated social phenomena such as ethnicity.

The Value of Case-Oriented Comparative Analysis

So far we have argued that comparative analysis is both centrally important to the study of race and ethnic relations (following See & Wilson, 1988) and remarkably problematic (following Ragin, 1987), to the point that such study seems to border on the impossible. However, it is not in the realm of strict empirical analysis of naturally occurring experimental designs that case-based comparative analysis offers returns to intellectual labor, but in the realm of conceptual development and elaboration. Specifically, it is through the use of what some have called "macrovariables" (see, e.g., the exchange between Elizabeth Nichols, 1986, and Theda Skocpol, 1986, regarding the analytic structure of Skocpol's *States and Social Revolutions*) that small-*N* case-based comparisons become valuable.

Consider again the fully elaborated comparison of two empirical cases displaying many discordant conditions in an attempted application of the method of difference:

Case 1: AbCDEFgHIjKLMN   O
Case 2: ABCdEFGHIJKlmn   o

For the sake of clarity, sort the causal conditions into concordant and discordant sets:

Case 1: ACEFHIK,bDgjLMN   O
Case 2: ACEFHIK,BdGJlmn   o

Assume that the cluster of conditions ACEFHIK displays conceptual coherence as a set and can be represented with a single macrovariable X and that the contrast bDgjLMN versus BdGJlmn also displays conceptual coherence and can be represented with a single macrovariable Z. The mapping of characteristics to cases now reduces to

Case 1: XZ   O
Case 2: Xz   o

This conceptual translation converts a fully elaborated but analytically indecisive comparison into a logically manageable proposition: In cases of X, macrovariable Z is the cause of O (i.e., if X, then Z → O). In effect, the macrovariable X defines relevant cases (and the relevant scope conditions; see Walker & Cohen, 1985); the macrovariable Z specifies causation. The key to the success of any such conceptual translation is found in the empirical plausibility and theoretical viability of the macrovariables. If the translation is compatible with existing knowledge and theory, or if it can be shown to advance existing knowledge or theory in meaningful ways, then the translation may be accepted. Otherwise, it fails.

Typically, the translation of sets of separate conditions into macrovariables is not the mechanical process of sorting and equating presented above. The translation, if it is to occur successfully, follows from an intensive dialogue between theoretical ideas and empirical evidence. Sometimes the fit between the macrovariable and relevant conditions is not perfect, but "more or less." This "more or less" fit is common in the use of ideal typic constructs, which Ragin and Zaret (1983) argue are central to the conduct of comparative historical inquiry. For example, an investigator might use an ideal typic specification of "the neocolonial situation" as the macrovariable for X in the example above. In different ways, the two cases might display most but perhaps not all of the characteristics subsumed under X (neocolonial situation: ACEFHIK), and the investigator would be required to argue or demonstrate that both cases conform sufficiently to ACEFHIK to be considered instances of X. In a similar manner, the causal conjunction represented in macrovariable Z may also be conceived ideal typically, and the fit of Case 1 to macrovariable Z and Case 2 to its absence (i.e., its fit to z) likewise might be "more or less." In many investigations this use of ideal types is an important part of the dialogue of ideas and evidence. Seen in this light, the ideal type can be considered a type of macrovariable: It displays more conceptual coherence than a mere colligation of related circumstances, but the fit of cases to the configuration specified by the ideal type may be imperfect due to the exaggerated or pure character of the ideal type (Weber, 1949).

In practical terms, the conceptual translation of sets of conditions into macrovariables occurs routinely in the work of comparative social scientists. However, these translations typically are conducted in haphazard, semiconscious, and inarticulated ways. It is rare for a comparative social scientist to articulate all the components of a macrovariable or an ideal type. Unfortunately, considerable truncation of a fully elaborated comparison is often made *before* conceptual translation is attempted, resulting in comparisons that may be rhetorically convincing, especially for nonspecialists, but analytically feeble. The truncation of the fully elaborated comparison is often invisible to audiences because no comprehensive articulation of conditions is offered and no direct mapping of the links between conditions and macrovariables is attempted.

More generally, contrast-oriented comparisons involving two cases that are paired on many characteristics yet also differing in important respects offer many useful avenues for developing concepts and elaborating ideal types (see also Amenta, 1991; S. L. Bailey, 1990). Although such analyses appear to be applications of Mill's method of difference (or, in some cases, of his method of agreement), they are not. They are more properly seen as "theoretical methods" (see Stinchcombe, 1978)—research strategies that focus on elaborating concepts through comparative inquiry. An early example of this use of paired cases is Turner's (1960) elaboration of the differences between "contest" and "sponsored" mobility using contrasts between stratification processes in the United States and Great Britain. The end product of his analysis is not a carefully argued empirical statement concerning the cause of some empirical outcome (e.g., the emergence of different perceptions of mobility), but the two ideal typic models of mobility. Such analyses clearly do not meet the strict logical requirements of the comparative method, especially as outlined above.

Case-Oriented Investigation
and Concept Elaboration: A Brief Illustration

As an illustration of the general approach to small-N case-oriented research we are advancing, consider the following brief sketch comparing the "civil rights era" of the United States (1954-1968) to that of France (1981-1990). (This discussion is based on Hein, 1991.) Clearly, it is not possible for us to provide a full elaboration of all the different causal conditions relevant to the contrasting outcomes in these two cases, nor is it possible to specify the different links between causal conditions and macrovariables (or between conditions and ideal types). A discussion providing this level of detail would require a book-length manuscript. Our goal is simply to provide a brief overview of the nature of the approach we are recommending for small-N comparative studies of ethnicity.

Our illustration begins with the specification of the relevant empirical category. This specification, in essence, requires elaboration of parallels and commonalities. From the perspective of comparative methodology and the natural experiment, this specification of commonalities indicates what conditions are being "held constant." At a more abstract level, the specification of commonalities answers the question: What is this a case of? (Ragin & Becker, 1992). Finally, from the perspective of formal theory, specifying commonalities establishes scope conditions—the limits set on any generalizations that might result from the study (Walker & Cohen, 1985). After discussing commonalities, we examine differences between the two cases in outcomes and differences in causally relevant features. This discussion of differences lays the foundation for the elaboration of ideal typic civil rights eras, which in turn are linked to broader perspectives to enhance further the dialogue between ideas and evidence.

Civil Rights Eras

There are many interpretations of the "civil rights era" in the United States, and considerable controversy still rages over its exact course. With this caveat in mind, one might describe the American civil rights era as follows. Changes in the economic and geographic position of

Blacks beginning in the 1920s and culminating in the 1950s elevated their place in the American social structure at the same time that international political pressures made racism less acceptable (Lemann, 1991; McAdam, 1982). Between 1953 and 1968, Black social movements in the South and North pushed the state to institute reforms that began to ameliorate Blacks' second-class citizenship. The southern pattern found Blacks using tactics of nonviolent direct action to stimulate aggression from whites, thus necessitating federal intervention to desegregate public facilities and ensure suffrage (Morris, 1984; W. J. Wilson, 1978). In the North, urban rebellions by Blacks increased state spending on public assistance and other social welfare programs (Isaac & Kelly, 1981; Piven & Cloward, 1971; Schram & Turbett, 1983). This shift away from nonviolent strategies reflected a change in movement goals from rights to resources (C. V. Hamilton, 1986). The movement slowed and then ended as it became geographically and politically diffuse (McAdam, 1982), white elites increasingly channeled the pace and direction of change (Jenkins & Eckert, 1986), and a white backlash undermined the Democratic party (Reider, 1985). Nevertheless, remarkable changes occurred in political participation (Button, 1989), economic advancement (Farley, 1984), and white prejudice (Schuman, Steeh, & Bobo, 1985) when measured against conditions prior to the movement.

The civil rights era in the United States was perhaps as important internationally as the American Revolution in shaping the meaning of equality, and issues surrounding civil rights for ethnic and racial minorities have become increasingly internationalized. Significant non-European minority populations emerged in Western European countries after World War II as a result of immigration and comparatively high minority fertility rates (Organization for Economic Cooperation and Development, 1988), and in many of these countries civil rights issues became major policy concerns (see Brubaker, 1989; Hammer, 1990; Layton-Henry, 1990). The single most extensive effort to address the civil rights of minorities in these countries was carried out in France between 1981 and 1990 following the election of a Socialist government.

The rise and fall of the Mitterrand reforms provides a possible case to compare with the American experience between 1954 and 1968. Between 1981 and 1986 the Mitterrand government initiated a series of laws to increase the political, economic, and social equality of foreigners, especially North Africans (Algerians, Moroccans, and Tunisians), the largest immigrant group (Safran, 1985, 1988). Liberalization of immigration laws allowed wives and children to join husbands and fathers, accelerating the development of ethnic communities (de Lay, 1983). During these reform years, mobilization in the form of collective protest and the establishment of formal ethnic organizations increased among North Africans and other ethnic minorities (de Wenden, 1988). However, a strong backlash in 1986 nearly forced the Socialists from power. By 1990, the Socialists had weathered the storm, but the racist National Front had gained a salient position in French politics (Messina, 1990; Schain, 1987).

If nothing else, this two-case comparison forces precise definition of the empirical category under study. The parallels between the two cases indicate that civil rights eras comprise complex relations among ethnic minorities, the dominant group, and the state, and they lead to the expansion and then contraction (or at least stabilization) of social, economic, and political equality for minorities within the framework of citizenship. They begin with changes in economic, social, and political institutions; in mid-course there is struggle among the minority, various groups within the dominant society, and the state; and they culminate with significant reforms, but also backlash.

Specifying Differences and Elaborating Ideal Types

The most substantively important difference in outcome of the two civil rights eras is their different degree of success in reducing inequality. By definition, civil rights eras produce some decrease in inequality, so one outcome is the relative gain as indicated by increased rights, resources, or some combination of the two. Similarly, civil rights eras end prior to achieving full equality for the minority—they are not social revolutions. Thus a companion outcome to consider is the nature of the dominant group backlash with respect to its strength, rapidity, and ultimately its ability to turn back reforms or to block further ones. To explain these differences in outcome, an investigator might consider differences between the two cases in changes in the underlying economic, demographic, and political contexts of race relations; relative strength of grass-roots mobilization of ethnic minorities; nature and strength of dominant group oppressors and dominant group allies; electoral alignments; and degree of state activism. One set of causes concerns structural conditions and the degree to which they have altered the minority's position in the society. The other set is relational and concerns links among ethnic movements and various components of the dominant group (oppressors, allies, the state, and so on).

Two-case comparisons can be used to elaborate contrasting ideal types when they emphasize differences between cases and argue that contrasting sets of conditions lead to contrasting outcomes. The comparison of civil rights in the United States (1954-1968) and France (1981-1990) can be used to elaborate contrasting types. The American case might be labeled an instance of "mobilized rights" because Black activism spurred the state to begin dismantling what was essentially a caste system. Conversely, one might label the French case an instance of "etatist rights." The French state implemented reforms to assimilate a population of immigrants, with little active participation on their part, at least initially. The major finding of this two-case comparison would be the elaboration of "bottom-up" versus "top-down" civil rights eras.

Elaborating contrasting ideal types is a well-recognized goal of the social sciences and contributes to theory building when the differences between the types are fully articulated. For example, the first round of Mitterrand reforms came largely in response to the oppressive policies of the previous government and a long-standing Socialist agenda, rather than to grass-roots mobilization. In addition, between 1981 and 1986 the primary struggle took place between the state and immigrant populations (a dyadic relationship), in contrast to the triadic relationship among Blacks, white oppressors, and the state in the United States. In the French case, gains primarily took the form of rights only, whereas in the American case gains took the form of rights and then resources. The backlash in France was comparatively swift but did not undo the reforms, whereas in the United States the backlash took longer to develop and many believe that it eroded Black gains. Based on these differences, we might want to argue that bottom-up civil rights eras produce stronger gains and backlashes, and those that work from the top down produce weaker gains and backlashes, and thus recast the contrasting ideal types as a causal argument.

Linking Ideal Types to Broader Perspectives

To further the dialogue of ideas and evidence, ideal types developed from case materials can be linked to broader perspectives and theories. For example, the bottom-up civil rights era suggested by the American case can be linked to the "social movement" perspective on political process and change. It suggests that attributes of civil rights eras, such as the degree of reform and extent of backlash, are primarily shaped by the extent of grass-roots mobilization of the ethnic minority. Conversely, the top-down approach to reform in France can be linked to the "state-centered theory." This perspective argues that the state is critical to the outcomes of civil rights eras because laws, political values, and interest groups remain embedded in state structures long after movements have dissipated. Obviously, these are competing claims about causal relationships, and they can be further elaborated and tested by crossing theories and cases. Specifically, by testing the social movement perspective against the French case and the state-centered perspective against the American case, it is possible both to refine the ideal types and to advance our understanding of the two cases. However, this crossing of cases and theories must be sensitive to differences in context. For example, in France, the national state is the main government actor in these struggles, whereas in the United States the interests of the national state and local states (e.g., Mississippi) often diverge and their actions conflict.

Testing the two perspectives against the two cases is likely to yield important insights into the expansion of citizenship for ethnic minorities in Western Europe and North America. For example, we might conclude that the Black movement in the United States shaped the types of reforms the national state instituted, but it was actually political dynamics produced by reforms in the context of a federalist, two-party political system that shaped the backlash, as recent historical discussions (e.g., Graham, 1990) and ethnographies (e.g., Reider, 1985) suggest. In France we might find that state structures determined the combination of rights and resources, but in so doing generated social movements among North Africans that sparked the backlash. For example, the Mitterrand reforms spurred the founding of mosques by North Africans (Commissariat General du Plan, 1987), which led to resentment among the French in many communities (de Wenden, 1988). Any of these findings would constitute major contributions to generalizations about equality for ethnic minorities in advanced industrial societies.

Conclusion

The analytic challenges for small-N comparative inquiry posed by the contextual and interactive nature of race and ethnic relations are considerable. Rather than forsaking small-N comparison altogether (as suggested, for example, by Lieberson, 1992) or resorting to the single-case study (Bradshaw & Wallace, 1991), we argue that small-N comparative analysis should be seen as a rich arena for the development and elaboration of concepts and ideal types, and for carrying on a rich and constructive dialogue between ideas and evidence.

The effectiveness of comparative study hinges on the development of competing theories, but theory remains a weakness in the literature on race and ethnicity. Certainly there are competing theories on the cultural, demographic, and historical causes of differential economic progress among ethnic groups (Model, 1988). And research on ethnic enclaves is challenging conventional theories of assimilation with an "ethnic resiliency" perspective (Portes & Bach, 1985). But much theoretical debate continues to be about whether or not race matters, such as reactions to the "declining significance of race" thesis (Feagin, 1991; Massey, 1990). And many studies make little or no attempt at generalization. As See and Wilson (1988) conclude, "The field of race relations, in comparison with other fields in sociology, has one of the severest imbalances between descriptive studies and studies grounded in theoretical principles" (p. 223). The undertheorized state of race and ethnic relations, combined with the diversity of ethnopolitical situations, indicates that comparative study is essential to the advancement of the field.

14

In the Archives

JOHN H. STANFIELD II

Archival research is the collection and analysis of personal and institutional documents. For years, scholars interested in race and ethnicity have utilized archival records to make their scholarly claims. Most of the archive-based literature in racial and ethnic studies has been produced by historians investigating forced and voluntary migration. The literatures dealing with the history of slavery and the qualitative European immigrant in America have contributed significantly to archival research in racial and ethnic studies.

This chapter addresses the value of archival materials in historically oriented social scientific studies of race and ethnicity (Stanfield, 1985, 1987). The researcher who uses archival materials must have not only a clear understanding of what archival materials are and where they can be found, but the ability to structure archival research processes and to assess data reliability and validity problems. These latter points are critical, because despite the extent to which historically oriented social scientists in general have utilized archival materials in their research, they have not addressed the structuring of the research process or data reliability and validity problems.

What Are Archival Materials?

When we say that archival materials are personal and institutional records, what do we mean? We mean personal and business correspondence,

273

financial statements, photographs, diaries, manuscript drafts, material artifacts, and other unpublished materials. Published archival records include official proceedings of organizations, vital statistics, and official institutional histories.

Unpublished archival materials can be found in any number of private or public settings. Private settings include households, corporations, and private academic and independent research organizations and associations. Public settings include government agencies and repositories, public libraries, public academic institutions, and independent research universities.

Whatever the setting, archival researchers must acquaint themselves with the legalities of literary heir rights. Even when using materials in a private household, the researcher should develop a contractual agreement to make sure the rights of all involved are protected in terms of access to materials and their utilization. When archives are housed in an institution, usually it is the archivist who supplies the contract on behalf of literary heirs (which may be the institution).

Historically oriented social scientists interested in racial and ethnic issues have gold mines of archival materials to consult in private households as well as in libraries. This is so because poor people, people of color, and immigrant families of European descent do not often cart their records to the local university archives. Also, academic institutions tend to be interested only in the archival records of the famous; thus the artifacts of ordinary people tend not to be sought after. In fairness to institutions, there is also the perennial problem of space, which means strict rules of selectivity must be abided by. Even when archivists are interested in the records of the plain and ordinary, there is only so much room. Thus archives of ordinary people remain in the homes of those people for the most part, in danger of being destroyed by natural disaster or by relatives who do not understand the value of records left behind by deceased loved ones. For the researcher who knows where to look and how to negotiate access rights, consulting the archives of ordinary people can be extraordinarily rewarding.

The Purpose of Archival Work
in the Historical Social Sciences

Archival materials contain data that allow social scientists to develop, test, and revise historically grounded theories of social processes and structures. This is what distinguishes social scientific uses of archival materials from those of historians, who tend to be interested in archival materials for their usefulness in the construction of narratives of past events and circumstances. When it comes to research on ordinary people, social scientists attempt to use archival records to reconstruct the processes of human development and the institutions, communities, and collective behavior of plain folks.

It is important to draw attention to the elite biases in historical writings based on the records of the affluent. Even the history of the less affluent—ordinary people, the plain folks—tends to be written from the archives of the affluent classes. The usual argument is that ordinary people rarely, if ever, keep records or have their perspectives recorded, and therefore all we have to rely upon are the archival remains of the affluent.

This argument was employed by slavery historians for years to justify their use of planter records to reconstruct the behavior and social organizations of slaves. Nowhere, it was claimed, did slaves leave records of their life historical experiences. This argument became a bone of contention in the American history profession when John Blassingame (1972) published *The Slave Community* in the early 1970s, in which he displayed voluminous slave autobiographical literature. It became apparent in the controversy Blassingame's seminal work generated and the new slavery literature it pioneered that certain "idols of the mind" prevented traditional slavery scholars from looking in other places for records that were the artifacts of the oppressed. This speaks to the general tendency in academic research to presume that the ordinary keep no records and therefore there is no need even to look for them. This perspective buys into the presumption that only the records of the affluent exist and survive.

When we survey the communities and institutions of ordinary people, however, it is more than apparent that they do indeed keep archival records. Personal letters, photo albums, diaries, church records, and household bills are only a few examples of archival materials produced by ordinary poor folks as well as by the rich and the powerful. Neighborhood newspapers and other media are also rich sources of information about nonaffluent communities and institutions.

When it comes to using the archival materials of powerful people, elites, there are a host of other problems. First, when studying the powerful, one must be mindful that the urge to distort and withhold information for the sake of image control and positive historical immortality is always a strong possibility. Second, another privilege of the powerful is their control of access. It is no coincidence that the heirs of powerful people more often than not contract with sympathetic researchers or family members to write *authorized* biographies. The legal knowledge and resources of heirs of powerful persons can result in archival access problems for researchers that can last years and decades. Third, even when access is relatively easy, those doing research on the rich and famous and otherwise powerful certainly risk legal suits or public ridicule if they happen to offer historical interpretations not in keeping with those of the subjects' heirs or with public taste.

Whether one prefers to study the powerful or the powerless, archival research can be immensely rewarding. Success in such research is a matter of developing the skills for knowing where to look for materials and how to utilize what one finds to make sound, empirically grounded, theoretical arguments. The first skill is related to the logic of inquiry; the second is related to matters of validity and reliability.

Logic of inquiry questions and problems in archival research do not differ very much from those of other methodologies. As in the case of survey research, experimental designs, and ethnographic investigations, archival research involves the construction of a research problem, the need for access, the effort to establish rapport, data sampling, and data analysis. For the archival researcher, the construction of the research problem involves identifying an interesting question for investigation and reviewing the pertinent literature. The pertinent literature comprises any historical and biographical studies related to the persons and/or social organizations on which the archival research will center. The tricky aspect of reviewing and mastering such literature is that the researcher must remember that historical and biographical interpretations are value-laden human activities. For instance, the archival data that form the basis of the traditional literature on the history of slavery are very much products of the assumptions of scholars about the inability of slaves to keep records or to have their experiences put down in writing by others. For decades, historians began their research on slavery by presuming that whatever they would find in the archives, it would be in planter records or in elite public or political institutions.

It is important for scholars to develop the paradoxical knack of mastering what has been written about a particular person, issue, event, or social organization while keeping an open mind. Otherwise, it is easy to stroll into an archive and look only for materials that conform with the norms of a discipline. What this means is that the researcher heading to the archive must remember that no matter how many others have published accounts out of the repository, there is always room for reinterpretation. For instance, when one has the occasion to go to Tuskegee University and to the Library of Congress, one is struck by noticeable gaps between what Booker T. Washington scholars have preferred to write about the man and what is actually there in his papers. While most scholars have preferred to place emphasis on Washington as a race leader, his papers certainly reveal a more complex, broader intellectual and political leader. The Washington papers as they lay in their archives also are gold mines for understanding how much more intricate and fluid racial caste issues were in the formation of segregated educational institutions and in the political economy of the South. Further, the papers reveal not only how Washington came to create and maintain political control in Afro-American affairs, but also the extent to which whites were beholden to him. Finally, it is more than apparent that Washington was not, as some of his contemporary historical interpreters claimed, a semiliterate leader dependent upon ghostwriters to do his thinking for him. Indeed, several of his summers were spent at Harvard.

Particularly when it comes to a powerful figure like Washington, who has been written about extensively, it is easy for the novice researcher or those with more experience to assume the final word has been said on the man, so they move on to another research topic. But, especially when archival materials are plentiful regarding the life and activities of an individual or a social organization, it pays to go and take a look.

The researcher should read and master what has been said about a research topic for two reasons. First, this activity helps the researcher to get ideas about where to start and what questions to raise. Second, good background work can help the researcher to gain respectable access to an archive. Archivists and potential subjects' next of kin are most impressed by researchers who have done their homework. It is appropriate for the researcher to send a letter to the archivist or to the literary heir, explaining in broad strokes what the research project is about and the initial work he or she has done. The researcher should follow this letter with a phone call to ask for an appointment to visit the archive site to consult materials.

If the researcher wishes to consult archives that are in private hands, it is important that he or she negotiate a contract of agreement regarding the rights of both parties. This point cannot be emphasized enough. I learned this the hard way, when several years ago the senile widow of a prominent Afro-American literary figure promised me verbally that I could have free, unchecked access to her husband's unprocessed papers, which were stored in her garage. After spending three days in stifling Florida heat going through mounds of papers and giving the widow park-bench advice about protecting her husband's archival materials, I managed to pack up a big suitcase full of documents. Since I thought we were on such good terms, I told the woman that I would take the papers back home to New Haven, look them over, and return them to her as soon as possible. I was not home for more than a day or so when she called me, claiming she did not mean for me to take the papers, and proceeding to mention advice she was getting from a friend. I did not hesitate to send the papers back to her quickly. In this case I not only wasted valuable time but ended up not being able to use the materials I collected to make some important points in an essay I was working on (which I subsequently published).

The researcher should develop rapport not only with the keeper of the records, but also with the materials themselves. If there is a register of the papers, the researcher should spend as much time as possible going through it and looking at sample files to get a general feel for the materials. If there is no register, the researcher should still do a random reading of boxes and files to get a general sense of what he or she may be in for. Also, it may be helpful to find out what other related collections a repository or household may have.

The major intellectual reason for becoming familiar with materials is that this step should help the researcher to determine how the archive may be helpful in contributing to theory building and testing. When a personal collection has abundant correspondence files, including both incoming and outgoing correspondence, it is probably a rich source for reconstructing social networks and their evolution and functions over time. When only the outgoing correspondence is present, the archive really is not an adequate data source for understanding how a particular person constructed and transformed networks. This is the basic problem with the James Weldon Johnson Papers at Yale and the E. Franklin Frazier Papers at Howard University (Stanfield, 1985). The incompleteness of personal correspondence files in the archives of these two eminent Afro-American intellectuals, and the scarcity of their correspondence in other collections, makes it very difficult for the researcher to utilize these archival materials in reconstructing their personal social networks.

The same can be said about the Charles S. Johnson Papers housed at Fisk University. Johnson, by reputation, was a man who kept things close to the vest. That is reflected in the scarcity of complete sets of correspondence in his extensive archive. One has to look through the archives of the numerous organizations in which he was involved to get even a faint glimpse of Johnson. Even when one finds outgoing correspondence in the Johnson papers or incoming Johnson correspondence in other archives, it is more than apparent Johnson always considered himself to be on stage and thus rarely let down his public guard. This is what made the *Bitter Canaan* (Johnson, 1987) project so fascinating. It involved peeling through layers of the public Johnson to find out why the private Johnson would write a work with such uncharacteristic passion. This involved consulting archives in private hands and in declassified government repository archival collections.

Although it is not prudent to enter into an archival research setting with preconceived ideas, the researcher should have in hand a metaphoric knife with which to cut into the materials in a systematic way—that is, a strategy for collecting and analyzing archival data drawn from one of several other kinds of methodologics. Survey questionnaire, experimental design, ethnography, oral history, ideal-type classification, and phenomenology are major methodological strategies that can be applied to archival research. Ethnography is applicable to reconstructing institutions and communities through the researcher's taking on the role of an anthropologist, observing some faraway village. It is also akin to the participant observation strategies that Erving Goffman employed in his total institution study. When I did my research on race philanthropists, for example, I imagined myself to be in their shoes as I reconstructed their steps through archival materials. And I find myself doing the same thing in my present work on late nineteenth-century British and American tropical medical experts assisting in the Western colonization of African subregions.

Validity and Reliability Issues

In this essay, *validity* refers to the adequacy of collected data for making theoretical statements that are isomorphic with empirical realities. When data analysis is *reliable,* this means it can be replicated under similar empirical conditions. Each metaphoric knife used in archival research has its own process problems and dilemmas related to data validity and reliability. In the case of ethnography, the researcher must be mindful of the ways in which a social setting potentially limits what and who he or she sees. Also, there is the danger of the researcher's going native or becoming overly biased toward or against the persons or roles he or she is investigating. Unlike dealing with real, live people, however, doing ethnographic work in the archives gives the researcher more time and space to sit back and reflect on what he or she is or is not doing, and to make appropriate adjustments.

There are validity and reliability problems that cut across the various metaphoric approaches to archival research. Validity problems come in two categories: internal and external.

Internal Validity

Internal validity problems relate to dilemmas that researchers experience in the process of collecting data that raise quality-control questions. Some of these problems are discussed below.

The single case dilemma. This problem occurs when there is only one personal letter or one entry in a diary that sheds significant light on an issue but cannot be confirmed with other archival materials or in external published sources. I remember once running across a letter from a correspondent in the archives of a prominent Afro-American intellectual that made me suspect an extramarital affair was in the works. As I could find no more evidence of this being the case, I left the issue alone rather than "shoot from the hip" and raise speculations.

The historical fame dilemma. There is sometimes a point at which persons or institutional decision makers become aware of their historical fame and begin to alter their records or to become more guarded in what they say in correspondence and in institutional record keeping. Usually, from that life historical point onward, the researcher should interpret and use archival records with much informed skepticism.

The researcher can usually tell when a person has become aware of his or her eventual historical fame and has attempted to control future public historical interpretations, because phrases such as "I will tell you the juicy parts when I see you" and "I would rather not put this in writing" begin to appear in correspondence. The person's correspondence becomes overly polite and civil. It begins to read as if the person lives a saintly life or is a being without deep if not serious personal opinion.

E. Franklin Frazier's papers are most adequate for data analysis prior to the early 1930s. After Frazier published his University of Chicago dissertation, *The Negro Family in Chicago,* in 1932, Frazier's professional status soared, a fact reflected in a decline in the candidness and quantity of his outgoing correspondence after that year.

Destroyed and forged documents. Perhaps the most frustrating data validity problem in archival research results from the destruction and forgery of documents. It is impossible to know how much correspondence and other records are destroyed in the course of a person's or an institution's life by accident, as a matter of routine practice, on purpose, or by protective or self-interested heirs. Charles S. Johnson of Fisk, for instance, was one who intentionally covered his tracks well. It is more than likely that Johnson routinely destroyed correspondence that was too revealing of his activities or inner thoughts. Document forgery by private persons, institutional decision makers, and heirs is an equally perplexing issue to untangle.

Life-cycle misplacement. This problem involves the potential for researchers to stretch data relevant to one life-cycle phase of an individual or institution to apply to one or more other life-cycle phases. For instance, just because Frazier's materials reveal he was a radical during the 1910s and 1920s does not mean he maintained the same degree of leftist thinking throughout the rest of his life. Even though the Johnson of the 1930s and 1940s was known for his congenial public presentation of self, it does not mean he was like that as a younger man. I recall a fascinating letter Johnson's recent bride wrote to him in the early 1920s while he was on the road, expressing disappointment in the gentleman she married for having torn a door off its hinges in a fit of anger. The same can be said about Booker T. Washington, William E. B. Du Bois, and other Afro-American intellectuals who tend to have their entire life histories interpreted on the basis of data drawn overwhelmingly from one or two life-cycle phases.

External Validity

External validity refers to the extent to which collected data can be confirmed with other data sources. Are there other archival collections housing materials that confirm what the researcher has found in a particular repository or attic? Are there secondary histories and other publications that indicate the researcher is on the right track? Are there other archives and secondary sources that shed light on gaps in the archive the researcher is consulting?

Of course, the basic external validity dilemma concerns the reliability of published sources and other archives. This is particularly the case when it comes to research on Afro-Americans and other people of color. Researchers beginning archival work are often surprised to find how much has been left out of or distorted in the published historical record. The cultural biases that influence interpretations about people of color in the press and in scholarship are legendary.

For example, take the study of pre-World War II race philanthropy. If one were to go by the official literature, one would think pre-World War II philanthropists through the years had been very progressive movers and shakers in the area of race relations. The autobiographies of philanthropists and the histories of their foundations promote the image of paternal benevolence in racial matters. But when one digs into the archives, a different impression emerges. It is more than apparent that even the most progressive pre-World War II philanthropists had social and political control motives for supporting race reform efforts. Thus using the published literature on race philanthropy to test external validity concerns is quite problematic.

On the other hand, triangulating archives in the historical study of race philanthropy is an effective way of sorting out external validity problems. This is because the more angles one has on a race philanthropy issue, the richer the data base to draw upon for doing analyses.

Reliability problems revolve around questions concerning the logical coherence of the available archival data for replication purposes. Archival materials must contain data that offer consistent if not systematic information. Inconsistencies in examined materials about age, educational background, birthplace, and so on must be resolved if accurate historical interpretation work is to be done. This is especially the case if a researcher is conducting cohort analysis, which requires pinpointing demographic characteristics as much as possible.

A most interesting internal reliability problem in race and ethnic studies is that of social identity. Although researchers for the most part are socialized to view socially defined racial populations in group identity terms, in reality racial and ethnic identity is much more complicated than the usual stereotypical categories would indicate. What really complicates things is that it is not unusual for people of color to change their ethnic identities to fit certain situations during the course of their lives. Archival materials, particularly personal correspondence and diaries, are valuable sources for reconstructing subjective shifts in the personal invention of racial and ethnic identities. But, unless the person under study has a reputation for having an "identity problem," there is a tendency for researchers to ignore "inconsistencies" in what the person calls him- or herself and to proceed to categorize the person in group terms. This certainly produces a subtle distortion of reality when the findings of a published researcher are replicated with no awareness of the fact that the person studied was much more complicated than a simple identification as Afro-American would make him or her seem. Such distorted analysis reproduces the myth of homogeneity in racial and ethnic identity formation that is both stagnant and singular rather than processual and plural (polyethnic identity).

Conclusion

Whether we are studying elites or ordinary people, archival research can be a valuable methodology. Perhaps the major value of archival research is that it allows the investigator to gather primary documents for possible reinterpretation of traditional historical assumptions about Afro-Americans and other people of color as well as about race and ethnic relations as historical processes embedded in the evolution of social organizations.

In the social sciences, the major purpose of archival research should be to develop historically grounded theories of social organizations and social stratification. This is in keeping with the view that history and social science are two sides of the same coin: process and structure. With this observation in mind, archival research offers a special challenge to the race and ethnic relations field, which tends to be both ahistorical and atheoretical.

References

Abrams, P. (1982). *Historical sociology*. Ithaca, NY: Cornell University Press.

Adair, J. (1968). *The history of the American Indians*. New York: Johnson Reprint.

Adams v. Wainwright, 709 F.2d 1443 (1988).

Adler, A. (1964). *Social interest: A challenge to mankind*. New York: Capricorn.

Agar, M. H. (1986). *Speaking of ethnography*. Beverly Hills, CA: Sage.

Alamprese, J. A., & Erlanger, W. J. (1988). *No gift wasted: Effective strategies for educating highly able, disadvantaged students in mathematics and science: Vol. 1. Findings*. Washington, DC: Cosmos.

Alamprese, J. A., Erlanger, W. J., & Brigham, N. (1989). *No gift wasted: Effective strategies for educating highly able, disadvantaged students in mathematics and science: Vol. 2. Case studies*. Washington, DC: Cosmos.

Alba, R. D. (1990). *Ethnic identity: The transformation of white America*. New Haven, CT: Yale University Press.

Alexander, J. C. (1983). *Theoretical logic in sociology* (4 vols.). Berkeley: University of California Press.

Alexander, J. C., & Colomy, P. (1985). Social differentiation and collective behavior. *Sociological Theory, 3*, 11-23.

Alvirez, D. (1973). The effects of formal church affiliation and religiosity on the fertility patterns of Mexican-American Catholics. *Demography, 10*, 19-36.

Amenta, E. (1991). Making the most of a case study: Theories of the welfare state and the American experience. *International Journal of Comparative Sociology, 32*, 172-194.

Andersen, M. L. (1988). Moving our minds: Studying women of color and re-constructing sociology. *Teaching Sociology, 15*, 123-132.

Anderson, B. (1986, August). *A report of the Study Group on Affirmative Action to the Committee on Education and Labor, U.S. House of Representatives*. Washington, DC: Government Printing Office.

Andreski, S. (1965). *The uses of comparative sociology.* Berkeley: University of California Press.

Asante, M. K. (1988). *Afrocentricity.* Trenton, NJ: Africa World.

Asante, M. K. (1987). *The Afrocentric idea.* Philadelphia: Temple University Press.

Ashley Montagu, M. F. (1952). *Man's most dangerous myth: The fallacy of race* (3rd ed., rev.). New York: Harper.

Atkinson, J. M., & Drew, P. (1979). *Order in court. The organization of verbal interaction in judicial settings.* London: Methuen.

Atkinson, J. M., & Heritage, J. (Eds.). (1984). *Structures of social action.* Cambridge: Cambridge University Press.

Baca Zinn, M. (1979). Field research in minority communities: Ethical, methodological and political observations by an insider. *Social Problems, 27,* 209-219.

Bailey, K. (1990). *Social entropy theory.* Albany: State University of New York Press.

Bailey, S. L. (1990). Cross-cultural comparison and the writing of migration history: Some thoughts on how to study Italians in the New World. In V. Yans-McLaughlin (Ed.), *Immigration reconsidered: History, sociology, and politics* (pp. 241-253). New York. Oxford University Press.

Baird, W. D. (1974). *The Chickasaw people.* Phoenix, AZ: Indian Tribal Series.

Baird, W. D. (1979). Peter Pitchlynn and the reconstruction of the Choctaw Republic. In H. G. Jordan & T. M. Holm (Eds.), *Indian leaders: Oklahoma's first statesmen* (pp. 12-28). Oklahoma City: Oklahoma Historical Society.

Baldwin, A. Y. (1984). *The Baldwin identification matrix 2 for the identification of the gifted and talented: A handbook for its use.* New York: Trillium.

Baldwin, J. A. (1991). African psychology and Black personality testing. In A. G. Hilliard (Ed.), *Testing African American students* (pp. 56-66). Morristown, NJ: Aaron.

Barden, G. B. (1953). The Gilberts and the Chickasaw nation. *Tennessee Historical Quarterly, 17,* 222-249, 318-335.

Baritz, L. (1988). *The good life: The meaning of success for the American middle class.* New York: Alfred A. Knopf.

Barth, F. (Ed.). (1969). *Ethnic groups and boundaries: The social organization of culture difference.* Boston: Little, Brown.

Baska, L. (1986). Alternatives to traditional testing: The use of the Raven Advanced Progressive Matrices for the selection of magnet junior high school students. *Roeper Review, 8*(3), 181-184.

Bean, F. D., & Frisbee, W. P. (Eds.). (1978). *The demography of racial and ethnic groups.* New York: Academic Press.

Bean, F. D., & Marcum, J. P. (1978). Differential fertility and the minority group status hypothesis: An assessment and review. In F. D. Bean & W. P. Frisbee (Eds.), *The demography of racial and ethnic groups* (pp. 189-212). New York: Academic Press.

Bean, F. D., et al. (1977). Familism and marital satisfaction among Mexican Americans: The effects of family size, wife's labor force participation, and conjugal power. *Journal of Marriage and the Family, 39,* 759-767.

Becker, G. S. (1971). *The economics of discrimination* (2nd ed.). Chicago: University of Chicago Press.

Becker, H. A. (1958). Problems of inference and proof in participant observation. *American Sociological Review, 23,* 652-660.

Bellisfield, G. (1973). White attitudes toward racial integration and the urban riots of the 1960s. *Public Opinion Quarterly, 36,* 579-584.

Belton, R. (1981). Burdens of pleading and proof of discrimination cases: Toward a theory of procedural justice. *Vanderbilt Law Review, 34*, 1205-1287.

Bendix, R. (1977). *Nation-building and citizenship.* Berkeley: University of California Press.

Benney, M., & Hughes, E. C. (1970). Of sociology and the interview. In N. K. Denzin (Ed.), *Sociological methods: A source book.* London: Butterworth.

Berger, C. R. (1985). Social power and interpersonal communication. In M. L. Knapp & G. R. Miller (Eds.), *Handbook of interpersonal communication* (pp. 439-496). Beverly Hills, CA: Sage.

Berger, P. L., & Luckmann, T. (1967). *The social construction of reality: A treatise in the sociology of knowledge.* Garden City, NY: Doubleday.

Berreman, G. D. (1972). Race, caste, and other invidious distinctions in social stratification. *Race, 13*(4), 385-414.

Berry, B., & Kasarda, J. (1977). *Contemporary urban sociology.* New York: Macmillan.

Bidney, D. (1964). *Theoretical anthropology.* New York: Columbia University Press.

Binet, A. (1909). *Les idees modernes sur les enfants.* Paris: Flammarion.

Binet, A., & Simon, T. (1912). *A method of measuring the development of intelligence of young children.* Lincoln, IL: Courier.

Binet, A., & Simon, T. (1916). *The development of intelligence in children: The Binet-Simon scale* (E. S. Kite, Trans.). Baltimore: Williams & Wilkins.

Blackwell, J. E., & Janowitz, M. (Eds.). (1974). *Black sociologists: Historical and contemporary perspectives.* Chicago: University of Chicago Press.

Blassingame, J. W. (1972). *The slave community: Plantation life in the antebellum South.* New York: Oxford University Press.

Blauner, R., & Wellman, D. (1973). Toward the decolonization of social research. In J. Ladner (Ed.), *The death of white sociology.* New York: Vintage.

Blood, R. O., & Wolfe, D. (1960). *Husbands and wives.* Glencoe, IL: Free Press.

Blum, D. E. (1990, October 10). Inquiry prompts professor to sue college and panel. *Chronicle of Higher Education,* p. 17.

Boas, F. (1920). The method of ethnology. *American Anthropologist, 22,* 311-321.

Boden, D., & Zimmerman, D. H. (Eds.). (1991). *Talk and social structure: Studies in ethnomethodology and conversation analysis.* Cambridge: Polity.

Bonacich, E. (1972). A theory of ethnic antagonism: The split labor market. *American Sociological Review, 37,* 547-559.

Bonacich, E., & Modell, J. (1980). *The economic basis of ethnic solidarity: Small business in the Japanese-American community.* Berkeley: University of California Press.

Bond, H. M. (1924). Intelligence test and propaganda. *Crisis, 28,* 61-64.

Booth, C. (1902). *Life and labour of the people in London.* London: Macmillan.

Boyd, C., & Hyman, H. (1975). Strategies of inquiry. In F. I. Greenstein & N. W. Rolsby (Eds.), *Handbook of political science* (pp. 265-350). Reading, MA: Addison-Wesley.

Boykin, A. W. (1983). The academic performance of Afro-American children. In J. Spence (Ed.), *Achievement and achievement motives.* San Francisco: W. H. Freeman.

Bradshaw, Y., & Wallace, M. (1991). Informing generality and explaining uniqueness: The place of case studies in comparative research. *International Journal of Comparative Sociology, 32,* 154-171.

Brilmayer, L. (1982). Comment. *Journal of the American Statistical Association, 77,* 789-790.

Broca, P. (1861). Sur le volume et forme du cerveau suivant les individus et suivant les races. *Bulletin Societe d'Anthropologique Paris, 2,* 139-207, 301-321, 441-446.

Brown, G., & Yule, G. (1983). *Discourse analysis.* London: Cambridge University Press.

Brown, P., & Levinson, S. C. (1987). *Politeness: Some universals in language use.* Cambridge: Cambridge University Press.

Brubaker, W. R. (Ed.). (1989). *Immigration and the politics of citizenship in Europe and North America.* Lanham, MD: University Press of America.

Burrell, G., & Morgan, G. (1979). *Sociological paradigms and organizational analysis.* London: Heinemann.

Burt, C. (1966). The genetic determination of differences in intelligence: A study of mono-zygotic twins reared together and apart. *British Journal of Psychology, 57,* 137-153.

Button, J. W. (1989). *Blacks and social change: Impact of the civil rights movement in southern communities.* Princeton, NJ: Princeton University Press.

Cahalan, D. (1960). Measuring newspaper readership by telephone: Two comparisons with face-to-face interviews. *Journal of Advertising Research, 1,* 1-6.

Campbell, A., & Schuman, H. (1968). *Racial attitudes in fifteen American cities: A report prepared for the National Advisory Commission on Civil Disorders.* Ann Arbor, MI. Institute for Social Research.

Campbell, T. (1984). Regression analysis in Title VII cases: Minimum standards, comparable worth, and other issues where law and statistics meet. *Stanford Law Review, 36,* 1299-1324.

Cannon, L. W., Higginbotham, E., & Leung, M. A. (1988). Race and class bias in qualitative research on women. *Gender & Society, 2,* 449-662.

Caplow, T., Bahr, H., Chadwick, B., Hill, R., & Williamson, M. H. (1982). *Middletown families.* Minneapolis: University of Minnesota Press.

Carbó, T. (1992). Towards an interpretation of interruptions in Mexican parliamentary discourse (1920-60). *Discourse and Society, 3,* 25-26.

Champagne, D. (1989). *American Indian societies: Strategies and conditions of political and cultural survival.* Cambridge, MA: Cultural Survival.

Champagne, D. (1990). Culture, differentiation and environment: Social change in Tlingit society. In J. C. Alexander & P. Colomy (Eds.), *Differentiation theory and social change: Comparative and historical perspectives* (pp. 52-87). New York: Columbia University Press.

Champagne, D. (1992). *Social order and political change: The constitutional governments among the Cherokee, the Choctaw, the Chickasaw and the Creek.* Stanford, CA: Stanford University Press.

Chase, A. (1980). *The legacy of Malthus: The social cost of the new scientific racism.* Chicago: University of Illinois Press.

Chilton, P. (Ed.). (1985). *Language and the nuclear arms debate: Nukespeak today.* London: Pinter.

Chomsky, N. (1957). *Syntactic structure.* The Hague: Mouton.

City of Richmond v. Croson, 488 U.S. 469 (1989).

CKN. (1977). [Chickasaw National Records, microfilm rolls 1, 4, 7, 8, 9.] Oklahoma City: Oklahoma Historical Society.

Clark, M. (1969). Mexican American aged in San Francisco: A case description. *Gerontologist, 9,* 90-95.

Cole, M., & Scribner, S. (1973). Cognitive consequences of formal and informal education. *Science Education, 182,* 553-559.

Collins, P. H. (1986). Learning from the outsider within: The sociological significance of Black feminist thought. *Social Problems, 33,* 14-32.

Collins, R. (1988). *Theoretical sociology.* San Diego, CA: Harcourt Brace Jovanovich.

Colombotos, J. (1969). Personal versus telephone interviews: Effects on responses. *Public Health Reports, 84,* 773-782.

Colomy, P. (1985). Uneven structural differentiation: Toward a comparative approach. In J. C. Alexander (Ed.), *Neofunctionalism* (pp. 131-156). Beverly Hills, CA: Sage.

Colomy, P. (1990a). Strategic groups and political differentiation in the antebellum United States. In J. C. Alexander & P. Colomy (Eds.), *Differentiation theory and social change: Comparative and historical perspectives* (pp. 222-264). New York: Columbia University Press.

Colomy, P. (1990b). Uneven differentiation and incomplete institutionalization: Political change and continuity in the early American nation. In J. C. Alexander & P. Colomy (Ed.), *Differentiation theory and social change: Comparative and historical perspectives* (pp. 119-162). New York: Columbia University Press.

Colvard, R. (1967). Interaction and identification in reporting field research: A critical reconsideration of protective procedures. In G. Sjoberg (Ed.), *Ethics, politics, and social research.* Cambridge, MA: Schenkman.

Commissariat General du Plan. (1987). *Immigrations: Le devoir d'insertion.* Paris: Documentation Française.

Conviction records in barriers to employment: Racial discrimination under Title VII—Green v. Missouri Pacific Railroad, 523 F.2nd 1290 (8th Circ. 1975). (1976). *Washington University Law Quarterly, 1976,* 122-134.

Conway, D. A., & Roberts, H. V. (1983). Reverse regression, fairness, and employment discrimination. *Journal of Business and Economic Statistics, 1,* 75-85.

Cornforth, M. (1947). *Science and idealism.* New York: International.

Cotton, J. (1988). On the decomposition of wage differentials. *Review of Economics and Statistics, 70,* 236-243.

Court, J. H., & Raven, J. (1982). *Research and references: 1982 update.* London: H. K. Lewis.

Crimshaw, A. (1973). Comparative sociology: In what ways different from other sociologies? In M. Armer & A. Crimshaw (Eds.), *Comparative social research: Methodological problems and strategies* (pp. 3-48). New York: John Wiley.

Cronbach, L. J. (1984). *Essentials of psychological testing.* New York: Harper & Row.

Cuellar, J. (1978). El senior citizens club: The older Mexican-American in the voluntary association. In B. Myerhoff & A. Simic (Eds.), *Life's career: Aging* (pp. 207-230). Beverly Hills, CA: Sage.

Dabney, M. (1983, July). *Perspectives and directions in assessment of the Black child.* Paper presented at the meeting of the Council for Exceptional Children, Atlanta, GA.

Dabney, M. (1988). An alternative model for identification of potentially gifted students: A case study. In R. L. Jones (Ed.), *Psychoeducational assessment of minority group children: A casebook* (pp. 273-294). Berkeley, CA: Cobb & Henry.

Davis, A., & Dollard, J. (1940). *Children of bondage: The personality development of Negro youth in the urban South.* Washington, DC: American Council on Education.

Davis, A., Gardner, B., & Gardner, M. (1941). *Deep South: A social anthropological study of caste and class.* Chicago: University of Chicago Press.

Davis, D. B. (1975). *The problem of slavery in the age of revolution, 1770-1823.* Ithaca, NY: Cornell University Press.

Davis, G. A., & Rimm, S. (1983). Group inventory for finding interests (GIFFI) I and II: Instruments for identifying creative potential in the junior and senior high school. *Journal of Creative Behavior, 16,* 50-57.

Davis, J. A., & Smith, T. W. (1983). *General Social Surveys 1972-1983: Cumulative code book.* Chicago: National Opinion Research Center.

Debo, A. (1934). *The rise and fall of the Choctaw Republic.* Norman: University of Oklahoma Press.

de Lay, M. (1983). French immigration policy since May 1981. *International Migration Review, 17,* 196-212.

Dennis, R. (1988). The use of participant observation in race relations research. In C. B. Marrett & C. Leggon (Eds.), *Research in race and ethnic relations* (Vol. 5). Greenwich, CT: JAI.

Dennis, R. (1991). Dual marginality and discontent among Black Middletown youth. In R. Dennis (Ed.), *Research in race and ethnic relations* (Vol. 6, pp. 3-25). Greenwich, CT: JAI.

Denzin, N. (1970). *The research act: A theoretical introduction to sociological methods.* Chicago: Aldine.

Deutscher, I. (1969). Looking backward: Case studies on the progress of methodology in sociological research. *American Sociological Review, 4,* 35-41.

de Wenden, C. W. (1988). *Les immigres et la politique: Cent cinquante ans d'evolution.* Paris: Presses de la Fondation Nationale des Sciences Politiques.

Dixon, V. J. (1976). World views and research methodology. In L. M. King, V. J. Dixon, & W. W. Nobles (Eds.), *African philosophy: Assumptions and paradigms for research on Black persons* (pp. 51-102). Los Angeles: Fanon Center.

Dogan, M., & Pelassy, D. (1984). *How to compare nations: Strategies in comparative politics.* Chatham, NJ: Chatham House.

Dollard, J. (1937). *Caste and class in a southern town.* New Haven, CT: Yale University Press.

Douglass, F. (1962). *The life and times of Frederick Douglass.* New York: Collier.

Dovidio, J. F., & Gaertner, S. L. (Eds.). (1986). *Prejudice, discrimination and racism.* New York: Academic Press.

Downing, J. D. H. (1980). *The media machine.* London: Pluto.

Drake, S. C., & Cayton, H. (1945). *Black metropolis: A study of Negro life in a northern city.* New York: Harcourt, Brace.

Draper, N. R., & Guttman, I. (1969). The value of prior information. In N. L. Johnson & H. Smith, Jr. (Eds.), *New developments in survey sampling* (pp. 305-325). New York: Wiley-Interscience.

Drew, C. (1973). Criterion-referenced and norm-referenced assessment of minority group children. *Journal of School Psychology, 11,* 323-329.

Du Bois, W. E. B. (1899). *The Philadelphia Negro.* Philadelphia: University of Pennsylvania Press.

Du Bois, W. E. B. (1961). *The souls of Black folk.* Greenwich, CT: Fawcett. (Original work published 1903)

Du Bois, W. E. B. (1968). *The autobiography of W. E. B. Du Bois.* New York: International.

Duncan, B., & Duncan, O. D. (1970). Family stability and occupational success. In C. Willie (Ed.), *The family life of Black people* (pp. 156-171). Columbus, OH: Merrill.

Durkheim, E. (1984). *The division of labor in society.* New York: Free Press.

Eaton, J. H. (1830). The progress made in civilizing the Indians for the last years and their present conditions. In *Report from the secretary of war* (21st Congress, 1st Session, vol. 2, p. 110). Washington, DC: Government Printing Office.

Edelman, M. J. (1977). *Political language: Words that succeed and policies that fail.* New York: Academic Press.

Eisenstadt, S. N. (1964a). Institutionalization and social change. *American Sociological Review, 29,* 235-247.

Eisenstadt, S. N. (1964b). Social change, differentiation, and evolution. *American Sociological Review, 29,* 375-386.

Eisenstadt, S. N. (1990). Modes of structural differentiation, elite structure, and cultural visions. In J. C. Alexander & P. Colomy (Ed.), *Differentiation theory and social change: Comparative and historical perspectives* (pp. 19-51). New York: Columbia University Press.

Ellison, R. (1964). *Shadow and act.* New York: Random House.

Ellison, R. (1967, March). A very stern discipline. *Harper's,* pp. 76-95.

Elsasser, N., MacKenzie, K., & Tixier y Virgil, Y. (1989). *Las mujeres: Conversations from a Hispanic community.* Old Westbury, NY: Feminist Press.

Esman, M. J. (1975). Communal conflict in Southeast Asia. In N. Glazer & D. P. Moynihan (Eds.), *Ethnicity: Theory and experience* (pp. 391-419). Cambridge, MA: Harvard University Press.

Essed, P. J. M. (1991). *Understanding everyday racism.* Newbury Park, CA: Sage.

Eubanks v. Louisiana, 356 U.S. 584 (1957).

Farley, R. (1984). *Blacks and whites: Narrowing the gap?* Cambridge, MA: Harvard University Press.

Farley, R., & Allen, W. (1989). *The color line and the quality of life in America.* New York: Oxford University Press.

Farris, B. E., & Glenn, N. (1976). Fatalism and familism among Anglos and Mexican Americans in San Antonio. *Sociology and Social Research, 60,* 393-402.

Feagin, J. R. (1991). The continuing significance of race: Antiblack discrimination in public places. *American Sociological Review, 56,* 101-116.

Feldman, D. (Ed.). (1983). *Developmental conceptions of giftedness.* San Francisco: Jossey-Bass.

Feuerstein, R. (1968). *The learning potential assessment device: A new method for assessing modifiability of the cognitive functioning of socioculturally disadvantaged adolescents.* Unpublished manuscript, Israel Foundation Trustees, Tel Aviv.

Feuerstein, R. (1977). Mediated learning experience: A theoretical basis for cognitive human modifiability during adolescence. In *Research to practice in mental retardation: Proceedings of the 4th Congress of IASMD: Vol. 2. Education and training* (pp. 105-116). Baltimore: University Park Press.

Fiske, S. T., & Taylor, S. E. (1984). *Social cognition.* Reading, MA: Addison-Wesley.

Foreman, G. (Ed.). (n.d.). *Indian-pioneer history collection* (120 vols.). Oklahoma City: Oklahoma Historical Society.

Franklin, V. (1976). Black social scientists and the mental testing movement, 1920-1940. In R. L. Jones (Ed.), *Black psychology* (pp. 201-215). Berkeley, CA: Cobb & Henry.

Frasier, M. (1989). A perspective on identifying Black students for gifted programs. In C. J. Maker & S. W. Schiever (Eds.), *Critical issues in gifted education: Defensible programs for cultural and ethnic minorities* (Vol. 2, pp. 213-255). Austin, TX: ProEd.

Frasier, M. (1990, April). *The equitable identification of gifted and talented children.* Paper presented at the annual meeting of the American Educational Research Association, Boston.

Frazier, E. F. (1932). *The Negro family in Chicago.* Chicago: University of Chicago Press.

Frazier, E. F. (1939). *The Negro family in the United States.* Chicago: University of Chicago Press.

Frazier, E. F. (1949a). *The Negro in the United States.* New York: Macmillan.

Frazier, E. F. (1949b). *Negro youth at the crossways: Their personality development in the middle states.* Washington, DC: American Council on Education.

Frazier, E. F. (1957). *Black bourgeoisie.* Glencoe, IL: Free Press.

Frazier, E. F. (1961). *The souls of Black folk.* Greenwich, CT: Fawcett.

Frazier, E. F. (1964). *Black bourgeoisie*: Public and academic reactions. In A. J. Vidich, J. Bensman, & M. R. Stein (Eds.), *Reflections on community studies.* London: John Wiley.

Frazier, E. F. (1968). *Black bourgeoisie.* New York: Collier. (Original work published 1957)

Freud, S. (1949). *Civilization and its discontents.* London: Hogarth.

Frey, W. (1985). Mover destination selectivity and the changing suburbanization of metropolitan whites and Blacks. *Demography, 22,* 223-244.

Frisbee, W. P., Bean, F. D., & Eberstein, I. (1978). Patterns of marital instability among Mexican Americans, Blacks, and Anglos. In F. D. Bean & W. P. Frisbee (Eds.), *The demography of racial and ethnic groups* (pp. 143-164). New York: Academic Press.

Fowler, R. (1991). *Language in the news: Discourse and ideology in the press.* London: Routledge.

Fowler, R., Hodge, B., Kress, G., & Trew, T. (1979). *Language and control.* London: Routledge & Kegan Paul.

Fuller, R. (1938). *A study of youth needs and services in Middletown.* Washington, DC: American Council on Education.

Galton, F. (1884). *Hereditary genius.* New York: D. Appleton.

Gardner, H. (1983). *Frames of mind.* New York: Basic Books.

Gay, J. (1978). A proposed plan for identifying Black gifted children. *Gifted Child Quarterly, 22,* 353-360.

Geertz, C. (1971). *Islam observed: Religious development in Morocco and Indonesia.* Chicago: University of Chicago Press.

Geertz, C. (1973). *The interpretation of cultures.* New York: Basic Books.

Geis, M. L. (1987). *The language of politics.* New York: Springer.

Gibson, A. (1971). *The Chickasaws.* Norman: University of Oklahoma Press.

Giles, H., & Coupland, N. (1991). *Language: Context and consequences.* Milton Keynes, UK: Open University Press.

Glaser, B. G., & Strauss, A. L. (1967). *Discovery of grounded theory: Strategies for qualitative research.* Chicago: Aldine.

Goddard, H. H. (1912). *Psychology of the normal and subnormal.* New York: Macmillan.

Goddard, H. H. (1919). *Psychology of the normal and abnormal.* New York: Dodd, Mead.

Goffman, E. (1967). *The presentation of self in everyday life.* Harmondsworth, UK: Penguin.

Goffman, E. (1974). *Frame analysis: An essay on the organization of experience.* New York: Harper & Row.

Goldscheider, C., & Uhlenberg, P. R. (1969). Minority group status and fertility. *American Journal of Sociology, 74,* 361-372.

Goodall, H., & Mitchell, J. P. (1976). *A history of Negroes in Muncie.* Muncie, IN: Ball State University Press.

Gordon, E. W. (1985). Social science knowledge production and minority experiences. *Journal of Negro Education, 54,* 117-133.

Gordon, E. W., Miller, F., & Rollock, D. (1990). Coping with communicentric bias in knowledge production in the social sciences. *Educational Researcher, 19*(3), 14-19.

Gossett, T. F. (1963). *Race: The history of an idea in America.* Dallas: Southern University Press.

Gould, S. J. (1977). *Ever since Darwin: Reflections in natural history.* New York: W. W. Norton.

Gould, S. J. (1981). *The mismeasure of man.* New York: W. W. Norton.

Graham, H. D. (1990). *The civil rights era: Origins and development of national policy, 1960-1972.* New York: Oxford University Press.

Green v. Missouri Pacific Railroad, 523 F.2d 1290 (1975).

Greenhouse, L. (1989, June 18). A changed court revises rules on civil rights. *New York Times,* sec. 4, p. 1.

Griggs v. Duke Power Co., 401 U.S. 424 (1971).

Guthrie, R. V. (1976). *Even the rat was white.* New York: Harper & Row.

Gwaltney, J. (1980). *Drylongso: A self-portrait of Black America.* New York: Random House.

Hagan, J., & Bumiller, K. (1983). Making sense of sentencing: A review and critique of sentencing research. In A. Blumstein, J. Cohen, S. E. Martin, & M. H. Tonry (Eds.), *Research on sentencing: The search for reform* (Vol. 2, pp. 1-54). Washington, DC: National Academy Press.

Hamilton, C. V. (1986). Social policy and the welfare of Black Americans: From rights to resources. *Political Science Quarterly, 101,* 239-255.

Hamilton, D. L. (1981). *Cognitive processes in stereotyping and intergroup behavior.* Hillsdale, NJ: Lawrence Erlbaum.

Hammer, T. (1990). *Democracy and the nation-state: Aliens, denizens and citizens in a world of international migration.* Aldershot, UK: Avebury.

Hansen, M. H., Hurwitz, W. R., Marks, E. S., & Mauldin, W. P. (1951). Response errors in surveys. *Journal of the American Statistical Association, 46,* 147-189.

Harbage, A. (1969). *William Shakespeare: The complete works.* Baltimore: Penguin.

Harding, S. (1986). *The science question in feminism.* Ithaca, NY: Cornell University Press.

Harris, J. J., & Ford, D. Y. (1991). Identifying and nurturing the promise of gifted Black American children. *Journal of Negro Education, 60,* 3-18.

Hartmann, P., & Husband, C. (1974). *Racism and the mass media.* London: Davis-Poynter.

Hartsock, N. (1983). The feminist standpoint: Developing the ground for a specifically feminist historical materialism. In S. Harding & M. Hintakka (Eds.), *Discovering reality: Feminist perspectives on epistemology, metaphysics, methodology, and philosophy of science* (pp. 283-310). Dordrecht, Netherlands: D. Reidel.

Haywood, H. C. (1988). Dynamic assessment: The learning potential assessment device. In R. L. Jones (Ed.), *Psychoeducational assessment of minority group children: A casebook* (pp. 39-63). Berkeley, CA: Cobb & Henry.

Hein, J. (1991). *Comparing civil rights eras in the U.S. and France.* Fellowship proposal funded by Centre National de la Recherche Scientifique, Paris.

Hess, I. (1985). *Sampling for social research surveys, 1947-1980*. Ann Arbor, MI: Institute for Social Research.

Hill, R. (1981). The economic status of Black Americans. In J. D. Williams (Ed.), *The state of Black America* (Vol. 5, pp. 1-59). New Brunswick, NJ: Transaction.

Hilliard, A. G., III. (1976). *Alternatives to I.Q. testing: An approach to the identification of "gifted" minority children.* Sacramento: California State Department of Education, Division of Special Education. (ERIC Document Reproduction Service No. ED 147 009)

Hilliard, A. G., III. (1984). I.Q. thinking as the emperor's new clothes: A critique of Jensen's bias in mental testing. In C. R. Reynolds & R. T. Brown (Eds.), *Perspectives in mental testing* (pp. 139-169). New York: Plenum.

Hintze, O. (1975a). Economics and politics in the age of modern capitalism. In F. Cohen (Ed.), *The historical essays of Otto Hintze* (pp. 422-452). New York: Oxford University Press.

Hintze, O. (1975b). Military organization and the organization of the state. In F. Cohen (Ed.), *The historical essays of Otto Hintze* (pp. 178-215). New York: Oxford University Press.

Hirschman, C. (1983). America's melting pot reconsidered. *Annual Review of Sociology, 9,* 397-423.

Hirschman, C., & Wong, M. (1984). Socioeconomic gains of Asian Americans, Blacks and Hispanics: 1960-1976. *American Journal of Sociology, 90,* 584-607.

Hochstim, J. R. (1962). Comparison of three information-gathering strategies in a population study of sociomedical variables. *Proceedings of the American Statistical Association (Social Statistics Section),* pp. 154-159.

Hochstim, J. R. (1967). A critical comparison of three strategies of collecting data from households. *Journal of the American Statistical Association, 72,* 976-989.

Hodge, R., & Kress, G. (1988). *Social semiotics.* London: Polity.

Hogan, D. P., & Kitagawa, E. M. (1985). The impact of social status, family structure, and neighborhood on the fertility of Black adolescents. *American Journal of Sociology, 90,* 825-855.

Hooks, B. (1989). *Talking back: Thinking feminist, thinking Black.* Boston: South End.

Hudson v. Palmer, 468 U.S. 517 (1984).

Hughes, H. S. (1958). *Consciousness and society.* New York: Random House.

Hymes, D. H. (1972). *Reinventing anthropology.* New York: Pantheon.

Inglis, K. M., Groves, R. M., & Heeringa, S. G. (1985, August). Telephone sample designs for the Black household population. *Proceedings of the American Statistical Association (Survey Section).*

Isaac, L., & Kelly, W. R. (1981). Racial insurgency, the state, and welfare expansion: Local and national level evidence from the postwar United States. *American Journal of Sociology, 86,* 1348-1386.

Isaacs, H. R. (1977). *Idols of the tribe: Group identity and political change.* New York: Harper Colophon.

Jackson, J., & Hatchett, S. (1985). Intergenerational research: Methodological considerations. In N. Data, A. L. Greene, & H. W. Reese (Eds.), *Intergenerational relations.* Hillsdale, NJ: Lawrence Erlbaum.

Jenkins, J. C., & Eckert, C. M. (1986). Channeling Black insurgency: Elite patronage and professional social movement organizations in the development of the Black movement. *American Sociological Review, 51,* 812-829.

Jenkins, M. D. (1936). A socio-psychological study of Negro children of superior intelligence. *Journal of Negro Education, 5,* 175-190.

Jenkins, R. (1986). *Racism and recruitment: Managers, organizations and equal opportunity in the labour market.* Cambridge: Cambridge University Press.

Jennings, J. (Ed.). (1947). Nutt's trip to the Chickasaw country. *Journal of Mississippi History, 9,* 34-61.

Jensen, A. R. (1969). How much can we boost IQ and scholastic achievement? *Harvard Educational Review, 33,* 1-123.

Jensen, A. R. (1979). *Bias in mental testing.* New York: Free Press.

Jiobu, R. M. (1988). Ethnic hegemony and the Japanese of California. *American Sociological Review, 53,* 353-367.

Johnson, C. S. (1934). *Shadow of the plantation.* Chicago: University of Chicago Press.

Johnson, C. S. (1941). *Growing up in the Black Belt: Negro youth in the rural South.* Washington, DC: American Council on Education.

Johnson, C. S. (1987). *Bitter Canaan: The story of the Negro republic.* New Brunswick, NJ: Transaction.

Johnson, S. T., Starnes, W. T., Gregory, D., & Blaylock, A. (1985). Program of Assessment, Diagnosis, and Instruction (PADI): Identifying and nurturing potentially gifted and talented minority students. *Journal of Negro Education, 54,* 416-430.

Johnson-Laird, P. N. (1983). *Mental models.* Cambridge: Cambridge University Press.

Jones, R. L. (1979). Protection in evaluation procedures: Criteria and recommendations. In Protection in Evaluation Procedures, *Developing criteria for the evaluation of protection in evaluating procedures provisions* (pp. 15-84). Philadelphia: Research for Better Schools.

Jordon, W. D. (1974). *The white man's burden: Historical origins of racism in the United States.* New York: Oxford University Press.

Jung, C. G. (1933). *Modern man in search of a soul.* New York: Harcourt.

Kamin, L. J. (1974). *The science and politics of I.Q.* Potomac, MD: Lawrence Erlbaum.

Kamin, L. J. (1975). Social and legal consequences of I.Q. tests as classification instruments: Some warnings from our past. *Journal of School Psychology, 13,* 317-323.

Kaplan, A. (1964). *The conduct of inquiry.* San Francisco: Chandler.

Katz, P. A., & Taylor, D. A. (Eds.). (1988). *Eliminating racism: Profiles in controversy.* New York: Plenum.

Kaufman, A. S., & Harrison, P. L. (1986). Intelligence tests and gifted assessment: What are the positives? *Roeper Review, 8*(3), 154-159.

Kaufman, A. S., & Kaufman, N. L. (1983). *Kaufman Assessment Battery for Children (K-ABC).* Circle Pines, MN: American Guidance Service.

Kaye, D. (1982). Statistical evidence of discrimination. *Journal of the American Statistical Association, 77,* 773-783.

Kedar, L. (Ed.). (1987). *Power through discourse.* Norwood, NJ: Ablex.

Kinder, M. (1990). *Going nowhere fast.* Englewood Cliffs, NJ: Prentice Hall.

Kish, L. (1961). Efficient allocation of a multi-purpose sample. *Econometrics, 29,* 363-385.

Kish, L. (1965). *Survey sampling.* New York: John Wiley.

Koo, H., & Janowitz, B. (1983). Interrelationships between fertility and marital dissolution: Results of a simultaneous logit model. *Demography, 20,* 129-145

Kramarae, C., Schulz, M., & O'Barr, W. M. (Eds.). (1984). *Language and power.* Beverly Hills, CA: Sage.

Kroeber, A. L. (1917). The superorganic. *American Anthropologist, 19,* 163-213.

Ladner, J. A. (1971). *Tomorrow's tomorrow.* Garden City, NY: Doubleday.

Ladner, J. A. (Ed.). (1973). *The death of white sociology.* New York: Random House.

Larsen, O. N. (1952). The comparative validity of telephone and face-to-face interviews in the measurement of message diffusion from leaflets. *American Sociological Review, 17,* 471-476.

Layton-Henry, Z. (1990). *The political rights of migrant workers in Europe.* London: Sage.

Lee v. Washington, 390 U.S. 333 (1968).

Lemann, N. (1991). *The promised land: The great Black migration and how it changed America.* New York: Alfred A. Knopf.

Levinson, S. (1983). *Pragmatics.* Cambridge: Cambridge University Press.

Lévi-Strauss, C. (1963). *Totemism.* Boston: Beacon.

Lévi-Strauss, C. (1966). *The savage mind.* Chicago: University of Chicago Press.

Lévi-Strauss, C. (1967). *Structural anthropology.* Garden City, NY: Doubleday.

Lévi-Strauss, C. (1969). *The raw and the cooked: Introduction to a science of mythology* (Vol. 1). New York: Viking.

Lévi-Strauss, C. (1979). *Myth and meaning.* New York: Schocken.

Lewis, H. (1955). *Blackways of Kent.* Chapel Hill: University of North Carolina Press.

Lewis, H. (1971). Culture of poverty? What does it matter? In E. B. Leacock (Ed.), *The culture of poverty: A critique* (pp. 345-363). New York: Simon & Schuster.

Lieberson, S. (1980). *A piece of the pie: Blacks and white immigrants since 1880.* Berkeley: University of California Press.

Lieberson, S. (1985). Unhyphenated whites in the United States. *Ethnic and Racial Studies, 8,* 159-180.

Lieberson, S. (1992). Small Ns and big conclusions: An examination of the reasoning in comparative studies based on a small number of cases. In C. C. Ragin & H. S. Becker (Eds.), *What is a case? Exploring the foundations of social inquiry* (pp. 105-118). New York: Cambridge University Press.

Lieberson, S., & Waters, M. C. (1988). *From many strands: Ethnic and racial groups in contemporary America.* New York: Russell Sage Foundation.

Liebow, E. (1967). *Tally's corner: A study of Negro street corner men.* Boston: Little, Brown.

Link, J. (1990). *Schönhuber in der Nationalelf: Halbrechts, rechtsaussen oder in Abseits? Die politische Kollektivsymbolik der Bundesrepublik und der Durchbruch der neorassistischen Schönhuberpartei* (DISS Texte 10). Duisburg: Duisburger Institut für Sprach- und Sozialforschung.

Linz, J. (1973). Early state building and late peripheral nationalism against the state. In S. Eisenstadt & S. Rokkan (Eds.), *Building states and nations* (Vol. 2, pp. 32-116). Beverly Hills, CA: Sage.

Litton, G. (Ed.). (1939). The negotiations leading to the Chickasaw-Choctaw agreement, January 17, 1837. *Chronicles of Oklahoma, 7,* 417-427.

Long, L. (1980). Back to the countryside and back to the city in the same decade. In S. Laska & D. Spain (Eds.), *Back to the city* (pp. 61-76). New York: Pergamon.

Lowie, R. H. (1922). Science. In H. E. Stearns (Ed.), *Civilization in the United States.* New York: Harcourt.

Lukes, S. (Ed.). (1986). *Power.* Oxford: Basil Blackwell.

Lynd, R. S., & Lynd, H. M. (1929). *Middletown: A study in contemporary American culture.* New York: Harcourt.

Lynd, R. S., & Lynd, H. M. (1937). *Middletown in transition: A study of cultural conflicts.* New York: Harcourt.

M234. (n.d.). [Letters received by the Office of Indian Affairs 1824-1881: Chickasaw Agency, 1824-1870, rolls 135-142; Choctaw Agency, 1824-1876, rolls 169-183]. Washington, DC: National Archives.

Malinowski, B. (1922). *Argonauts of the Western Pacific.* New York: E. P. Dutton.

Malone, J. (1922). *The Chickasaw nation: A short sketch of a noble people.* Louisville, KY: John P. Morton.

Manheim, H. L. (1977). *Sociological research: Philosophy and methods.* Homewood, IL: Dorsey.

Marable, M. (1984). *Race, reform and rebellion: The second reconstruction in Black America, 1945-1982.* London: Macmillan.

Marks, C. (1989). *Farewell—we're good and gone: The great Black migration.* Bloomington: Indiana University Press.

Marsh, R. (1967). *Comparative method: A codification of cross-societal analyses.* New York: Harcourt, Brace & World.

Martindale, C. (1986). *The white press and Black America.* Westport, CT: Greenwood.

Martindale, D. (1960). *The nature and types of sociological theory.* Boston: Houghton Mifflin.

Massey, D. (1990). American apartheid: Segregation and the making of the underclass. *American Journal of Sociology, 96,* 329-357.

Maurier, H. (1979). Do we have an African philosophy? In R. A. Wright (Ed.), *African philosophy: An introduction* (M. McDevitt, Trans.). Washington, DC: University of America Press.

Mbiti, J. (1969). *African religion and philosophy.* Garden City, NY: Anchor.

McAdam, D. (1982). *Political process and the development of Black insurgency, 1930-1970.* Chicago: University of Chicago Press.

McCleskey v. Kemp, 753 F.2d 877 (1985).

McDonnell Douglas Corp. v. Green, 411 U.S. 792 (1973).

McIntosh, P. (1983). *Interactive phases of curriculum revision* (Working Paper). Wellesley, MA: Wellesley College, Center for Research on Women.

McIntosh, P. (1988). *White privilege and male privilege: A personal account of coming to see correspondences through work in women's studies* (Working Paper No. 189). Wellesley, MA: Wellesley College, Center for Research on Women.

Messina, A. M. (1990). Political impediments to the resumption of labour migration to Western Europe. *West European Politics, 13,* 31-46.

Michael, R., & Tuma, N. B. (1985). Entry into marriage and parenthood by young men and women: The influence of family background. *Demography, 22,* 515-544.

Miles, R. (1989). *Racism.* London: Routledge.

Miller, E. (1986). *Street woman.* Philadelphia: Temple University Press.

Model, S. (1988). The economic progress of European and East Asian Americans. *Annual Review of Sociology, 14,* 363-380.

Montagu, M. F. A. (1952). *Man's most dangerous myth: The fallacy of race.* New York: Harper.

Morgan, E. S. (1975). *American slavery, American freedom: The ordeal of colonial Virginia.* New York: W. W. Norton.

Morris, A. (1984). *The origins of the civil rights movement: Black communities organizing for change.* New York: Free Press.

Moynihan, D. P. (1965). *The Negro family: The case for national action.* Washington, DC: Government Printing Office.

Munch, P. A. (1957). Empirical science and Max Weber's *Verstehen Soziologie.* In M. Truzzi (Ed.), *Verstehen: Subjective understanding in the social sciences.* Reading, MA: Addison-Wesley.

Myers, S. L., Jr. (1985a). Methods of measuring and detecting discrimination in punishment. *Proceedings of the Business and Economic Statistics Section, American Statistical Association,* pp. 41-50.

Myers, S. L., Jr. (1985b, Summer). Statistical tests of discrimination in punishment. *Journal of Quantitative Criminology, 1,* 191-218.

Myrdal, G. (1944). *An American dilemma: The Negro problem and modern democracy.* New York: Harper & Row.

Naglieri, J. A. (1985a). *Matrix Analogies Test: Expanded form.* New York: Psychological Corporation.

Naglieri, J. A. (1985b). *Matrix Analogies Test: Short form.* New York: Psychological Corporation.

Naglieri, J. A., & Prewett, P. N. (1990). Nonverbal intelligence measure: A selected review of instruments and their use. In C. R. Reynolds & R. W. Kamphaus (Eds.), *Handbook of psychological and educational assessment of children: Intelligence and achievement* (pp. 348-370). New York: Guilford.

Nairne, T. (1988). *Nairne's Muskhogean journals: The 1708 expedition to the Mississippi River* (A. Moore, Ed.). Jackson: University Press of Mississippi.

National Urban League. (1980). *A periodic national survey of the Black community in America.* New York: Author.

Nichols, E. (1986). Skocpol and revolution: Comparative analysis versus historical conjecture. *Comparative Social Research, 9,* 163-186.

Nichols, E. J. (1976). *The philosophical aspects of cultural difference.* Unpublished table, University of Ibadan, Nigeria.

Nkrumah, K. (1973). *Autobiography of Kwame Nkrumah.* London: Panaf. (Original work published 1957)

Nobles, W. W. (1983). *Critical analysis of scholarship on Black family life.* Washington, DC: United Church of Christ Commission for Racial Justice.

Nobles, W. W. (1987). Psychometrics and African American reality: A question of cultural antimony. *Negro Educational Review, 38,* 45-55.

Oakley, A. (1981). Interviewing women. In H. Roberts (Ed.), *Doing feminist research* (pp. 30-61). New York: Routledge & Kegan Paul.

Oberschall, A. (1973). *Social conflict and social movements.* Englewood Cliffs, NJ: Prentice Hall.

Ogbu, J. (1988). Human intelligence testing: A cultural-ecological perspective. *National Forum, 68*(2), 23-29.

Omi, M., & Winant, H. (1986). *Racial formation in the United States: From the 1960s to the 1980s.* New York: Routledge.

Organization for Economic Cooperation and Development. (1988). *Continuous reporting system on migration.* Paris: Author.

Ortner, S. B. (1974). Is female to male as nature is to culture? In M. Z. Rosaldo & L. Lamphere (Eds.), *Woman, culture, and society* (pp. 67-87). Stanford, CA: Stanford University Press.

Park, R. E. (1950). *Race and culture.* Glencoe, IL: Free Press.

Parkins, F. (1979). *Marxism and class theory*. New York: Columbia University Press.

Parsons, T. (1937). *The structure of social action*. New York: McGraw-Hill.

Parsons, T. (1956). *Economy and society*. New York: Free Press.

Parsons, T. (1977a). *The evolution of societies*. Englewood Cliffs, NJ: Prentice Hall.

Parsons, T. (1977b). *Social systems and the evolution of action theory*. New York: Free Press.

Patton, J. P., Prillaman, D., & VanTassel-Baska, J. (1990). The nature and extent of programs for the disadvantaged gifted in the United States and territories. *Gifted Child Quarterly, 34*(3), 94-96.

Petersilia, J. (1983). *Racial disparities in the criminal justice system*. Santa Monica, CA: RAND Corporation.

Peterson, M. A., & Braiker, H. B., with Polich, S. (1980). *Doing crime: A survey of California inmates* (Publication No. R-2200-DOJ). Santa Monica, CA: RAND Corporation.

Pettigrew, T. (1985). New black-white patterns: How best to conceptualize them. *Annual Review of Sociology, 11,* 329-346.

Piven, F. F., & Cloward, R. A. (1971). *Regulating the poor: The functions of public welfare*. New York: Vintage.

Planet of the year: Endangered Earth. (1989, January 2). *Time.*

Pope, C. E. (1979). Race and crime revisited. *Crime & Delinquency, 25,* 347-357.

Popper, K. R. (1972). *Objective knowledge*. Oxford: Clarendon.

Portes, A., & Bach, R. (1985). *Latin journey: Cuban and Mexican immigrants in the United States*. Berkeley: University of California Press.

Portes, A., & Walton, J. (1981). *Labor, class, and the international system*. New York: Academic Press.

Powdermaker, H. (1939). *After freedom: A cultural study of the Deep South*. New York: Viking.

Prejean v. Blackburn, 743 F.2d 1092 (1984).

Price, D. (1969). *Changing characteristics of the Negro population*. Washington, DC: Government Printing Office.

Przeworski, A., & Teune, H. (1970). *The logic of comparative social inquiry*. New York: Wiley-Interscience.

Punch, M. (1986). *The politics and ethics of fieldwork*. Beverly Hills, CA: Sage.

Ragin, C. C. (1987). *The comparative method: Moving beyond qualitative and quantitative strategies*. Berkeley: University of California Press.

Ragin, C. C. (1991). Introduction: The problem of balancing discourse on cases and variables in comparative social science. *International Journal of Comparative Sociology, 32,* 1-8.

Ragin, C. C., & Becker, H. S. (Eds.). (1992). *What is a case? Exploring the foundations of social inquiry*. New York: Cambridge University Press.

Ragin, C. C., & Zaret, D. (1983). Theory and method in comparative research: Two strategies. *Social Forces, 61,* 731-754.

Rainwater, L. (1970). *Behind ghetto walls*. Chicago: Aldine DeGruyter.

Rapp, R. (1983). *Anthropology: The science of man?* Address presented at the University of Delaware.

Rappaport, R. A. (1971). Nature, culture, and ecological anthropology. In H. L. Shapiro (Ed.), *Man, culture, and society*. New York: Oxford University Press.

Raven, J. C. (1938). *Standard progressive matrices*. London: H. K. Lewis.

Raven, J. C. (1947a). *Advanced progressive matrices*. London: H. K. Lewis.

Raven, J. C. (1947b). *Coloured progressive matrices.* London: H. K. Lewis.

Redfield, R. (1955). *The little community.* Chicago: University of Chicago Press.

Reeves, F. (1983). *British racial discourse.* Cambridge: Cambridge University Press.

Reider, J. (1985). *Canarsie: The Jews and Italians of Brooklyn against liberalism.* Cambridge, MA: Harvard University Press.

Reinharz, S. (1983). Experiential analysis: A contribution to feminist research. In G. Bowles & R. Duelli-Klein (Ed.), *Theories of women's studies* (pp. 162-191). New York: Routledge & Kegan Paul.

Remmling, G. (1967). *Road to suspicion.* New York: Crofts.

Renzulli, J. S. (1983). Rating the behavioral characteristics of superior students. *Gifted Child Today, 29,* 30-35.

Renzulli, J. S., & Hartman, R. K. (1971). Scale for rating behavioral characteristics of superior students. *Exceptional Children, 38,* 243-248.

Reschly, D. J. (1980). *Nonbiased assessment.* Des Moines: State of Iowa Department of Public Instruction.

Reschly, D. J., & Ross-Reynolds, J. (1982). An investigation of WISC-R item bias with four sociocultural groups. *Journal of Consulting and Clinical Psychology, 51,* 144-146.

Rich, P. D. (1986). *Race and empire in British politics.* Cambridge: Cambridge University Press.

Richert, E. S., Alvino, J., & McDonnel, R. (1982). *The national report on identification: Assessment and recommendations for comprehensive identification of gifted and talented youth.* Sewell, NJ: Educational Improvement Center—South.

Rimm, S. (1976). *GIFT: Group Inventory for Finding Talent.* Watertown, WI: Educational Assessment Service.

Rimm, S., & Davis, G. A. (1976). GIFT: An instrument for the identification of creativity. *Journal of Creative Behavior, 10,* 178-182.

Rimm, S., & Davis, G. A. (1980). Five years of international research with GIFT: An instrument for the identification of creativity. *Journal of Creative Behavior, 14,* 35-46.

Robinson, D. L. (1971). *Slavery in the structure of American politics, 1765-1820.* New York: Harcourt Brace Jovanovich.

Rogers, A. R. (1988). Does biology constrain culture? *American Anthropologist, 90,* 819-831.

Rokkan, S. (1975). Dimensions of state formation and nation-building: A possible paradigm for research on variations with Europe. In C. Tilly (Ed.), *The formation of national states in Western Europe* (pp. 562-600). Princeton, NJ: Princeton University Press.

Rose, D. (1990). *Living the ethnographic life.* Newbury Park, CA: Sage.

Rosenthal, R. (1966). *Experimenter effects in behavioral research.* New York: Appleton-Century-Crofts.

Roth, G. (1971). Max Weber's comparative approach and historical typology. In I. Vallier (Ed.), *Comparative methodology in sociology* (pp. 75-93). Berkeley: University of California Press.

Rothschild, J. (1981). *Ethnopolitics: A conceptual framework.* New York: Columbia University Press.

Rubin, M. (1951). *Plantation county.* New Haven, CT: College and University Press.

Safran, W. (1985). The Mitterrand regime and its policies of ethnocultural accommodation. *Comparative Political Studies, 17,* 41-63.

Safran, W. (1988). Rights and liberties under the Mitterrand presidency: Socialist innovations and post-socialist revisions. *Contemporary French Civilization, 12,* 1-35.

Salvia, J., & Ysseldyke, J. E.(1988). *Assessment in special and remedial education.* Boston: Houghton Mifflin.

Sattler, J. M. (1982). *Assessment of children's intelligence and special abilities.* Boston: Allyn & Bacon.

Sattler, J. M., Hilliard, A., Lambert, N., Albee, G., & Jensen, A. (1981, August). *Intelligence tests on trial: Larry P. and PASE.* Paper presented at the annual meeting of the American Psychological Association, Los Angeles.

Schaeffer, N. C. (1982). A general social survey experiment in generic words. *Public Opinion Quarterly, 46,* 572-581.

Schain, M. (1987). The National Front in France and the construction of political legitimacy. *West European Politics, 10,* 229-252.

Scherer, K. R., & Giles, H. (Eds.). (1979). *Social markers in speech.* Cambridge: Cambridge University Press.

Schermerhorn, R. A. (1978 [1970]). *Comparative ethnic relations.* Chicago: University of Chicago Press.

Schram, S. F., & Turbett, J. P. (1983). Civil disorder and the welfare explosion: A two-step process. *American Sociological Review, 48,* 408-414.

Schulz, D. (1969). *Coming up Black: Patterns of ghetto socialization.* Englewood Cliffs, NJ: Prentice Hall.

Schuman, H., & Hatchett, S. (1974). *Black racial attitudes: Trends and complexities.* Ann Arbor, MI: Institute for Social Research.

Schuman, H., Steeh, C., & Bobo, L. (1985). *Racial attitudes in America: Trends and interpretations.* Cambridge, MA: Harvard University Press.

See, K. O., & Wilson, W. J. (1988). Race and ethnicity. In Neil J. Smelser (Ed.), *Handbook of sociology* (pp. 223-242). Newbury Park, CA: Sage.

Seidel, G. (Ed.). (1988). *The nature of the right: A feminist analysis of order patterns.* Amsterdam: Benjamins.

Sharma, S. (1986). Assessment strategies for minority groups. *Journal of Black Studies, 17,* 111-124.

Shuy, R. (1977). Quantitative language data: A case for and some warnings against. *Anthropology and Education Quarterly, 8,* 78-82.

Sica, A. (1988). *Weber, irrationality, and social order.* Berkeley: University of California Press.

Skocpol, T. (1979). *States and social revolutions.* New York: Cambridge University Press.

Skocpol, T. (1984a). Emerging agendas and recurrent strategies in historical sociology. In T. Skocpol (Ed.), *Vision and method in historical sociology* (pp. 356-391). New York: Cambridge University Press.

Skocpol, T. (Ed.). (1984b). *Vision and method in historical sociology.* Cambridge, MA: Cambridge University Press.

Skocpol, T. (1986). Analyzing configurations in history: A rejoinder to Nichols. *Comparative Social Research, 9,* 187-194.

Smelser, N. J. (1959). *Social change in the Industrial Revolution.* Chicago: University of Chicago Press.

Smelser, N. J. (1963). *The theory of collective behavior.* New York: Free Press.

Smelser, N. J. (1976). *Comparative methods in the social sciences.* Englewood Cliffs, NJ: Prentice Hall.

Smelser, N. J. (1985). Evaluating the model of structural differentiation in relation to educational change in the nineteenth century. In J. C. Alexander (Ed.), *Neofunctionalism* (pp. 113-130). Beverly Hills, CA: Sage.

Smelser, N. J. (1990). The contest between family and schooling in nineteenth-century Britain. In J. C. Alexander & P. Colomy (Eds.), *Differentiation theory and social change: Comparative and historical perspectives* (pp. 165-186). New York: Columbia University Press.

Smith v. Balkcom, 671 F.2d 858 (1982).

Smith, A. D. (1986). *The ethnic origin of nations.* New York: Basil Blackwell.

Smith, A. W. (1984). *Evaluating the products of alternative sampling methods.* Paper presented at the annual meeting of the American Sociological Association, San Antonio, TX.

Smith, A. W. (1985). Social class and racial cleavages on major social indicators. *Research in Race and Ethnic Relations, 4,* 33-65.

Smith, D. E. (1987). *The everyday world as problematic: A feminist sociology.* Boston: Northeastern University Press.

Sotomayor, M. (1973). *A study of Chicano grandparents in an urban barrio.* Unpublished doctoral dissertation, University of Denver, School of Social Work.

Spearman, C. (1923). *The nature of "intelligence" and the principles of cognition.* London: Macmillan.

Stanfield, J. H., II. (1985). *Philanthropy and Jim Crow in American social science.* Westport, CT: Greenwood.

Stanfield, J. H., II. (1987). Archival methods in race relations research. *American Behavioral Scientist, 30,* 366-380.

Stanfield, J. H., II. (1988). Not quite in the club. *American Sociologist, 19,* 291-300.

Stanfield, J. H., II. (1991). Racism in America and other race-centered societies. *International Journal of Comparative Sociology, 32,* 243-260.

Sternberg, R. (1985). *Beyond I.Q.* Cambridge, MA: Cambridge University Press.

Sternberg, R. (1991). Giftedness according to the triarchic theory of human intelligence. In N. Colangelo & G. A. Davis (Eds.), *Handbook of gifted education* (pp. 45-53). Boston: Allyn & Bacon.

Stinchcombe, A. (1978). *Theoretical methods in social history.* New York: Academic Press.

Stolnitz, G. (1983). Three to five main challenges to demographic research. *Demography, 20,* 415-432.

Stryker, S. (1980). *Symbolic interactionism.* Menlo Park, CA: Benjamin Cummings.

Sudman, S. (1967). *Reducing the cost of surveys.* Chicago: Aldine.

Sudman, S., & Bradburn, N. (1974). *Response effects in surveys.* Chicago: Aldine.

Taeuber, K. E. (1975). Racial segregation: The persisting dilemma. *Annals of the American Academy of Political and Social Science, 422,* 87-96.

Taeuber, K. E., & Taeuber, A. (1965). *Negroes in cities.* Chicago: Aldine.

Taylor, R. J. (1986). Receipt of support from family among Black Americans: Demographic and familial differences. *Journal of Marriage and the Family, 48,* 67-77.

Tedeschi, J. T. (Ed.) (1981). *Impression management: Theory and social psychological research.* New York: Academic Press.

Terman, L. M. (1916). *Human nature and the social order.* New York: Macmillan.

Texas Department of Community Affairs v. Burdine, 450 U.S. 248 (1981).

Thomas, W. I., & Znaniecki, F. (1918-1920). *The Polish peasant in Europe and America.* New York: Alfred A. Knopf.

Thompson, E. P. (1966). *The making of the English working class.* New York: Vintage.

Thompson, E. T. (1975). *Plantation societies, race relations and the South.* Durham, NC: Duke University Press.

Thorndike, E. L. (1940). *Human nature and the social order.* New York: Macmillan.

Tienda, M., & Glass, J. (1985). Household structure and labor force participation of Black, Hispanic, and white mothers. *Demography, 22,* 381-344.

Tilly, C. (1984). *Big structures, large processes, huge comparisons.* New York: Russell Sage Foundation.

Time Magazine. (1989, January 2). Planet of the year: Endangered Earth. (p. 24).

Tobias, C. (1986). *Identifying Anglo, Mexican-American and American Indian respondents for a study of recent widows: Suggestions for future researchers* (Working Paper). Tucson: University of Arizona, Southwest Institute for Research on Women.

Tolnay, S. (1981). Trends in total and marital fertility for Black Americans, 1886-1899. *Demography, 18,* 443-463.

Torrance, E. P. (1969). Creative positives of disadvantaged children and youth. *Gifted Child Quarterly, 13*(2), 71-81.

Torrance, E. P. (1977). *Discovery and nurturance of giftedness in the culturally different.* Reston, VA: Council for Exceptional Children.

Torrance, E. P. (1987). *Using tests of creative thinking to guide the teaching of creative behavior.* Bensenville, IL: Scholastic Testing Service.

Torrance, E. P. (in press). *The blazing drive: The creative personality.* Buffalo, NY: Bearly.

Tourangeau, R., & Smith, A. W. (1985). Finding subgroups for surveys. *Public Opinion Quarterly, 49,* 351-369.

Tuddenham, R. D. (1962). The nature and measurement of intelligence. In L. Postman (Ed.), *Psychology in the making: Histories of selected research problems* (pp. 469-525). New York: Alfred A. Knopf.

Turner, R. H. (1960). Sponsored and contest mobility in the school system. *American Sociological Review, 25,* 855-867.

Turner, R. H., & Killian, L. (1972). *Collective behavior.* Englewood Cliffs, NJ: Prentice Hall.

Uya, O. E. (1981). Using federal archives: Some problems in doing research. In R. L. Clarke (Ed.), *Afro-American history sources for research* (pp. 19-29). Washington, DC: Howard University Press.

Valencia, R. R. (1979). Comparison of intellectual performance of Chicano and Anglo third grade boys on the Raven's Coloured Progressive Matrices. *Psychology in the Schools, 16,* 448-453.

van den Berghe, P. L. (1981). *The ethnic phenomenon.* New York: Elsevier.

van Dijk, T. A. (1984). *Prejudice in discourse.* Amsterdam: Benjamins.

van Dijk, T. A. (1985a). Cognitive situation models in discourse processing: The expression of ethnic situation models in prejudiced stories. In J. P. Forgas (Ed.), *Language and social situations* (pp. 61-79). New York: Springer.

van Dijk, T. A. (Ed.). (1985b). *Handbook of discourse analysis* (4 vols.). London: Academic Press.

van Dijk, T. A. (1987a). *Communicating racism.* Newbury Park, CA: Sage.

van Dijk, T. A. (1987b). Episodic models in discourse processing, 1983. In R. Horowitz & S. J. Samuels (Eds.), *Comprehending oral and written language* (pp. 161-196). New York: Academic Press.

van Dijk, T. A. (1987c). *Schoolvoorbeelden van racisme. De reproduktie van racisme in maatschappijleerboeken* [Textbook examples of racism: The reproduction of racism in social science textbooks]. Amsterdam: Socialistische Uitgeverij Amsterdam.

van Dijk, T. A. (1988a). *News analysis: Case studies of international and national news in the press.* Hillsdale, NJ: Lawrence Erlbaum.

van Dijk, T. A. (1988b). The Tamil panic in the press. In T. A. van Dijk, *News analysis: Case studies of international and national news in the press* (pp. 215-254). Hillsdale, NJ: Lawrence Erlbaum.

van Dijk, T. A. (1989). Structures of discourse and structures of power. In J. A. Anderson (Ed.), *Communication yearbook 12* (pp. 18-59). Newbury Park, CA: Sage.

van Dijk, T. A. (1990). Social cognition and discourse. In H. Giles & R. P. Robinson (Eds.), *Handbook of social psychology and language* (pp. 163-183). Chichester, UK: John Wiley.

van Dijk, T. A. (1991). *Racism and the press.* London: Routledge.

van Dijk, T. A. (1992). Stories and racism. In D. Mumby & J. Turow (Eds.), *Narrative and social control.* Newbury Park, CA: Sage.

van Dijk, T. A. (1993). *Elite discourse and racism.* Unpublished manuscript.

van Dijk, T. A., & Kintsch, W. (1983). *Strategies of discourse comprehension.* New York: Academic Press.

VanTassel-Baska, J., Patton, J., & Prillaman, D. (1989). Disadvantaged gifted learners at-risk for educational attention. *Focus on Exceptional Children, 22*(3), 1-16.

Veblen, T. (1927). *The theory of the leisure class: An economic study of institutions.* New York: Vanguard.

Vernon, P. E. (1969). *Intelligence and cultural environment.* London: Methuen.

Vidich, A., & Bensman, J. (1968). *Small town in mass society.* Princeton, NJ: Princeton University Press.

Waksberg, J. (1978). Sampling methods for random digit dialing. *Journal of the American Statistical Association, 73,* 40-46.

Walker, H. A., & Cohen, B. P. (1985). Scope statements: Imperatives for evaluating theory. *American Sociological Review, 50,* 288-301.

Wallerstein, I. (1974). *The modern world-system.* New York: Academic Press.

Wards Cove Packing v. Atonio, 490 U.S. 642, 109 S.Ct. 2115 (1989).

Warner, W. L., Junker, B. H., & Adams, W. A. (1941). *Color and human nature: Negro personality development in a northern city.* Washington, DC: American Council on Education.

Washington v. Davis, 426 U.S. 229, 96 S.Ct. 2040 (1976).

Waters, M. C. (1990). *Ethnic options: Choosing identities in America.* Berkeley: University of California Press.

Weber, M. (1949). *The methodology of the social sciences.* Glencoe, IL: Free Press.

Weber, M. (1958). *The Protestant ethic and the spirit of capitalism.* New York: Charles Scribner's Sons.

Weber, M. (1963). *The sociology of religion.* Boston: Beacon.

Weber, M. (1968). *Economy and society* (G. Roth & C. Wittich, Eds.). New York: Bedminster.

Weber, M. (1981). *General economic history.* New Brunswick, NJ: Transaction.

Wellman, D. T. (1977). *Portraits of white racism.* Cambridge: Cambridge University Press.

White, L. A. (1949). *The science of culture.* New York: Farrar, Straus & Giroux.

White, L. A. (1973). *The concept of culture.* Minneapolis: Burgess.

Whyte, W. F. (1943). *Street corner society: The social structure of an Italian slum.* Chicago: University of Chicago Press.

Williams, M. D. (1979). The harvesting of "Sluckus" (*Porphyra perforata*) by the Straits Salish Indians of Vancouver Island. *Syesis, 12,* 63-70.

Williams, M. D. (1981a). Observations in Pittsburgh ghetto schools. *Anthropology and Education Quarterly, 12,* 211-220.

Williams, M. D. (1981b). *On the street where I lived.* New York: Holt, Rinehart & Winston.

Williams, M. D. (1984). *Community in a Black Pentecostal church: An anthropological study.* Prospect Heights, IL: Waveland.

Williams, M. D. (1989). Children's games and play of the Straits Salish Indians of Vancouver Island. In R. Bolton (Ed.), *The content of culture: Constants and variants* (pp. 19-32). New Haven, CT: HRAF.

Williams, M. D. (1990). The Afro-American in the cultural dialogue of the United States. In G. Spindler & L. Spindler (Eds.), *The American cultural dialogue and its transmission* (pp. 144-162). New York: Falmer.

Williams, M. D. (1992a). *The Black middle class and social transformations: The production and reproduction of social inferiority.* Ann Arbor, MI: Author.

Williams, M. D. (1992b). *The human dilemma.* New York: Harcourt Brace Jovanovich.

Willis, W. S., Jr. (1974). Skeletons in the anthropological closet. In E. D. Dell Hymes (Ed.), *Reinventing anthropology.* New York: Vintage.

Wilson, C. C., & Gutiérrez, F. (1985). *Minorities and the media.* Beverly Hills, CA: Sage.

Wilson, J. (1990). *Politically speaking.* Cambridge, MA: Basil Blackwell.

Wilson, W. J. (1978). *The declining significance of race: Blacks and changing American institutions.* Chicago: University of Chicago Press.

Wilson, W. J. (1987). *The truly disadvantaged: The inner city, the underclass and public policy.* Chicago: University of Chicago Press.

Windisch, U. (1978). *Xenophobie? Logique de la pensee populaire* [Xenophobia? Logic of popular thought]. Lausanne: L'Age d'Homme.

Wodak, R. (Ed.). (1989). *Language, power and ideology.* Amsterdam: Benjamins.

Wodak, R., Nowak, P., Pelikan, J., Gruber, H., De Cillia, R., & Mitten, R. (1990). *"Wir sind unschuldige Täter": Studien zum antisemitischen Diskurs im Nachkriegösterreich.* Frankfurt am Main: Suhrkamp.

Wolf, E. (1982). *Europe and the people without history.* Berkeley: University of California Press.

Wolfgang, M. E. (1983). Delinquency in two birth cohorts. In K. T. Van Dusen & S. A. Mednick (Eds.), *Prospective studies of crime and delinquency* (pp. 7-16). Boston: Kluwer Nijhoff.

Wolfgang, M. E., & Cohen, C. (1970). *Crime and race: Conceptions and misconceptions.* New York: Institute of Human Relations Press, American Jewish Committee.

Woodson, C. (1918). *A century of Negro migration.* New York: AMS.

Wright, M. H. (1929). Brief outline of the Choctaw and Chickasaw nations in the Indian Territory 1820 to 1860. *Chronicles of Oklahoma, 7,* 388-418.

Yeric, J. L., & Todd, J. R. (1983). *Public opinion: The visible politics.* Itasca, IL: Peacock.

Yerkes, R. M. (1917). The Binet version versus the point scale method of measuring intelligence. *Journal of Applied Psychology, 1,* 111-112.

Yinger, M. (1985). Ethnicity. *Annual Review of Sociology, 11,* 151-180.

Young, C. (1976). *The politics of cultural pluralism.* Madison: University of Wisconsin Press.

Zavella, P. (1979). *Women's work and Chicano families.* Ithaca, NY: Cornell University Press.

Zimmer, B. G. (1981). The impact of social mobility on fertility: A reconsideration. *Population Studies, 35,* 120-131.

Index

About the Contributors

Margaret L. Andersen is Professor of Sociology and Women's Studies at the University of Delaware, where she also serves as Vice Provost for Academic Affairs. She is the author of *Thinking About Women* (Macmillan, 1993); coeditor, with Patricia Hill Collins, of *Race, Class, and Gender: An Anthology* (Wadsworth, 1992); and coauthor, with Frank Scarpitti, of *Social Problems* (Harper Collins, 1992). She is currently the editor of *Gender & Society* and Vice President of the Eastern Sociological Society.

Duane Champagne is a member of the Turtle Mountain Chippewa Tribe of North Dakota, and is Associate Professor of Sociology at the University of California, Los Angeles. He also is Director of the UCLA American Indian Studies Center, and editor of the *American Indian Culture and Research Journal*. He has published numerous books and articles on comparative history and social change among Native American societies. He is author of *American Indian Societies: Strategies and Conditions of Political and Cultural Survival* (Cultural Survival, 1989) and *Social Order and Political Change: The Constitutional Governments Among the Cherokee, the Choctaw, the Chickasaw and the Creek* (Stanford University Press, 1992).

Rutledge M. Dennis received his B.A. from South Carolina State University and his M.A. and Ph.D. from Washington State University. He is currently Professor of Sociology at George Mason University and was Director of Afro-American Studies and Professor of Sociology at Virginia Commonwealth University from 1971 to 1978. His research has focused on community studies, W. E. B. Du Bois, political sociology, social stratification, and social theory. He is Past President of the Association of Black Sociologists and is Editor of the JAI Press Series in Race and Ethnic Relations.

Elisa Facio is Assistant Professor in the Sociology Department at the University of Colorado, Boulder. She conducts research on aging, health care policy, and Chicana feminist studies. She is currently completing a manuscript for Sage Publications on Chicana elderly. She received her B.A. from Santa Clara University and her M.A. and Ph.D. from the University of Colorado, Boulder.

Jeremy Hein is Assistant Professor of Sociology at the University of Wisconsin—Eau Claire. He conducts research on comparative historical sociology, race and ethnic relations, international migration, and social policy. The National Science Foundation and the Centre National de la Recherche Scientifique (the French equivalent of NSF) have supported his research. His publications include articles in *Sociological Quarterly, Sociological Perspectives, Ethnic Groups,* and *International Migration Review.* His book *States and International Migrants: The Incorporation of Indochinese Refugees in the United States and France* completes a decade of research on the role of government in shaping the adaptation of refugees from Vietnam, Laos, and Cambodia. His current research is a comparison of civil rights eras in the United States (1954-1968) and France (1981-1990). This research tests a social movement and a state-centered theory of cross-national variation in periods of politically initiated change in racial inequality.

Carole C. Marks, Associate Professor of Black American Studies and Sociology at the University of Delaware, received a Ph.D. in sociology from New York University. She has been awarded an NIMH Postgraduate Fellowship, a Mellon Faculty Fellowship and a Sloan Fellowship. She is a member of the Board of Managers of Haverford College. In addition, she was Codirector of the Minority Opportunity Summer

Training Program sponsored by the American Sociological Association and the University of Delaware (1990-1991). She has also held the Division Chair of Racial and Ethnic Minorities of the Society of the Study of Social Problems. She has published extensively in scholarly journals and currently serves on the Advisory Board of *Gender & Society*. Her book *Farewell, We're Good and Gone* was published by Indiana University Press in 1989.

Samuel L. Myers, Jr., is the Roy Wilkins Professor of Human Relations and Social Justice at the Hubert H. Humphrey Institute of Public Affairs, University of Minnesota. As Chairholder, he directs teaching, research, and citizen education in the areas of human relations and social justice. Educated at Morgan State University and the Massachusetts Institute of Technology, where he earned his doctorate in economics, he is a specialist in the impacts of social policies on the poor. He has pioneered in the use of applied econometric techniques to examine racial disparities in crime, to detect illegal discrimination in credit markets, to assess the impacts of welfare on family stability, and to evaluate the effectiveness of government transfers in reducing poverty. He has authored or coauthored four books and monographs and numerous journal articles and technical papers. Prior to joining the Humphrey Institute, he was Professor in the Department of Economics and Director of the Afro-American Studies Program at the University of Maryland, College Park.

James M. Patton, Ed.D., is Associate Professor of Special Education and Associate Dean of Academic Programs at the College of William and Mary of Virginia. He is Director of Project Mandala, a federally funded gifted research and development project aimed at identifying and serving selected students and their families who exhibit at-risk and at-promise characteristics. Formerly, he directed professional development and teacher education and evaluation programs for the Commonwealth of Virginia. He has served also as Dean of the School of Education and Chairperson of the Department of Special Education at Virginia State University and as Chair of the Special Education Program at Hampton University. He has taught in the public schools of Louisville, Kentucky, where he also directed the Career Opportunities Program, a federally funded effort to increase the number of indigenous inner-city teachers in the Louisville Public Schools. His major research interests include the educational and psychosocial development of African

Americans, particularly those with gifts and talents, enhancing the development of African American males, and analysis of policies that affect people of color and those from low socioeconomic circumstances.

Charles C. Ragin is Professor of Sociology and Political Science and Research Fellow, Center for Urban Affairs and Policy Research, at Northwestern University. His writings on methodology span macrosociology and comparative politics and address both the gulf and the links between qualitative and quantitative approaches; his substantive work addresses ethnicity, political mobilization, and political economy. His book *The Comparative Method: Moving Beyond Qualitative and Quantitative Strategies* (University of California Press, 1987) won the Stein Rokkan Prize for comparative research. He is the editor of *Issues and Alternatives in Comparative Social Research* (E. J. Brill, 1991) and coeditor, with Howard S. Becker, of *What Is a Case? Exploring the Foundations of Social Inquiry* (Cambridge University Press, 1992). With John Stephens and Evelyne Huber, he is currently conducting an NSF-funded study of the welfare state in 19 advanced capitalist societies.

A. Wade Smith is Professor and Chair of Sociology at Arizona State University. He received his doctorate from the University of Chicago. He has held positions at the University of South Carolina, Center for the Study of Youth Development (Boys Town), and continues intermittently to be a Research Associate at the National Opinion Research Center. His grant from the National Science Foundation produced the Black oversample in the 1982 General Social Survey. Over the course of his career, he has been awarded a dozen grants for national and international research. He has presented scores of papers at professional meetings, and has published even more refereed journal articles and book chapters. He has served as an associate editor for the *American Sociological Review* and for *Social Forces*. Currently, his research focuses on analyses of race and class cleavages in attitudes and values, as well as analyses of the effects of the media on people's attitudes toward violence, especially police violence.

John H. Stanfield II is the Frances and Edwin Cumming Professor of American Studies and Sociology, Scholar in Residence, Commonwealth Center for the Study of American History and Culture, College of William and Mary. His research interests include sociology of knowledge approaches to the study of race and sciences. His current research focus is on the comparative sociological history of race and colonialism in the formation of nineteenth- and early twentieth-century sciences.

Teun A. van Dijk is Professor of Discourse Studies at the University of Amsterdam. After earlier work in literary studies, text grammar, and the psychology of text comprehension, his research in the 1980s focused on the study of news in the press and the propagation of racism through various types of discourse. He has published several books in each of these domains, and his work has been translated into a dozen languages. His present research in critical discourse studies focuses on the relationships among power, discourse, and ideology. He holds two honorary doctorates and is founder-editor of the international journals *TEXT* and *Discourse & Society,* and editor of the four-volume *Handbook of Discourse Analysis.* He has lectured at many universities in Europe and the Americas, and has served as a visiting professor at the Universities of Bielefeld (FRG), Mexico City, Puerto Rico, and Campinas and Recife (Brazil).

Melvin D. Williams is Professor of Anthropology at the University of Michigan, Ann Arbor, and Ombudsperson for the College of Literature, Science and the Arts. He has served on the Dean's Council of the College and as the Director of the Comprehensive Studies Program. He held the Olive B. O'Connor Chair in American Institutions at Colgate University in 1976-1977. He received his A.B., M.A., and Ph.D. from the University of Pittsburgh. He has published in numerous professional journals and in edited volumes, and his books include *Community in a Black Pentecostal Church: An Anthropological Study* (Waveland, 1984) and *The Human Dilemma* (Harcourt Brace Jovanovich, 1992).